ISRAEL
AND THE CHURCH

RONALD E. DIPROSE

ISRAEL
AND THE CHURCH

THE ORIGINS
AND EFFECTS OF
REPLACEMENT THEOLOGY

Ronald E. Diprose

Biblica Books
from InterVarsity Press

InterVarsity Press
P.O. Box 1400, Downers Grove, IL 60515-1426
ivpress.com
email@ivpress.com

Original title of the Italian version: Israele e la Chiesa
Italian Version Copyright © 1998, Istituto Biblico Evangelico Italiano, Rome, Italy

InterVarsity Press® is the book-publishing division of InterVarsity Christian Fellowship/USA®, a movement of students and faculty active on campus at hundreds of universities, colleges and schools of nursing in the United States of America, and a member movement of the International Fellowship of Evangelical Students. For information about local and regional activities, visit intervarsity.org.

All Scripture quotations, unless otherwise indicated, are taken from the Holy Bible, New International Version®. NIV®. Copyright ©1973, 1978, 1984 by International Bible Society. Used by permission of Zondervan Publishing House. All rights reserved.

While any stories in this book are true, some names and identifying information may have been changed to protect the privacy of individuals.

Originally published by Biblica.

This book is available in Italian from:
Istituto Biblico Evangelico Italiano,
Via del Casale Corvio, 50, 00132 Rome, Italy Fax 0039-06-2070151
Email: amministrazione@ibei.it

This volume contains parts of a dissertation for which Ronald E. Diprose was awarded the PhD in Theology by the Evangelische Theologische Faculteit, Heverlee (Louvain), Belgium, in September, 1997. The Evangelische Theologische Faculteit has given permission for this material to be published.

Cover design: Paul Lewis

ISBN 978-0-8308-5689-3 (print)
ISBN 978-0-8308-5911-5 (digital)

Library of Congress Cataloging-in-Publication Data
A catalog record for this book is available from the Library of Congress.

P 25 24 23 22 21 20 19 18 17 16 15 14 13 12 11 10 9 8 7 6 5 4 3 2 1
Y 36 35 34 33 32 31 30 29 28 27 26 25 24 23 22 21 20 19 18 17 16 15 14

CONTENTS

Abbreviations vii

Foreword by Donald Tinder xi

Preface xiii

Introduction 1

1. A Unique People 5

2. Replacement Theology and the New Testament 29

3. The Development of Replacement Theology 69
   in Post-Apostolic Times

4. Replacement Theology and Ecclesiology 99

5. Replacement Theology and Eschatology 137

6. Lessons for Christian Theology 169

Appendix: Israel and Christian Theology: 175
   Some Effects of the New Majority View

Notes 193

Bibliography 237

Subject Index 257

ABBREVIATIONS

1. Books of the Bible

The same abbreviations are used as are found in the New International Version (1985).

2. Ancient works

Augustine

	Civ.	*City of God*
	Barn.	Barnabas, (pseudonymous) Epistle of

Clement of Alexandria

	Strom.	*Stromata*

Cyprian

	Testimonies	*Three Books of Testimonies Against the Jews*
	Unit. eccl.	*On the Unity of the Church*

Cyril of Jerusalem

	Cat.	*Catechetical Lectures*

Eusebius

	Hist. eccl.	*Ecclesiastical History*

Hippolytus

	Antichr.	*On Antichrist*

Irenaeus

    Haer.   *Against Heresies*

Justin Martyr

    Tryph. Jud.   *Dialogue with Trypho*

Origen

    Cant.   *Exposition of the Song of Songs*
    Cels.   *Against Celsus*
    Princ.   *On First Principles*

Tertullian

    Adv. Jud.   *Against the Jews*
    Marc.   *Against Marcion*
    bap.   *On Baptism*

3. Collections, modern publications, and journals

ANF   *Ante-Nicene Fathers*, Alexander Roberts and James Donaldson, eds., American reprint, A. Cleveland Coxe and Allan Menzies, eds., 10 vols. Grand Rapids, MI: Eerdmans, 1986.

CH   *Church History*

IBMR   *International Bulletin of Missionary Research*

ICC   International Critical Commentaries

JEH   *Journal of Ecclesiastical History*

JES   *Journal of Ecumenical Studies*

NIDCC   *The New International Dictionary of the Christian Church*, J.D. Douglas, ed., Exeter: The Paternoster Press, 1978.

NIDNTT   *New International Dictionary of New Testament Theology*, translated and revised, with additions, Colin Brown,

	ed., 3 vols., Exeter: Paternoster Press, 1975-1978.
NPNF fs	*Nicene and Post-Nicene Fathers*, First Series, 14 vols, Philip Schaff, ed., Reprint, Grand Rapids, MI: Eerdmans, 1979-1987.
NPNF ss	*Nicene and Post-Nicene Fathers*, Second Series, 14 vols. Philip Schaff and Henry Wace, eds., Grand Rapids, MI: Eerdmans, 1983.
PG	*Patrologia Graeca*, 162 vols., Paris: J.P. Migne, 1856–1866.
PL	*Patrologia Latina*, 221 vols., Paris: J.P. Migne, 1862–1865; Reprint, Turnbolti, Belgium: Typographi Brepols Editores Pontifichi, n.d.
TCJP	*The Theology of the Churches and the Jewish People: Statements by the World Council of Churches and its member churches.* Comments by Allan Brockway, Paul van Buren, Rolf Rendtorff and Simon Schoon, eds., Geneva: WWC Publications, 1988.
TDNT	*Theological Dictionary of the New Testament.* Gerhard Kittel and Gerhard Friedrich, eds., Translated by Geoffrey W. Bromiley, 9 vols., Grand Rapids, MI: Eerdmans, 1964–1972.

4. Other abbreviations

1:459	volume 1, page 459 or volume 1, column 459

Comm.	Commentary
Ep.	Epistle, Epistles
Hom.	Homily, Homilies
sec.	section
Serm.	Sermon, Sermons
WCC	The World Council of Churches

FOREWORD

Modern Israel, especially in its relations with its Arab neighbors, has been continually and conspicuously in the daily news ever since World War II. Less well known, but amply demonstrated by Dr. Diprose, is the contrasting fact that the concept of "Israel," and the continuing existence and role of the Jewish people has been hovering in the background while Christians have shaped their doctrinal expressions and the practical consequences resulting from them.

The early church was challenged as to whether Israel's sacred writings were to be considered as Sacred Scripture. The triumphant professing church of the Middle Ages assumed (without bothering to prove) that it had taken over the promises and blessings (but not the curses) that God had promised Israel. Our own time has seen the culmination of centuries of Christian Anti-Semitism in the German Holocaust and the subsequent debate as to whether Jewish people are considered to be saved—as Christians would understand it—by virtue of God's covenant with Israel. Dr. Diprose demonstrates that major areas of Christian doctrine have been shaped by the Church's attitudes towards Israel. But tragically for the Jewish people and for the Christian theological tradition, this crucial role of Israel has not been systematically, publicly, and generally reflected upon.

Dr. Diprose is to be commended for undertaking this wide-ranging study in order to demonstrate the need for such reflection. And it is especially fitting that he lives and works in the ancient city of Rome, to whose early Christians the apostle Paul wrote his own sustained reflection on the place of Israel. Sadly, Christians have all too rarely reflected upon the implications of Paul's conclusion in his epistle to the Roman Church: "Just as you . . . have now received mercy because of their disobedience, so . . . by the mercy shown to you, they too may now receive mercy" (Romans 11:30, 31). In repeated and various ways over the centuries, most Christians, and the Church in its theology, have been anything but merciful to Israel.

May this publication of Dr. Diprose's study be one small step toward correcting this ancient and continuing error.

Donald Tinder Ph.D.
Professor, Evangelische Theologische Faculteit, Louvain,
Belgium and Tyndale Theological Seminary, Amsterdam,
Netherlands

PREFACE

I have always been aware that Israel is important for Christian theology. However, for a long time it had seemed to me that the question of Israel had become some kind of theological football that two opposing teams of theologians kicked about in accordance with their particular agendas. For dispensationalists it was apparently important that ethnic Israel be given a high profile while for reformed theologians it was apparently important to show that, with the advent of the Church, ethnic Israel's significance had been irrevocably eclipsed. The result was that to affirm that there are institutional distinctions between Israel and the Church was tantamount to declaring oneself to be a dispensationalist while denial of such distinctions was a sign of reformed orthodoxy.

A few years ago I decided to consider Israel as a question in its own right and not as an adjunct to a given theological position. Following that decision, I made some interesting discoveries. For example, I discovered that two very different views concerning Israel have held sway in Christendom. During the early centuries, Israel was thought to be a renegade nation that should be treated with contempt. However, after the *Shoah*[1] and the birth of the modern State of Israel in 1948, a new view developed according to which Israel's status as a visible, elect nation exonerated its members from the need to exercise faith in Jesus Christ in order to be saved.

The antithetical nature of these two views puzzled me and suggested that factors other than the clear biblical message had determined their development. This was confirmed as I read many of the Church Fathers and then the literature pertaining to the current Jewish-Christian dialogue. I also noticed that the neglect of the biblical message concerning Israel had repercussions on Christian theology in general. While both views have important implications for hermeneutics, the effects of the earlier view were particularly evident in ecclesiology and eschatology, whereas the new view is having serious repercussions in soteriology and missiology.

Many people have helped—both directly and indirectly—to make this investigation possible. A conversation while walking with Patrick Sookhdeo around a lake in southern Italy prodded me to think more deeply into some of the relevant issues. Interaction with Professor Donald Tinder was also very fruitful. The footnotes bear witness to my great debt to numerous other scholars. On a more practical level special thanks is due to the Board of the Italian Bible Institute for granting me a brief sabbatical in which I was able to begin the project. In particular I wish to thank Bernard Oxenham who generously shouldered many of my responsibilities thus allowing me to engage in uninterrupted research for weeks at a time.

This project would not have been possible without adequate library facilities. In this regard I am grateful to Professor Daniele Garrone for the freedom he gave me to use the excellent Library of the Waldensian Faculty, Rome.

Special thanks also goes to the editorial staff of Authentic Media for their friendly attitude and their scrupulous attention to detail in the course of preparation of the manuscript for publication.

Last, but not least, special thanks is due to my wife Eunice and to our sons, Andrew and Jonathan, who not only accepted that I be unavailable to them for long hours but who have also offered encouragement and practical assistance during the various phases of the work.

INTRODUCTION

*". . . we realize that in this question [of the
relationship of the Church to Israel] the entire self-
understanding of the Church is at stake."[1]*

Since the tragic events of the *Shoah*[2] and the birth of
the modern State of Israel on May 14, 1948,[3] the interest
shown in God's ancient people has been sustained
and widespread. Awareness of the importance of the
minuscule State of Israel for the general well-being of
mankind was shown by the presence of seventy prime
ministers and heads of state at the funeral of Israeli Prime
Minister Yitzhak Rabin in November 1995. Furthermore,
large sectors of Christendom, such as those represented
by the World Council of Churches and the Roman
Catholic Church, are now involved in dialogue with the
Jewish people. Richard Harries speaks of the "existence
of an identical hope of the kingdom, a common mission
aimed at sanctifying God's name and . . . equal dignity in
dialogue."[4]

Considering the importance of Israel in the
Hebrew and Christian Scriptures, Christian theology
could be expected to give particular attention to these
developments. However, while the *Shoah* and the birth

1

of the modern State of Israel have led some Christian theologians to rethink the question of Israel's relationship to the Church, works of systematic theology continue to be produced which omit Israel altogether or include only marginal mention of her theological significance.[5] In the words of Gordon Lewis and Bruce A. Demarest, "the notion of institutional Israel is a missing link in much systematic theology."[6]

The absence of Israel in much of Christian theology has a long history. During the formative period of the Christian tradition,[7] the common view was that what was promised to Israel found its ultimate fulfillment in Jesus, the Israelite *par excellence*. It follows that the Church completely and permanently replaced ethnic Israel in the working out of God's plan as the recipient of Old Testament promises originally addressed to Israel. Although this view, variously known as "supersessionism" or "replacement theology,"[8] is now widely rejected, both popular opinion and Christian theology remain profoundly influenced by it.

It is conceivable that some avoid theologizing about Israel for quite a different reason. They fear that any attempt to take Israel seriously runs the risk of being labeled "dispensationalist." While it is true that Israel occupies an important place in dispensational theology, it is also true that reflection concerning the place of Israel in God's plan predates this school of thought by many centuries. The apostle Paul himself engaged in an in-depth study of the relationship of Israel to the rest of the divine program in the ninth, tenth, and eleventh chapters of Romans. In the Reformation era, Puritan theologians such as Henry Finch and Thomas Goodwin attributed great importance to Israel.[9] Moreover, the seminal works that led to the reconsideration of the place of Israel in the divine plan at the beginning of the nineteenth century came from very different sectors of Christianity than those generally associated with dispensationalism.[10]

I believe that Christian theology should consider Israel for her own sake and not as an adjunct to a particular theological system. It is my intention, therefore, to show that when Christian theology has failed to take into account all of the biblical data concerning Israel, much damage has been done to Christian thought and practice.[11]

After considering the evidence for Israel's uniqueness among the nations, I will address the thorny question of how the radical concept known as replacement theology originated. This will be followed by an investigation into the link between replacement theology and other aspects of Christian thought, particularly ecclesiology and eschatology.

Before proceeding, however, I must note here that ecclesiology and eschatology are not the only areas of Christian theology to have been affected by the Church's views concerning Israel. In fact, the omission of Israel in Christian theology has had detrimental, yet deterministic effects on a wide variety of theological issues.

For example, the basic assumption that the interpretation of the Old Testament was exclusively the prerogative of the Church, linked with the normalization of the allegorical method, led to the neglect of the Hebrew world view. This resulted in theological thought being set in an essentially Greek philosophical frame of reference.[12] This in turn led to, among other things, the polarization of the sovereignty of God and the free will of man. As Jaroslav Pelikan writes, "the Augustinian tradition has been affected by the loss of contact with Jewish thought, whose refusal to polarize the free sovereignty of God and the free will of man has frequently been labeled Pelagian."[13]

Another serious effect of the loss of constructive contact with the Hebrew world was the position which the Medieval Church assumed in the iconoclastic controversy. A person who favored the destruction of images was discredited as "one who thought like a Jew."[14] The result was that the Medieval Church supported the use of images in worship despite Scriptural prohibitions to do so.

Following the Shoah and the birth of the modern State of Israel, a very different view regarding Israel has gained widespread acceptance. Advocates of the new view claim that God's original covenant with Israel is equivalent to Christian salvation and discourage sharing the good news of their Messiah with Jewish people. This raises important questions for Christian soteriology and missiology. Underlying the development of both the old and new views is a common shortcoming: a selective use of Scripture.[15]

I have chosen to quote extensively from primary sources so that the reader can readily discern the relationship between the Church's view concerning Israel and the development of Christian thought. Although this approach may prove to be a little tedious at times, it has the considerable advantage of permitting the reader to participate in the evaluation of the data.

1

A UNIQUE PEOPLE

Israel in the Old Testament

The Origin of Israel

The term "Israel" appears over two thousand times in the Old Testament and seventy times in the New Testament. This term refers to a specific ethnic group[1] who believed itself to be united by a covenant with Yahweh, the only true God.[2] The name *Yisra'êl* was conferred on Jacob (Genesis 32:28), Abraham's grandson, and means "soldier of God"[3] or "God persists."[4] The significance of Abraham's offspring for general history is explained more fully in the words which God addressed to the patriarch at the moment of his call:

> Leave your country, your people and your father's
> household and go to the land I will show you.
> I will make you into a great nation
> and I will bless you;
> I will make your name great,
> and you will be a blessing.
> I will bless those who bless you,
> and whoever curses you I will curse;

> and all peoples on earth
>> will be blessed through you. (Genesis 12:1–3)

The call of Abram and the promises that God made to him at that time were ratified as a solemn covenant described as everlasting (Genesis 15:1–20; cf. 17:1–10; 22:17–18; 28:13–15). Thus the personal and family history of Abram would always be governed by covenant promise and divine sovereignty. This was immediately evident in the personal history of Abram and his wife Sarai. One year before Isaac, the son of promise, was born, God renamed the patriarch Abraham, meaning "father of many" (17:1–19). As for Sarai (renamed Sarah or "princess"), her sterility through the age of childbearing and her great age when Isaac was born (11:30; 18:11; 21:6–7), confirmed that Abraham's descendants through her were to be God's elect people and not simply a natural offspring. God's special relationship with Abraham and his descendants was soon recognized by surrounding peoples despite their human imperfections (Genesis 18–20; cf. 26:25–29; 28:15; 31:25–29).

Personal blessing under the promises was conditioned upon obedience to the God who made the covenant.[5] Those blessings contained in the covenant with Abraham did not include eternal salvation. Rather, according to the terms of the Abrahamic covenant, Israel as a whole was to be the special object of God's love and through them blessing was to flow to the whole earth.

Because of the promissory,[6] unconditional nature of God's covenant with Abraham, Isaac, and Jacob, this covenant was not abrogated when God stipulated a second, conditional, covenant with Israel at the time of Moses (Exodus 19:5–8; 24:4–8; cf. Galatians 3:15–18).

Thus the unconditional covenant remained operational, and the blessings promised to Abraham and to his descendants provide a key to understanding the history of this people, who, despite blatant transgression of the Mosaic covenant and the consequent application of its sanctions, continued to be the object of God's love (see Hosea chapters 1–3).

From being a patriarchal clan which gained the respect of neighboring peoples (Genesis 20; 26; 31), Jacob's descendants developed into a nation while living in Egypt, where they eventually became slaves of the Egyptian Pharaohs (see Genesis 47–50; Exodus 1). Following the Exodus,[7] in which God revealed his power and faithfulness to his elect people, the twelve tribes of Israel lived as wandering nomads for forty years. Later, following the partial conquest of the Promised Land, these tribes remained loosely associated with the tabernacle at Shiloh being the main element of national unity. At the time of the prophet Samuel, Israel became a powerful monarchy. However, there was a sharp decline in Israel's fortunes following the death of Solomon, David's son. It was characterized by the division of the nation into a northern and southern kingdom, the institutionalization of idolatry in the northern kingdom, fratricidal wars, and two disastrous exiles.

The second exile was followed by the partial restoration of the southern kingdom which enjoyed varying degrees of political independence. It was made up of the tribes of Judah and Simeon and those descending from members of the other ten tribes who had either remained in the territory of Judah at the time of the division of the kingdom or had defected to the southern kingdom during the reigns of Rehoboam and Asa (1 Kings 12:16–17;

2 Chronicles 11:13–17; 15:9). Presumably, their choice to identify with the southern kingdom was related to the association of both orthodox religious practice and the royal line of David in Jerusalem.

A Nation Set Apart

After the name "Israel" was conferred on the patriarch Jacob, the two names were used interchangeably (Genesis 46:29–30; Numbers 24:17; Psalm 146:5; 147:2). Moreover, Jacob's descendants were referred to both as "the house of Jacob" (Isaiah 2:2–5; Psalm 114:1) and "the house of Israel" (Genesis 31:33; Isaiah 5:7) or simply "Israelites" (Genesis 47:27; Exodus 14:28). This shows that the ethnic identity was closely related to the divine purpose in the history of the Jewish people.

This was clearly demonstrated shortly after Jacob's arrival in Egypt when he blessed the reigning pharaoh (Genesis 47:7). Inasmuch as the lesser person is blessed by the greater (Hebrews 7:7), this act highlights Israel's crucial role in God's plan as an instrument of blessing (Genesis 47:7; cf. 12:3). Subsequently, in a prophetic utterance, the aged Jacob went so far as to specify that it would be someone arising from the tribe of Judah that would eventually gain "the obedience of the nations" (49:8–12).

Israel's unique identity was further confirmed when God identified her as his "firstborn" at the time of Moses (Exodus 4:22–23). It received further, surprising confirmation when the pagan prophet Balaam was compelled by God to utter blessings upon Israel even though hired by Balak, king of Moab, to curse them. In his divinely inspired oracle, Balaam declared, "From the rocky peaks I see them, from the heights I view them. I see a people who live apart and do not consider themselves one of the nations" (Numbers 23:9; cf. Deuteronomy 23:4–5).

The reason why Israel was not included among the nations is explained by Moses: "The LORD your God . . . has declared that he will set you in praise, fame and honor high above all the nations he has made and that you will be a people holy to the LORD your God, as he promised" (Deuteronomy 26:19).

Because God chose to put his name upon Israel, this people had the possibility of being either more blessed or more severely castigated than the nations into whose destinies she could never be fully assimilated. Moreover, Moses taught that Israel would never be irreversibly assimilated into other nations (Deuteronomy 27–28), in fact, because of their particular relationship with God, the Israelites were not allowed to enter into mixed marriages (Deuteronomy 25:5–9; Joshua 23:12). Furthermore, because of God's close association with Israel, the attitude of other nations towards her had a direct bearing upon their national fortunes. Thus when Balaam looked out and saw Israel encamped tribe by tribe, the Spirit of God came upon him and he uttered this oracle: "May those who bless you be blessed and those who curse you be cursed!" (Numbers 24:2, 9; cf. Isaiah 54:17).

Awareness of Israel's uniqueness, which depended on her unique relationship with Yahweh, is a recurring theme on the lips of non-Israelites in the course of Old Testament history. For example, Rahab summarized the reaction of the population of Jericho to the mighty acts of God on behalf of Israel, with these words: "When we heard of it, our hearts melted and everyone's courage failed because of you, for the LORD your God is God in heaven above and on the earth below" (Joshua 2:11).

In the fifth century BC, Haman the Agagite, a high-ranking official in the court of the Persian King Xerxes, requested that Israel be annihilated. The terms with which he communicated his request show that the pagan nations of his day perceived Israel's uniqueness. Haman introduced his request to Xerxes with the following statement: "There is a certain people dispersed and scattered among the peoples in all the provinces of your kingdom whose customs are different from those of all other people and who do not obey the king's laws; it is not in the king's best interest to tolerate them" (Esther 3:8).

Besides affirming Israel's uniqueness, Haman's words imply the impossibility of adopting a neutral attitude towards this people. Either her uniqueness gained her the respect of the nations or she was likely to experience their intolerance. This is further seen in the sudden turn in fortunes in which Xerxes honored the Jew, Mordecai, for having revealed an assassination plot and at which Haman's wife Zeresh made this significant statement: "Since Mordecai, before whom your downfall has started is of Jewish origin, you cannot stand against him—you will surely come to ruin!" (Esther 6:13).

The Survival of Israel

It is not part of our purpose to rehearse all the Old Testament prophetic oracles concerning a future messianic age and their implications for Israel, so we will limit our attention to the question of whether or not the Hebrew Scriptures envisage a situation in which the special relationship which God had established with Israel could be revoked. We may begin by noting that God's decision to set his affection on Israel was in no way determined by their performance or national greatness but rather by his free will and sovereign purposes (Deuteronomy 7:7–8; 9:4–5). Similarly the survival of the kingdom of Judah, despite the blatant disobedience of kings such as Jehoram and Ahaziah (2 Kings 8:16–27), depended entirely on the covenant promises which God made to David (2 Samuel 7:16; 23:5; Psalm 89:3–4; 132:10–18).[8]

The unconditional nature of these earlier statements is paralleled in a surprising statement pronounced by the prophet Jeremiah. After insisting on the inevitability of the exile of Judah to Babylon and exhorting those who were already in exile to settle down and serve Nebuchadnezzar, Jeremiah turned to the constructive phase of his ministry. This began with a prophecy concerning the restoration of Israel and Judah to the land which God had given as an inheritance to Israel (Jeremiah 30:3; cf. 16:18; 31:10–11, 27–28). There follows what must be rated as one of the most important Old Testament prophecies (31:31–34).[9] It concerns a new covenant which God intends to make with Israel and Judah following a period of national repentance (vv. 18–19). The main characteristics of this new covenant are complete forgiveness for sins, the writing of God's law on the hearts of his people, and God becoming "their God" in a way not yet experienced (vv. 33–34). What interests us at this point is the statement which undergirds the prophecy, making its fulfillment certain:

> This is what the LORD says,
> he who appoints the sun to shine by day,
> who decrees the moon and stars to shine by night,
> who stirs up the sea so that its waves roar—
>   the LORD Almighty is his name:

> "Only if these decrees vanish from my sight,"
>> declares the LORD,
> "will the descendants of Israel ever cease to be a
>> nation before me."
> This is what the LORD says:
> "Only if the heavens above can be measured
>> and the foundations of the earth below be
>> searched out
> will I reject all the descendants of Israel
>> because of all they have done," declares the
>> LORD. (Jeremiah 31:35–37)

Earlier in his prophetic ministry, Jeremiah insisted that the sin of Judah had made judgment by exile certain just as the northern kingdom of Israel had been duly judged. However, he now says that Israel's failure to perform according to expectations cannot upset God's plans. Israel's sin can no more thwart God's future purposes for the nation than can the heavens be measured and all the secrets of the earth be known. Thus it is clear that God will not reject the descendants of Israel because of the nation's unfaithfulness. But there is more: only in the case of the collapse of God's sovereign control over the physical universe would Israel cease to exist as a nation.

God makes a similar statement through the prophecy of Malachi, in a context which affirms the immutability of God: "I the LORD do not change. So you, O descendants of Jacob, are not destroyed" (Malachi 3:6). Thus, though from the time of the patriarchs Israel continually turned away from God's decrees, there is still hope for her future (v. 7).

It may be argued that, in the Old Testament, expressions suggesting permanence, such as we find here, can refer to a lengthy but limited time.[10] However, what cannot be doubted is that the words of Jeremiah mean that Israel will continue to exist as a nation until they enter into the new covenant relationship described in the preceding verses. Moreover, it is impressive that in Isaiah 66:22 the permanence of Israel, as a distinct nation, is put in relation to the permanence of the new heavens and new earth.

The New Testament Witness to Israel's Uniqueness

The Problem Posed by Israel's Unbelief

The fact that Jesus restricted his own ministry almost exclusively to Israel (Matthew 10:5; 15:24) is another strong indication of their uniqueness in the counsels of God. It is not surprising that Jesus' contemporaries were more interested in gaining political advantage from his supernatural powers than they were in taking to heart his insistence on the need for spiritual renewal (John 6:14–69). What nation, living under political oppression, would have reacted differently? However, despite the failure of the majority of the Jewish nation to listen to Jesus, some Jews did become sincere disciples and their number increased significantly after the Pentecost event.

The number of Jews who accepted the message preached by Jesus' apostles, though considerable (Acts 2:41; 4:4; 5:14; 6:1; 21:20), was not noticeably different from that of converts to Israel's Messiah from other nations (Acts 11:19–26; 17:1–4; 1 Thessalonians 1:6–9; Acts 18:9–10; 19:8–10). According to the New Testament writers, the unbelief of the majority of the Jews was without excuse, as the ministry of both Jesus and his apostles had been authenticated by the miraculous signs which the Old Testament had taught Israel to expect with the coming of the Messiah (Matthew 11:2–6 [Isaiah 35:4–6; 61:1]; John 15:22–24; Acts 2:16–22, 32–33; Hebrews 2:1–4). What is more, unbelieving Jews sought to prevent the Gentiles, who had previously been excluded from the privileges enjoyed by Israel (Ephesians 2:11–12), from hearing the gospel in order that they might be saved (Acts 13:44–45; 17:5–9; 1 Thessalonians 2:14–16).

Israel's unbelief has the potential to lead to two diverse but equally troubling conclusions. First, the gospel of God's grace could be the product of the imagination of the followers of Jesus of Nazareth, and second, God may have abandoned Israel because of their unbelief. The second of these conclusions is hardly less serious than the first because in Jeremiah's day God had promised that he would not abandon Israel because of her sin (Jeremiah 31:31–37). If it could be shown that he has now done so, not only would that imply the end of Israel's uniqueness, it would also raise questions concerning God's faithfulness. Paul grapples with these two conclusions in Romans chapters 9–11.

The Grounds of Israel's Uniqueness: Election in Romans 9–11
One of the key concepts in these chapters is the election of Israel which is seen in the apostle's paradoxical statement in 11:28. We will begin with a brief consideration of this statement and then seek to clarify the apparent paradox by contextually studying the other uses of the word *eklogē* ("election") in these chapters.

"Enemies of the Gospel" Yet "Elect" 11:28–29. "As far as the gospel is concerned, they are enemies on your account" (v. 28a). It is clear from their description as enemies that "they" refers to the part of Israel which has been temporarily hardened because of their refusal to believe in Jesus as the Messiah of Israel (see v. 25). Here Paul repeats the concept, already affirmed earlier in verse 13, that unbelieving Israel's opposition to the gospel represents an advantage for the Gentile nations. The apostle then makes a statement which, because it contrasts so strongly with the first half of the verse, must be understood as a basic assumption of Paul's thought: "but as far as election is concerned, they are loved on account of the patriarchs, for God's gifts and his call are irrevocable" (vv. 28b–29).

According to Paul, unbelieving Israel retains her status as an elect people. Does this assertion mean that the majority of ethnic Israelites, although unbelieving, possess salvation? According to the Jewish scholar Raphael Jospe, chosenness and the obtaining of salvation are not identical concepts.[11] Likewise, the apostle Paul, following the prophet Isaiah, distinguishes between being members of God's elect people and possessing salvation (Romans 9:27). Yet some Christian scholars treat election and salvation as though they were synonyms.[12] One purpose of our survey of the use of *eklogē* in these chapters is to find out whether this is justified.

What Paul Teaches in Romans 9 Concerning the Election of Israel. The word "election" first occurs in the opening section of this chapter to illustrate the existence of a more authentic Israel within historical Israel (v. 6b).

Paul then elaborates on God's elective purpose within the context of Abraham's physical descendants (vv. 7–13).[13]

The apostle could have illustrated the concept of an Israel within Israel by appealing to examples taken from the history of his nation, as when some members of the northern kingdom defected to Judah during the times of the reforms promoted by kings Asa and Jehoshaphat (see 2 Chronicles 15:9; 19:4).[14] However, Paul prefers to ground his more nuanced definition of Israel in divine election (*eklogēn*, v. 11). Paul makes the point that not all natural children (*ta tekna tēs sarkos*) are to be considered "children of God," but only the descendants of Isaac, whose existence depends upon divine promise. In other words, a special family relationship exists between God and the children of promise. This relationship held good even when Israel transgressed God's commands. Thus God declared through his prophet Amos, "You only have I chosen of all the families of the earth; therefore I will punish you for all your sins" (Amos 3:2).

God's purpose of election is further seen in the terms of the covenant which he confirmed with Isaac and Jacob (v. 7; cf. Genesis 21:12; 26:23–24; 28:13–14). These included the promise of national greatness, a land, and the role of bringing blessing to all nations (Genesis 12:1–3; 13:14–15). Because God uniquely became "the God of Israel," Isaac and his descendants were put in a position of particular privilege so far as receiving salvation was concerned. However, nowhere is it suggested that Israel's advantageous position guaranteed salvation to all members of the nation, neither did it exclude that Ishmael and those who did not descend from Isaac and Jacob, could experience salvation. On the contrary, according to the terms of the covenant, the blessing of salvation was to become available to all families of the earth through the elect nation of Israel (Genesis 12:3; Isaiah 49:5–6; Galatians 3:8–14).

The election of Jacob and his descendants gave expression to God's sovereign will (*prothesis* Romans 9:11). The fact that it was already determined "before the twins were born or had done anything good or bad" demonstrates that the election of Jacob rather than of Esau did not depend in any way on the merits or demerits of the persons concerned. The corollary of this truth, often repeated by the Hebrew prophets, is that the full outworking of God's purpose through Israel will not depend upon their faithfulness (Isaiah 54:10–17; 65:1–8; Jeremiah 5:10–11, 18; 31:35–37; Ezekiel 16:59–63; Hosea 1–14; cf. Romans 11:28–29).

Paul brings together two Old Testament passages in order to show that God's way of dealing with Israel is the fruit of sovereign choice: "'The older will serve the younger' (see Genesis 25:22–23). Just as it is written, 'Jacob have I loved but Esau have I hated,'" (Romans 9:12–13; cf. Malachi 1:1–3).

When the contexts of these two quotations are kept in mind, it becomes evident that the prediction—"The older will serve the younger"—concerns two nations, Israel and Edom, and not the twins as persons. The fact that Esau never served Jacob (in fact it was Jacob who bowed before Esau (Genesis 33:1–4)) confirms that it is the nations which descended from the two brothers that are being discussed here. Not until the time of David would descendants of Esau serve descendants of Jacob (2 Samuel 8:14).

The subject of the second prophecy, pronounced about 1500 years after the birth of Jacob and Esau, is clearly the nation of Edom and its territory (Malachi 1:2–5). During the intervening centuries, the descendants of Esau not only had shown hostility toward Israel, they had also tried to prevent the realization of God's plan through Israel (Numbers 20:14–21; cf. Ezekiel 25:12–14). While it is true that God's love for Israel was the result of sovereign choice, Israel had also experienced just judgment and chastisement because of her transgressions. Yet, because God had put his name on Israel and made solemn covenant promises to Abraham, Isaac, and Jacob, he always returned to bless the nation when chastisement induced repentance (2 Chronicles 7:13–14; Hosea 11:7–11; 14:1–9).

We have noted that the last clause of the Abrahamic covenant, "and all peoples on earth will be blessed through you" (Genesis 12:3), implied that Israel's election was to be in some way instrumental.[15] However, Israel did not always understand her election in these terms.[16] Thus in the continuation of Romans chapter nine, Paul develops the theme of God's mercy, which has in view the blessing of the Gentile nations as well as Israel (9:15–16, 22–24; cf. 11:30–32).

What Paul Teaches in Romans 11 Concerning the Election of Israel. Paul opens the chapter by confronting the widespread idea that God had turned his back on the Jews: "I ask then: Did God reject his people?"[17] His answer is emphatic: "By no means!"[18] Paul confirms this negation with a biographical note: he himself is at the same time an apostle and servant of Christ Jesus, an Israelite, a descendant of Abraham from the tribe of Benjamin (11:1). He then adds a more general consideration: "God did not reject his people whom he foreknew" (v. 2). In other words, God intentionally loves the Jews, and is reserving a special destiny for them. Consequently, it is unthinkable that he would reject them.[19]

Having excluded categorically that God has repudiated Israel, Paul immediately describes an element of continuity between present events involving the nation and its past history. He utilizes Elijah the prophet, who, in a moment of discouragement, thought that he was the only believer left in Israel. In reality there were seven thousand Israelites who had not "bowed the knee to Baal" (1 Kings 19:10–18). Paul then affirms, "So too, at the present time there is a remnant chosen by grace" (*leimma kat' eklogēn*, v. 5).

According to Refoulé, the remnant chosen by grace corresponds to the true Israel of which Paul speaks in 9:6b; moreover the *pas Israēl* of 11:26 corresponds to this elect remnant viewed in its entirety.[20] However, Cranfield observes that, if the expression "all Israel will be saved" referred to the sum of the elect chosen by grace during the present time, the statement would repeat something already spelled out in the chapter, which would make verses 25–27 an anticlimax, whereas in Paul's argument these verses clearly form a climax.[21]

The attribution of the same value to *eklogē* (election) in 11:1–10 as in 9:11 is based on the conviction that these passages contain parallel treatments of the theme of election.[22] In reality chapter nine affirms the election of the nation, through Isaac. The choice of Isaac, and consequently the existence of Israel as the people of the covenant, depends only on the free will of God. In chapter 11, on the other hand, the term *eklogē* is qualified by the words "by grace" (*charitos*, v. 5). This is the first and indeed only time in Paul's writings that he qualifies "election" in this way. Moreover, it is clear from the context (9:31–11:7a) that election which is the product of a work of grace is linked with faith and is election unto salvation.[23] That Paul here intends election unto salvation is confirmed by his emphatic statement in verse six which links the present discussion with his teaching in the earlier part of Romans, that salvation is by grace through faith and not by works (see especially 3:21–31 and 9:30–10:13). Thus, whereas in 9:11 "election" refers to God's sovereign choice concerning the national destiny of Israel, in 11:5 and 11:7 "election" concerns a relatively small number of Israelites who have obeyed the Gospel in the way described in 10:9–13.

There is undoubtedly a tension between the way *eklogē* is used in 9:11 and its more restrictive use in 11:5 and 7. We may ask: What now of "the others" in verse seven, are they no longer included in the special election of Israel? In other words, does Israel's status as an elect nation now depend on her own faithfulness and no longer on the sovereign purpose of God? Paul was evidently aware that his words concerning the election "according to grace" could be construed as limiting God's interest in Israel to those Jews who had become members of the Church. Thus, after distinguishing between "the elect [according to grace]" and "the others" (*hoi de loipoi*), he applied himself to defining the present and future status of "the others"—the unbelieving majority of Israel. One of his purposes in pursuing this theme was to prevent his Gentile readers from becoming arrogant (vv. 13, 19–21). In light of the conclusion in verse 28, we can safely say that Paul also is confirming the election of Israel despite the nation's failure to recognize Jesus as their Messiah. Nothing, not even their opposition to the gospel, could cancel the special love of God for his people. It is this election of Israel which makes her eschatological salvation certain. Likewise, her status as an elect people explains why, in the present time, even in her unbelief, Israel contributes to the enrichment and the reconciliation with God of the other nations of the world (vv. 11–15).

The Witness of History from AD 70 to the Present

The survival of the people of Israel and of their culture over three millennia and in almost impossible conditions requires an explanation. In the preceding sections of this chapter, we have considered some biblical evidence for Israel's uniqueness. We have seen that Paul affirmed this uniqueness, grounding it in their special election which was not rescinded despite the refusal of many of the Jews to recognize Jesus as their Messiah. In subsequent centuries, however, the uniqueness of the Jewish people was contested by some of the most influential members of the Christian Church. Canon law, for instance, degraded the Jews to a status much lower than that of other peoples. Thus it is appropriate to ask whether there continued to be any evidence of Israel's uniqueness during the Christian era.[24]

Most of the nineteen centuries which have run their course from the destruction of the temple in Jerusalem have been marked by intense conflict between rabbinical Judaism and Christendom.[25] Sheer inequality of numerical strength has meant that the Jews have been constrained to play the part of the underdog vis-à-vis a triumphant Church. Contempt and abuse meted out by representatives of Christendom have often fostered uprisings in which instigations, like those of Chrysostom "to hate them and long for their blood,"[26] have inspired massacres.

There is a fascinating testimony to the link between the Christian religion and persecution of the Jews in the eleventh century in Sir Walter Scott's famous novel *Ivanhoe*:

> Except perhaps the flying-fish, there was no race existing on the earth, in the air, or the waters, who are the object of such an unintermitting, general, and relentless persecution as the Jews of this period. Upon the slightest and most unreasonable pretences, as well as upon accusations the most absurd and groundless, their persons and property were exposed to every turn of popular fury; for Norman, Saxon, Dane, and Briton, however adverse these races were to each other, contended which should look with greatest detestation upon a people, whom it was accounted a point of religion to hate, to revile, to despise, to plunder, and to persecute.[27]

For their part, the Jewish people have maintained their own traditions and "have taken to the whole world the witness, often heroic, of their faithfulness to the one God."[28] Furthermore, in spite of the contempt in which they have been held and repeated waves of aggressive anti-Semitism,[29] they have found the energy to make significant contributions to human well-being and culture. One example of this is their cultural contribution during the period known as "the Golden Age of Spain"—the eleventh, twelfth, and thirteenth centuries. Another is the rapid rise of Jewish scholars to positions of influence in England after Oliver Cromwell gave tacit permission for Jewish resettlement in 1656. The celebrated career of Isaac Abendana at Oxford University (1663–1699) is but one example of Jewish integration into many different spheres of English life in the seventeenth century. Interestingly enough, the first Jewish knighthood was awarded as early as 1700.[30]

But the phenomenon is even more general. For example, the Jews, often constrained to uproot and resettle, were mediators for different civilizations, philosophical concepts, and scientific knowledge. Jews were primarily responsible for the translation of ancient Greek and Roman texts first into Arabic and later into Latin on the eve of the Renaissance.[31]

The quality and extent of the cultural contribution of the Jews is reflected, in recent times, in the number of Nobel Prize[32] winners of Jewish origin. A survey of the period from 1910 to 1960 shows that during that half century more than thirty Jews, mostly of German origin, received the Nobel Prize in fields such as medicine, physics, and chemistry.[33] In subsequent years, further Nobel Prizes in science and literature have been awarded to persons of Jewish origin. Moreover, in 1960 no less than thirty-two Jews were members of the Royal Society of the English Academy of Science.[34]

This is all the more remarkable when it is remembered that most of these Jewish contributions were made in a climate of anti-Semitism. Many of the Jewish members of the Royal Society were Jews who had found refuge from anti-Semitic persecution in England.[35] Even Albert Einstein, who was awarded the Nobel Prize for physics in 1922 and was declared the man of the twentieth century by Time magazine,[36] drew upon himself a continual stream of verbal abuse and was forced into exile, by reason of his race.[37]

All attempts to exterminate the Jews, whether perpetrated in God's name or not,[38] have met with failure. However, there have been other threats to their survival including the physical and cultural constrictions of ghetto existence,[39] the pressure put on them to convert to Christianity *en masse* during the twelfth, fourteenth, and fifteenth centuries,[40] repeated expulsions,[41] and attempts to assimilate them into Christian or secular society.

A particularly dangerous development for the survival of Jewry was the achievement of the great Jewish scholar Moses Mendelssohn (1729–1786) in the breaking down of the cultural and social barrier between Jew and Gentile in Germany. Roth summarizes his influence as follows: "In the years following Mendelssohn's death, hundreds of his followers and admirers carried his principles to their logical conclusion by going over to the dominant religion, as he himself had gone over to the dominant culture."[42] Thus in the latter part of the eighteenth century, wholesale assimilation began to be seen in Europe as a viable solution to an age-long problem, a solution that was reflected in the political policies of Joseph II of Austria, Louis XVI of France, and the Granduca of Tuscany, Leopoldo I.

However, assimilation was to prove impossible. While the French Revolution held the promise of greater emancipation for the Jews, the *Code Napoléon*, by creating a Jewish Sanhedrin and sundry laws for Jewish citizens, prepared the way for more persecution after the fall of the Napoleonic Empire.[43]

The acme of all attempts to destroy the Jews, and at the same time, the ultimate demonstration that the policy of assimilation had failed, was reached with the policies of the Third Reich (1934–1945). Jewish families, who for generations had been assimilated in German society, were listed among those to be exterminated. Adolf Hitler was so convinced that he was about to exterminate the Jewish race that he ordered the concentration of objects of Jewish cultural interest in the city of Prague, where he planned to construct a large Jewish museum, in order that Jewish culture would not be totally forgotten by humanity.[44]

While the perpetrators of the pogroms and the Third Reich were bent on destroying the Jewish communities within their reach, a very different movement called Zionism[45] was gaining momentum within Jewry itself. This movement had the ultimate aim of "securing for the Jewish people a home in Palestine guaranteed by public law."[46] This was finally achieved with the birth of the modern State of Israel on May 14, 1948. The subsequent history of this elect people is common knowledge and it is no longer possible to ignore the surprising survival of the Jewish nation.

The Place of Israel in God's Plan

At the conclusion of this brief survey of evidence of Israel's uniqueness, it seems appropriate to summarize what the Scriptures teach concerning the purposes which God is working out through his elect people. Israel's special status as an elect nation was never intended to be an end in itself. One of the terms of God's covenant promise to Abraham, Isaac, and Jacob was that "all peoples on earth will be blessed through you" (Genesis 12:3; 26:4; 28:14). In reiterating this covenant promise to Jacob, God explicitly stated his plan to bless the world "through [Israel] and [her] offspring" (Genesis 28:14).

Even in Old Testament times, while the nation of Israel was in the process of learning to know and obey God, God so ordered their existence as to bring blessing to others through them. To mention just a few examples, Israel was instrumental in making known the true God to the Egyptians at the time of the Exodus, to the Ninevites at the time of Jonah, and to all those living under the dominion of the Babylonian king Nebuchadnezzar at the time of Daniel (Exodus 1–15, Jonah, Daniel 1–4).

The supreme example of the offspring of Abraham, Isaac, and Jacob bringing blessing to the whole of mankind is, of course, the saving work of Jesus the Messiah, "son of David, the son of Abraham," accomplished during his first advent (Matthew 1:1, 21; cf. Isaiah 49:1–7). No blessing can compare with the gift of eternal salvation which is offered to all peoples on the basis of the Jewish Messiah's substitutionary death and resurrection (Romans 3:21–4:25). In this connection it should not be forgotten that it was Jesus himself who insisted that "salvation is from the Jews" (John 4:22).

Even the present hardening of unbelieving Israel has, according to Paul, the positive purpose of enriching the Gentile world by favoring its reconciliation to God (Romans 11:15a), much as the Babylonian captivity brought blessing to pagan kings and their subjects (Daniel chapters 2, 4, and 6). It is no accident that Gentiles who respond in faith to the gospel thereby become "fellow citizens with God's people" (Ephesians 2:19). In fact, by means of their relationship with Israel's Messiah, Jews and Gentiles are joined together, sharing the blessing promised to Abraham. The Bible further predicts that the return of unbelieving Israel to the Lord will be a means of exceptional blessing for the rest of the world (Romans 11:12–27).

Finally, if Jeremiah 31:35–37 and Isaiah 66:22 are read in light of the survival of Israel, it becomes apparent that the history of Israel also constitutes a powerful sign of God's faithfulness.

Conclusion

The biblical and historical evidence for Israel's uniqueness fully justifies the following statement which emanated from the inaugural assembly of the World Council of Churches: "In the design of God, Israel has a unique position. It was Israel with whom God made His covenant by the call of Abraham. It was Israel to whom God revealed His name and gave His law. It was to Israel that He sent His prophets with their message of judgment and of grace. It was Israel to whom He promised the coming of His Messiah. By the history of Israel God prepared the manger in which in the fullness of time He put the Redeemer of all mankind, Jesus Christ."[47]

Whatever our conviction concerning the present significance of Israel in the divine plan, we are bound to admit that the nation which God called into being through Abraham, Isaac, and Jacob, continues to be a protagonist on the world stage. The best explanation for this is her continuing status as God's elect people. It is because Israel retains her elect status that the Church, in order to not become presumptuous, is obliged to seriously consider the place of this nation in God's plan.[48]

2

REPLACEMENT THEOLOGY AND THE NEW TESTAMENT

The Present Debate

For over nineteen centuries the Jewish people have been an object of contempt and suspicion. What has come to be called "replacement theology" is widely perceived as being one of the causes of this attitude.[1] According to this concept, Israel has been repudiated by God and has been replaced by the Church in the working out of his plan.[2] A variation of this idea is that true Israel always has been the Church.[3]

It is clear from the New Testament writings that much which was formerly true of Israel is in fact true of the Church. Israel enjoyed a special relationship with God based on election, so does the Church. Just as Israel was called to be a light to the nations, so Christ has entrusted a missionary mandate to the Church. It also seems clear that Jesus' decision to choose twelve disciples had the purpose of convincing Israel that the continuation of salvation history, during the period beginning with the coming of the Holy Spirit at Pentecost, was to be linked primarily with the Church. Thus no one can deny that the Church stands in continuity with Israel in the working out of God's plan. The question is whether this implies the cessation of Israel's special elective status and thus the eclipse of her significance in salvation history. It is to this claim that we will be referring when using the expression "replacement theology" in the following pages.

According to some scholars, the roots of replacement theology are to be found in the New Testament. According to others, its origin is to be sought in post-apostolic times. Which of these two positions is correct? Can it be demonstrated that the New Testament itself teaches the cessation of Israel's special election now that God is calling his people from all nations, or that being part of true Israel does not entail a physical relationship with Abraham?

If replacement theology is taught in the New Testament, we must either accept this concept as an aspect of Christian orthodoxy or adopt a critical attitude towards the New Testament writings themselves. On the other hand, if it turns out that replacement theology developed in post-apostolic times, we would expect that its acceptance into the Christian tradition would modify other aspects of Christian theology as well.

To keep our investigation in focus, it is helpful to remember that replacement theology was the majority position within Christendom from post-apostolic times until the middle of the nineteenth century. However, just three months after the founding of the modern State of Israel in May 1948 the First Assembly of the World Council of Churches issued a cautious repudiation of the concept.[4] Subsequent statements emanating from ecumenical circles have included either an implicit or an overt admission that the Church was partly to blame for the Holocaust due to the fomentation of anti-Judaic attitudes through its theology of contempt.[5] In 1965, in the context of the Vatican II Council, the Roman Catholic Church also made a statement[6] judged by Jaroslav Pelikan to be "the most forceful official Christian affirmation of the permanence of the covenant with Israel, at least since the ninth, tenth, and eleventh chapters of the Epistle to the Romans."[7]

Official repudiation of replacement theology implied the need to reflect on the origin of the concept. An influential contribution to this discussion was made by the Roman Catholic scholar Rosemary R. Ruether with the publication of her book *Faith and Fratricide*.[8] According to Ruether, Christology was the key factor in the development of Christian anti-Judaism.[9] The way Ruether builds her case shows the importance of distinguishing between "gospel" and "theological embroidery."[10] In fact the form of Christology criticized by Ruether is colored by the realized eschatology of later centuries, in particular the claim of the Church to be the normative expression of the Kingdom of God.

A variety of reactions to Ruether's work were published together under the title *Anti-Semitism and the Foundations of Christianity*.[11] In his Preface to this book, James Parkes wrote, "the foundations of anti-Semitism, and the responsibility for the holocaust, lie ultimately in the New Testament."[12] However, John Meagher, author of the first essay, does not agree with him. While admitting that there is something very amiss in the way Christian theology understands the Jews, he believes that its function was "to whitewash and justify an antagonism that sprang mainly from other sources."[13] Monika K. Hellwig[14] also denies that anti-Semitism is rooted in New Testament Christology. She affirms, "It is rather a series of unquestioned ethnocentric assumptions arising out of the particular patterns of our history (anachronistically) to read back into the story of Jesus and into the doctrine that he is Christ and Lord [and that this implies] a divinely ordained ending of the covenant of Israel, giving way to the new era of the covenant of Christians."[15]

Debate has continued into the present. In an important contribution, Jeffrey Siker traces the use made of Abraham in New Testament and post-apostolic writings up to the time of Justin Martyr.[16] He concludes that some New Testament writings, in particular the Gospel of John, do anticipate what became the common understanding: that Gentile inclusion in the new covenant implies Jewish exclusion.[17] We will consider the evidence of John's Gospel later in this chapter. At this point it suffices to mention that when considering the New Testament evidence it is important to bear in mind that Jewish particularism and God's universal purpose already coexist in the promise of God to Abraham as recorded in Genesis 12:1–3. It follows also that an emphasis on either Jewish particularism or God's universal purpose for mankind elsewhere in Scripture does not in itself imply the exclusion of the other aspect.

In another important work published about the same time as Siker's book, James Dunn argued that most if not all of the conflict between the Church and the Synagogue witnessed to in the New Testament was in reality an in-house debate comparable to other such debates within Second Temple Judaism.[18] However, reputable evangelical theologians continue to consider some form of replacement theology axiomatic to a correct interpretation of Scripture.[19] For this reason and considering the role of this concept in the general development of Christian thought,[20] it is appropriate to re-examine the evidence for its origin in apostolic and post-apostolic times. In the present chapter we will consider some New Testament passages thought to contain evidence for replacement theology. In the next chapter we will consider the tensions which developed between the Church and unbelieving Jews in the years following the fateful Jewish war of AD 66–70 as well as the post-canonical writings, beginning with pseudo Barnabas and terminating with Origen.[21]

The New Testament and the Present Status of the Jewish People

New Testament Passages Thought to Support Replacement Theology

John 8:30–59. Jeffrey Siker believes that "the contrast between *sperma Abraam* ("descendants of Abraham") and *tekna Abraam* ("children of Abraham") points to the heart of the dispute in John 8:31–47."[22] The Jews describe themselves as *sperma Abraam* in 8:33 and Jesus concedes this (v. 37). But in Siker's opinion, by describing his Jewish opponents as "descendants of Abraham" while excluding that they are "children of Abraham" (v. 39), Jesus denies that Abraham is their father "in any meaningful way" (cf. v. 15). Siker then proceeds to link 8:39 with 1:12 and suggests that in the fourth Gospel *teknon Abraam* ("child of Abraham") and *teknon theou* ("child of God") are equivalent terms. Thus anyone who meets the conditions of 1:12, whether a physical descendant of Abraham or not, becomes both a child of God and a child of Abraham. Unbelieving Jews on the other hand, are "children of the Devil" (v. 44).[23] Siker concludes that according to the fourth Gospel,

Jewish opponents of the Johannine community "have no legitimate claim to being children of Abraham."[24]

Some comment is called for. The Greek text of John 8:44, which links Jesus' Jewish opponents with the Devil, does not contain the word *tekna* ("children") as Siker avers.[25] The text reads *humeis ek tou patros tou diabolou este* (lit. "out of your father the devil you are"). Second, it is an exaggeration to say that Jesus denies that Abraham is the father of these Jews "in any meaningful way" considering that Jesus addresses them with the words *Abraam ho patēr humōn* ("Abraham your father") in verse 56. While the Jews who opposed Jesus were not, according to John, "children of God" (1:12) and could not be described as *spiritual* "children of Abraham,"[26] there still was a real sense in which they could legitimately call Abraham their father (8:56).

When evaluating what some contemporary writers consider anti-Judaic attitudes in the fourth Gospel, it should be remembered that it was no novelty to deny the status of "children of God" to disobedient Jews. In Deuteronomy 14:1–29 Moses makes it clear that being "children of God" implies obedience to the covenant. Moreover, the "Song of Moses" contains the following statement: "They have acted corruptly toward him; to their shame they are no longer his children, but a warped and crooked generation" (Deuteronomy 32:5). So the issue turns not on language but rather on whether Jesus is really the Christ, as the writer of the fourth Gospel has set out to demonstrate (John 20:30–31). If he is, those who fail to recognize this fact are disobedient and thus cannot be considered children of God according to Deuteronomy 32:5. Moreover, if the words "you belong to your father, the devil" (John 8:44)[27] are understood in light of the

Jewish way of speaking in Jesus' time, they no longer appear to be anti-Judaic nor a sign that unbelieving Israel has been repudiated by God. In fact a little later in the same conversation, Jesus' Jewish opponents express the conviction that he has a demon (v. 52).

A wider study of Johannine terminology concerning unbelievers confirms that the words attributed to Jesus in John 8:44 are not anti-Judaic. In 1 John 3:10 all of humanity, not just the Jewish people, are divided into *tekna theou* ("children of God") and *tekna tou diabolou* ("children of the devil") to indicate those who are born of God and those who are not (v. 9). Further on in the same letter, John affirms, "We know that we are children of God, and that the whole world is under the control of the evil one" (5:19). Thus it is faulty exegesis to take Jesus' phrase "you belong to your father, the devil," in isolation and read anti-Judaic attitudes into it while failing to consider the parallel expressions used elsewhere in John's writings.[28] It is certain that the words "children of the devil" used in 1 John 3:10 do not have anti-Judaic connotations. Neither is John the only one to report Jesus' use of strong language. In Matthew 16:23 we read of Jesus using the word "Satan" to describe, not opponents, but the apostle Peter.

Perhaps the most significant of all references to "the Jews" in John's Gospel are those found in chapter four. Here Jesus refers to himself as a Jew (v. 9); moreover his answer to the Samaritan woman's question concerning the right place to worship includes this significant statement: "we [Jews] worship what we do know, for salvation is from the Jews" (v. 22). According to Jesus, the Jews have a unique knowledge of God; furthermore, only as a Jew could Jesus contribute to God's saving work (cf. v. 42).

Thus the fourth Gospel, which contains the clearest statements concerning the incarnation (1:14; 16:28), also contains the clearest statement concerning the whole world's indebtedness to the Jewish nation.

Matthew 21:42–44. Jesus addressed the Jewish leaders who rejected him with these words: "Therefore I tell you that the kingdom of God will be taken away from you and given to a people who will produce its fruit." According to Chrysostom, the whole parable of the tenants and this conclusion in particular, teaches the repudiation of the Jews.[29] In reality, the subject of the sentence is not the Jews themselves but rather the kingdom with which they had enjoyed a special relationship.

According to Scot McKnight, this announcement reflects the thrust of Matthew's Gospel: "the message of the kingdom is for all, and one of the major foundations for this offer is the suspension of national privilege."[30] On the other hand, David Hill agrees with Chrysostom when he writes, "the Jewish nation, as a corporate entity, had now forfeited its elect status."[31] Hill reaches this conclusion in spite of having previously observed that "Matthew intentionally differentiates between the eschatological kingdom (which the Jews never possessed, in any case) and the 'sovereignty of God' over Israel, expressed in terms of the special covenantal relationship."[32]

The denial that Israel possesses the eschatological kingdom does not imply that her special covenantal relationship with God has terminated. D.A. Carson understands the announcement to refer to Israel's role as agent in the administration of the kingdom: "Strictly speaking, then, verse 43 does not speak of transferring the locus of the people of God from Jews to Gentiles, though it may hint at this insofar as that locus now extends far beyond the authority of the Jewish rulers (cf. Acts 13:46; 18:5–6; 1 Peter 2:9); instead, it speaks of the ending of the role the Jewish religious leaders played in mediating God's authority."[33]

The post-resurrection mandate which Jesus entrusted to his followers spelled out the exact nature of the authority conferred upon them and their mediatorial role in the administration of God's rule (Matthew 28:18–20). Although the Jewish people, as such, do not feature in this mandate, the overwhelming majority of the first generation of Christ's witnesses were Israelites. Moreover, we are reminded in various parts of Acts that the Church's role in the present administration of the kingdom must not be confused with the eschatological kingdom (Acts 1:6–8; 3:19–31; 14:21–23).

Acts 15:1–18. The question addressed at the Jerusalem Conference was whether Gentile converts were required to accept circumcision and embrace the Mosaic law in order to be saved (Acts 15:1–5). Peter's negative answer (vv. 7–11) was based on the way he had seen God work in the house of Cornelius where he had witnessed the purification of the hearts of Gentiles who had believed the Gospel through a direct work of the Holy Spirit. It is significant that Peter does not mention water baptism in the place of Jewish circumcision as essential to salvation, although he had in fact baptized the converts at Caesarea (10:47–48).

The distinctiveness of James' contribution to the discussion (vv. 14–18) lies in his use of the term *laos* ("people") and in the fact that he puts the Gentile mission into eschatological perspective. According to

Kevin Giles, the fact that James "can transfer the title [*laos*] to Christians, irrespective of their nationality, shows that a theological transition in his thinking on the status of Christians is well under way."[34] According to Giles, the understanding of the New Testament writers concerning the status of Christians was paralleled by the corresponding demise of ethnic Israel's status as the people of God.[35]

There is no doubt that James' description of those called from the Gentile nations as a people (*laon*) for his name "was for Jewish ears an astounding and even a revolutionary saying."[36] This is due to the unprecedented juxtaposition of *ethnōn* and *laon*, which in Jewish thinking had been mutually exclusive terms (Exodus 19:5; 23:22; Deuteronomy 14:2; 28:9–10; Amos 3:1; Isaiah 43:1). However, this need not imply that the Church supplants Israel. According to Strathmann, "The circle of the word *laos* is given a new center. Only faith in the Gospel decides. The title is not herewith taken from Israel. But another *laos* now takes its place along with Israel on a new basis."[37]

Strathmann's observation—that the use of *laon* to describe Gentile believers does not imply disinheriting Israel of the title—finds support in the fact that the definite article is not used with *laon* in Acts 15:14 whereas the definite article is still used to describe Israel in Acts 28:17, 26–27. Furthermore, we know from other passages in Acts and the New Testament Epistles that the new people that God is calling to himself is composed of Jewish as well as Gentile converts.[38]

James' statement in verse 15 that "the words of the prophets are in agreement with this," is clearly a generalization. The fact that God is calling from the

Gentiles a people for his name, should not come as
a surprise to readers of the Old Testament. After all,
the Abrahamic covenant and the Hebrew prophets had
envisaged Israel being a means of blessing to all peoples.
As an example of the agreement between "the words
of the prophets" and God's work of "taking from the
Gentiles a people for himself," James quotes part of a
prophecy relating to the re-establishment of the Davidic
dynasty (vv. 16–18, [Amos 9:11–12]). The modification
of the Amos prophecy from "so that they may possess
the remnant of Edom" to "that the remnant of men may
seek the Lord" (v. 17a) tends to confirm that Israel's
involvement in history, whatever form it may take, is
in view of the furthering of God's salvation purpose
(cf. Genesis 12:3 [Galatians 3:8]; Isaiah 49:5–6).[39] The
identification of Jesus as "the son of David" and Israel's
promised messianic king in Matthew 1:1–2:6; 21:9;
27:37 fully justifies James' conviction that "David's
tent" was being rebuilt by the victorious conclusion of the
Messiah's first advent. The continuation of the prophecy
in the book of Amos (9:13–15) and such New Testament
passages as Matthew 23:39 and Acts 1:6–7; 3:19–21,
suggests that the rebuilding of David's tent will also have
positive significance for Israel as a nation at the time of
Messiah's second advent.

James' concluding words, "For Moses has been
preached in every city from the earliest times and is read
in the synagogues on every Sabbath" (v. 21), suggest that
the attention he gives to God's wider purpose does not
imply unawareness of the particular role of his own race
in God's program. It must be remembered that James'
primary concern was to give his opinion concerning "the
Gentiles who are turning to God," whether or not they

should be asked to accept circumcision and to observe the Law of Moses (vv. 5, 19). According to James, such a request ignored an important part of the purpose which God was working out through the Davidic line. In the benevolent plan of God, there was room for the Gentile nations as well as the people of Israel.

Galatians 3:26–29; 6:16. Galatians is a particularly polemical letter; in fact the reason Paul wrote it was to refute the error of Jewish Christians who attributed a similar importance to "the works of the law" as the apostle attributed to justification "by grace through faith in Christ." Paul met this challenge first with an appeal to his personal history and the experience of the Galatians themselves (1:11–3:5), and second by considering some key elements of salvation history (3:6–18). The passage which interests us concludes with this important statement: "There is neither Jew nor Greek, slave nor free, male nor female, for you are all one in Christ Jesus. If you belong to Christ, then you are Abraham's seed, and heirs according to the promise" (3:28–29).

According to H.D. Betz the thrust of Paul's argument is that unbelieving Jews are excluded from the Abrahamic promises. In other words the Church has taken the place of Israel.[40] Is this so? A straightforward reading of Galatians does not require this conclusion. The question being discussed is not the status of Israel as such, but whether justification can be attained by "the works of the law" as Paul's opponents believed. Siker, who examines Paul's polemic in Galatians as possible evidence of the disinheriting of the Jews, writes "Paul's fight in Galatians is not with non-Christian Jews but with a rival group of Christians whom he views as opponents because of their understanding of the law's centrality to the gospel. Indeed, Paul's dispute with the Teachers appears to have been primarily over the necessity of law observance for Gentile Christians."[41]

The idea that by contrasting "God's grace" (*charin tou theou*) with the "righteousness of the law" (*nomou dikaiosunē*) Paul is also proclaiming the demise of Israel as an elect people is based on too narrow an understanding of first century Judaism. Dieter Georgi has discovered parallels to Paul's teaching on grace in Galatians[42] and his polemic with Torah-centered Judaism within first-century Judaism.[43] Dunn concurs that Paul's argument and appeal in Galatians "reflect the concerns and language of intra-Jewish polemic."[44]

In order to understand Paul's argument in 3:26–29, it is necessary to consider his statement in verse 16 concerning Abraham's seed (*spermati*). F.F. Bruce writes: "There is no need to make heavy weather of Paul's insistence that the biblical text has *spermati* (singular) and not *spermasin* (plural). The essence of his argument can be expressed quite acceptably if it is pointed out that the biblical text uses a collective singular ("offspring") which could refer either to a single descendant or to many descendants."[45]

That "seed" can have a plural connotation as well as refer to a single individual is evident from several passages in Genesis (12:7; 13:15; 17:7; 24:7) as well as Isaiah (chapters 42–53). Thus the word "seed" in Galatians 3:16 can be understood as referring to a single descendant, Christ, without excluding reference to the people to which he belonged (cf. 4:4 and John 4:22). The idea, then, is that through Jesus the Jew the promised blessing comes to all the Gentile nations (Galatians 3:8).

The second use of the term (v. 29) refers to all who receive this blessing, that is, to all who belong to Christ and are thereby included in Abraham's spiritual offspring. Thus Paul can write, "You are all sons of God through faith in Christ Jesus, for all of you who were baptized into Christ have clothed yourselves with Christ" (vv. 26–27). Being "clothed with Christ" is the secret of Gentiles becoming heirs of the promise made to Abraham.

At this point Paul writes, "There is neither Jew nor Greek, slave nor free, male nor female, for you are all one in Christ Jesus" (v. 28). In Christ, believers feature neither as Jews (people whose standing depends on privileges, such as those mentioned in Romans 9:1–5), nor as Greeks (people without any standing before God according to Ephesians 2:11–12), but rather as Abraham's seed and, as such, heirs of the promise. Thus the attempt of Paul's opponents to put the Gentile converts of Galatia under law was ill-conceived.

It is instructive to consider the other distinctions (slave/free and male/female) which are eclipsed by the relationship of believers in Christ (v. 28). Both of these distinctions still subsisted even though the social distinctions did not carry over into the relationship of these various categories of people in Christ. It follows from a comparison of these three pairs (Jew/Greek, slave/free, male/female) that Paul is not insinuating the demise of Israel as a nation. What is new is that the distinction between Jew and Gentile does not carry over to the standing of believers in the grace of Christ.

We conclude, therefore, that this passage does not allude to the Church substituting Israel. Rather, Paul's purpose here, as elsewhere in Galatians, is to demonstrate to his Jewish-Christian opponents, as well as to those

Galatians who had been influenced by their teaching, that Gentiles, as well as Jews, become "heirs according to the promise" by placing their faith in Jesus the Messiah (cf. Acts 15:10–11).

We must now consider one of the concluding statements of Paul's letter to the Galatians. The expression *kai epi ton Israēl tou theou,* which appears only in Galatians 6:16, is variously interpreted "and upon the Israel of God" (KJV), "even to the Israel of God" (NIV), and "They are the new people of God" (NLT). E. D. Burton understands the Greek text to mean that Paul invokes peace on those who walk according to the rule summarized in Galatians 6:14–15 and mercy upon the Israel of God, understood as "those within Israel who even though as yet unenlightened are the true Israel of God."[46] Bruce compares Paul's desire that Israel experience "peace and mercy" both with his teaching concerning the hope of Israel in Romans 11:26 and with the closing words "Peace be upon Israel" of Psalm 125:5, which is the eighteenth ascription of the Eighteen Benedictions, used as a prayer in Jewish synagogues.[47] According to Bruce the phrase is to be understood as having an eschatological connotation. He writes, "For all his demoting of the law and the customs, Paul held good hope of the ultimate blessing of Israel."[48] On the other hand, J.B. Lightfoot understands the statement *kai epi ton Israēl tou theou* to contrast with the expression "Israel after the flesh" found in 1 Corinthians 10:18, giving it the following sense: "spiritual Israel generally, the whole body of believers whether Jews or Gentiles."[49]

Several recent writers insist that we read the words *kai epi ton Israēl tou theou* in light of Paul's polemic with the Judaizers. Harvey Graham writes, "Since 'Israel' has always been associated with 'the people of God' it will now, in this polemic, serve to demonstrate that when all the barriers are down God has one people regardless of their origin. Outside of this polemic 'Israel' is not used of the new group. In as much as this polemic interacts with other uses of 'Israel' the name cannot be said to have been usurped by the Christian group at this date."[50]

James D. G. Dunn's position is similar: "It will have been no accident, then, that Paul concludes this, his most polemical letter, with a blessing on 'the Israel of God'" (6:16), itself a final polemical shot summing up the claim (chapters 3–4) that the Israel of covenant promise is the Israel defined by that promise as including Gentiles as well as Jews."[51]

Gutrod concludes that "the expression is in a sense to be put in quotation marks."[52] On the other hand, Kevin Giles maintains that the Church can properly be called "the Israel of God" and that Paul is stating as much here, polemics apart.[53]

We may sum up the evidence as follows: the expression *kai epi ton Israēl tou theou* appears only once in the New Testament writings. The letter in which it appears is admittedly polemical and the translation "even upon the Israel of God," although possible, is not the most straightforward rendering of *kai*, otherwise translated "and" or "also." Thus we conclude that Galatians 6:16 is insufficient grounds on which to base an innovative theological concept such as understanding the Church to be the new and/or true Israel.

Ephesians 2:11–22. This section of Ephesians treats the change in status of Gentiles who have become part of the Church. Our question is, Does this mean any significant change in status for the Jewish nation? Commenting on the term *tōn hagiōn* ("of the saints") in verse 19, T. K. Abbott wrote a century ago, "The clear reference to the *politeia* of Israel shows decisively that the *hagioi* are those who constitute the people of God. Such formerly had been the Jews, but now are all Christians. These are now the Israel of God. . . . The *hagioi*, then, are not the Jews, nor specially the patriarchs or Old Testament saints."[54]

Markus Barth, commenting on the same passage three quarters of a century later, had a different perspective on the matter. He writes: "First the Gentiles are reminded that they are received into the house of God, the community of Israel."[55]

Abbott's comment reflects the majority view of the Church before the Shoah and the birth of the modern State of Israel—that the Church has entirely replaced Israel. Barth's comment, on the other hand, reflects the renewed attention given to "the place of Israel and the Jew in God's purpose for the salvation of the world, and . . . the relationship of Israel to the Christian Church" which followed these events.[56] But is this all there is to it? Which of the two comments reflects more closely the meaning and flow of the Greek text?

Abbott's statement only apparently follows the text. The word *politeia* does not occur in verse 19, where the new status of Gentile Christians is defined, but rather in verse 12, where it is affirmed that, in former times, the Gentiles "were . . . excluded from citizenship (*politeia*) in Israel and strangers to the covenants of promise." The word in verse 19 is *sumpolitai*, meaning "fellow-citizens." The whole phrase, *sumpolitai tōn hagiōn* means "fellow-citizens of the saints." In other words, Gentile Christians were accepted in the community of saints which was already in existence. In this way they also become "members of God's household," which is "the household of faith" (Galatians 6:10).

In v. 17 Israel is characterized as being "near" (*engus*) while the pagan nations are characterized as being "far away" (*makran*). But being near did not mean that all Israelites were "saints." Both before and after the advent of Christ and the subsequent birth of the spiritual temple of the Church (John 4:21–24; Matthew 16:18b), only believing, obedient Israelites were counted among the saints (Ephesians 2:18; cf. Hebrews 3:7–19; 11:1–38; Malachi 3:16). What is new is the realization of God's eternal purpose of uniting Jews and Gentiles in the Church (Ephesians 3:1–12). This "mystery" had only been partially revealed in former times, for example in the last clause of the Abrahamic covenant (Genesis 12:3; cf. Isaiah 49:5–6). But with Christ it was revealed in full; for in Christ, believing Gentiles came to share in the honor of being part of God's household. All in this household have greater privileges than in former times, having become the temple of the Holy Spirit (vv. 21–22; cf. Hebrews 11:39–40). Dunn's comment on vv. 17–19 sums it up: "The point is that Israel has not been cast off; its blessings have not been taken away from them and given to others (contrast even Mark 12:9). Rather the Gentiles have been brought in to share the blessings previously confined to Israel."[57]

There is further confirmation of this in verse 20. Besides Christ himself, the foundation of the new temple consists of twelve Jewish apostles together with the prophets. So it is incorrect to speak of a Gentile church. Rather, God, through the preaching of the gospel, calls people from among the Gentiles (Acts 15:14) as well as the Jews, to salvation and sanctification. So far as those not belonging to the Church are concerned, Paul does not suggest that Israel has lost her privileged status among the nations.

Hebrews 8:1–13. If the traditional opinion concerning the addressees of Hebrews is assumed,[58] this book appears irrelevant to the question of the origin of replacement theology. Siker notes that this letter does not contain either "any direct critique of non-Christian Judaism" or "any explicit appeal to Abraham to argue for Gentile inclusion."[59] That is not to say that there is no room for Gentile inclusion in the Church, the question is simply not raised. Robert W. Wall and William L. Lane write, "The pastoral strategies adopted in Hebrews were all designed to stir the members of a Jewish-Christian assembly to recognize that they could not turn back the hands of the clock and deny their Christian understanding and experience; . . . this is not anti-Judaism; it is the reflection of a distinctive reading of Scripture in light of the writer's convictions about Jesus."[60]

However, not everyone agrees with Wall and Lane. Clark M. Williamson writes, "Whatever its purpose, Hebrews put forth a supersessionist argument against Judaism, claiming that the covenant between God and the Israel of God had been abolished."[61] This statement is not fair to the writer to the Hebrews; for right at the center of his homily he makes it clear that he is describing the fulfillment of Old Testament prophecy (Hebrews 8:8–12; cf. Jeremiah 31:31–34).

Readers who were acquainted with the book of Jeremiah knew, that in a moment of extreme weakness in the life of Judah, God had announced that he would, in the future, make a new covenant with the whole house of Israel. In the same context God spoke of the unconditional nature of promised blessing on the nation (Jeremiah 31:35–37). This prophecy is quoted at length in Hebrews 8:8–12 and again at the conclusion of the writer's discussion of the new covenant (10:15–17). Wall and Lane observe that "the argument developed in Hebrews on the basis of Jeremiah 31:31–34 exhibits the writer's ability to recognize a significant hint in Scripture that was overlooked by contemporary writers."[62]

The concern of the author of Hebrews is that his readers grasp the nature of this new, better covenant of which Christ is the great high priest (8:1–2). While he shows great respect for all that has preceded the new covenant, he insists that the new is better, as indeed does Jeremiah. The chief purpose of his "hortatory discourse" (*tou logou tēs paraklēseōs*, 13:22) is to warn his own generation against making the same mistake as the generation of Israelites which Moses led out of Egypt, namely, failing to believe God (see 2:1–4; 3:7–19; 6:4–6; 10:26–29).

It is true that much of the book is devoted to showing that the new covenant, and what pertains to it, are better than the old Levitical covenant. However, it is crucial to realize that this difference depends upon a solid fact of salvation history: the new covenant is based on the better, final sacrifice of Jesus the Messiah. Williamson takes particular issue with the biblical author's conviction that the old covenant has been abolished, a position which he describes as "supersessionist."[63] But, as Bruce observes, "The very words 'a new covenant' antiquate the previous one. In saying this our author does not go beyond

Jeremiah, who explicitly contrasts the new covenant of the future with the covenant made at the time of Exodus, and implies that when it comes, the new covenant will supersede that earlier one."[64]

What needs to be stressed is that this is not a case of the Church pretending to supersede the Israel of God, but rather of one (presumably Jewish) Christian seeking to convince his fellow Jews that the new covenant has been established through Jesus and that there is no turning back. His readers are encouraged to join those of their own nation who have already entered the new covenant through faith. It is not part of his purpose to consider the status of non-Jews who are admitted into the new covenant by virtue of their relationship with Israel's Messiah.

While claiming that "we are receiving a kingdom that cannot be shaken" (12:28), the writer is aware that not all kingdom promises have yet been fulfilled (10:12–13). Thus he envisages Christ appearing "a second time to bring [complete] salvation to those who are waiting for him" (9:28).

1 Peter 2:4–10. Similar to James' speech in Acts 15:14–18, this passage attributes the dignity of "people of God" (*laos*) to converts to the Christian faith. Because of the deliberate way in which this is done (v. 10), it has been taken as evidence for replacement theology. For example, in view of all that God is said to have bestowed on the followers of Christ in verses 4–10, Wayne Grudem concludes his comment with this rhetorical question: "What more could be needed in order to say with assurance that the church has now become the true Israel of God?"[65]

Peter H. Davids agrees with Grudem, but goes further by suggesting that the apostle's interest in these verses is exclusively in the experience of the Gentile component of the churches to which he writes. Davids writes, "Unlike Israel these Christians never experienced themselves as unfaithful to a covenant, but they did realize that they were once outside God's favor, that is, rejected. . . . But now these Christians know they are elect—not just a people of God, but the people of God."[66] Certainly the transposition of titles of honor in verses 9–10 is impressive: "But you are a chosen people, a royal priesthood, a holy nation, a people belonging to God, that you may declare the praises of him who called you out of darkness into his wonderful light. Once you were not a people, but now you are a people of God; once you had not received mercy, but now you have received mercy."[67]

In considering the apostle's transposition of titles of honor used by the prophet Hosea (Hosea 2:23; cf. 1:6, 9–10) to the Church, it must be remembered that Christian Jews were among the addressees to whom the letter was written (1 Peter 1:1–2; cf. Galatians 2:8–9).[68] For these Jewish Christians, the words of Hosea would have had much the same meaning as they had for the Israelites of Hosea's own time. The name *Lo-Ammi* (Hosea 1:9), meaning "not my people," stood for a severing of the covenant relationship between God and Israel through Israel's acting like an unfaithful wife. However, God's faithfulness toward unfaithful Israel meant that there was a future for the nation. Thus Hosea prophesied, "Yet the Israelites will be like the sand of the seashore, which cannot be measured or counted. In the place where it was said to them, 'you are not my people,' they will be called 'sons of the living God,'" (Hosea 1:10).

To understand how Peter could legitimately apply this prophecy to Jews who had come to faith in Christ, it is helpful to bear in mind the theme of repentance and forgiveness in Hosea (14:1–4) and the following parts of Jeremiah's prophecy concerning the new covenant: "I will be their God, and they will be my people. . . . For I will forgive their wickedness and will remember their sins no more" (Jeremiah 31:33–34).

John the Baptist, the forerunner of Jesus, addressed the nation of Israel, calling them to repentance in the spirit of Hosea 14: 1–4. Many of his countrymen flocked to hear him preach. While the first part of Jesus' earthly ministry was similar to that of his predecessor (John 3:22–30; Mark 1:14–15), it concluded with the stipulation of the new covenant by means of the shedding of his own blood, (Luke 22:14–20; cf. Mark 10:45; 1 Peter 3:18a).

After his resurrection, Jesus entrusted the Good News to his apostles and Joel's prophecy began to be fulfilled at Pentecost (Acts 2:1–21). To those Jews who believed the gospel, God became their God in a new, more intimate way and they became his people in a new way, just as Hosea and Jeremiah had prophesied (Acts 2:38–47; 3:19–26; 4:23–31). These Jews, born again of the Spirit, gained a new standing with God based on the finished work of Christ (John 1:12–13; 3:3–8; Romans 8:1–16; cf. Ezekiel 36:26). Georgi writes, "The Jesus believers identified themselves as the beginning and center of the eschatological people of God; Israelites and Jews knew this idea from the prophetic predictions of the end times when a renewed covenantal community would grow out of the people of Israel."[69]

We may presume that there were also Gentile Christians among the first readers of Peter's letter. Both Grudem and Davids feel that the application of the Hosea prophecy to these non-Jews is proof that the Church has, for all intents and purposes, replaced Israel as the people of God. But this is not a necessary conclusion. Peter knew that Gentile Christians had been admitted into the new covenant. We are informed concerning the occasion in which "the apostle to the Jews" was constrained by God to recognize Gentiles who believe in Christ as having the same status as their Jewish brothers (Acts 10:1–11:18; 15:7–11). By applying the Hosea prophecy to the whole Church, Peter gave further demonstration of having accepted this fact.

It is not part of Peter's purpose to force a decision that either the Church or Israel is to be understood as the people of God. While Davids is emphatic that the Church is "the people of God," Peter himself carefully avoids using the definite article in verses 9–10.[70] It would seem then that Peter uses Old Testament titles of honor analogically, without attributing exclusiveness to them. If we bear in mind what Peter himself said elsewhere about the future fulfillment of God's promises to Israel (Acts 3:19–21), his avoidance of the definite article when describing the nature of the Church as a people of God appears to be deliberate.

Finally, nowhere does Peter state "that the Church is the new/true Israel." Such statements have to be added by commentators. In my opinion, Peter himself would not have made such a statement despite his recognition that the Church, as God's people, had much in common with Israel.

Philippians 3:4–9 and 1 Thessalonians 2:15–16. It has been suggested that these two Pauline passages are radically anti-Semitic.[71] However, this assumes that Paul should have always used the kind of diplomatic language which is more in vogue in our pluralistic society than it was in the first century. In reality, the radical nature of Paul's language is paralleled in Romans 11:28 where he describes the unbelieving majority of Israel as enemies of the gospel (11:28a). In the same letter he writes, "Pray that I may be rescued from the unbelievers in Judea" (15:31). The strong language used in Paul's letter to the Thessalonians was well known to readers of the Hebrew prophets. Such invective was actually a confirmation of the special love of God for unfaithful Israel (Amos 3:1–2).[72]

According to Williamson, Paul's negative evaluation of his former life in Philippians 3:4–9 is directed against pious Jews.[73] This reading of the passage neglects the fact that Paul continued to consider himself a devout Jew even after his conversion on the Damascus road (Acts 21:20–26; 24:10–18). Paul's polemic is actually with those who sought to construct a personal righteousness derived from the law rather than "the righteousness that comes from God and is by faith" (Philippians 3:9). Thus the real question—as in the case of Jesus' polemic in John eight—becomes whether or not Jesus is the promised Messiah. According to Ruether, the root cause of replacement theology is the conviction that Jesus of Nazareth is the Messiah and the consequent obligation that Israel accept him as such.[74] In reality, the fact that the head of the Church is Israel's Messiah constitutes a strong element of continuity between Judaism and Christianity and a strong affirmation of the uniqueness of the Jewish people.

Passages Which Seem to Exclude Replacement Theology

Romans 9–11. In this section of Romans, Paul conducts a thorough examination of Israel's place in the outworking of the divine plan, so it follows that no serious examination into the legitimacy of replacement theology can ignore these chapters.[75] This is not the place to attempt a full-scale exegesis of these chapters, rather we will consider one of their leading features, the repeated use of the term "Israel." In fact while the term "Israel" is used eleven times in Romans 9–11, it does not appear elsewhere in Romans and is used only six times in the rest of Paul's writings. The question we need to answer, then, is, Did Paul use the term Israel deliberately in these chapters in order to maintain the sense of Israel's uniqueness, or was it his purpose to enlarge its field of reference to include the Church and Gentile Christians?

There is no doubt that in Paul's opening statement (9:1–5) the term Israel refers to the ethnic people with whom the plan of God is closely associated in the Hebrew Scriptures.[76] The passionate nature of this statement finds correspondence in Paul's prayer "for the Israelites . . . that they may be saved" (10:1). After listing the privileges enjoyed by Israel, Paul denies that the Word of God has failed. In order to prove this he makes the following statement: "For not all who are descended from Israel are Israel" (9:6). According to Ulrich Luz, the second use of the term indicates the extension of Israel's privileges to the Christian community without implying that the Church takes Israel's place in the divine plan.[77] Arethas, in his comment on the Greek text, substantially expresses the same conviction. He interprets the words "not all who descended from Israel are Israel" in light of the preceding statement, "It is not as though God's Word had failed" (v. 6a). He adds this exhortation: "Let no-one, observing the entrance of the Gentiles, suppose that God's Word has fallen to the ground."[78] Thus for Arethas it is the entrance of the Gentiles which ensures that the Word of God does not fail. However, in order to demonstrate that Israel denotes the entrance of the Gentiles in verse six, Arethas finds it necessary to add the word *monoi*, modifying the phrase as follows: "In fact not all descendants of Israel are, only they, Israel."

Arethas' addition of *monoi* to the text throws some doubt on the claim that Gentile Christians, understood as the true Israel, are alluded to in the latter half of verse six. There is, in fact, no concrete evidence in the immediate context corroborating the interpretation according to which Israel includes those converted from paganism. Gutbrod is of the opinion that "the distinction at Romans 9:6 does not go beyond what is presupposed at John 1:47 ("Here is a true Israelite in whom there is nothing false")."[79] According to François Refoulé, Paul's more restrictive use of Israel in verse six corresponds to elect Israel which is to be found within physical Israel.[80]

R. Mayer approaches this restrictive use of the term Israel by comparing it with a wider phenomenon within first century Judaism. Different groups made the claim to be the true Israel while at the same time refraining from identifying themselves with eschatological total-Israel.[81] He writes, "Each individual group relied on the fact that it was the separated remnant of Israel which would lead to the eschatological community of the saved."[82]

Mayer understands Paul's treatment of Israel in Romans 9–11 to reflect that of first century Jewish sects. In this case the restrictive use of the term Israel in 9:6b does not exclude the notion that the same term can be used to describe a wider category corresponding to the eschatological total-Israel.[83] C. E. B. Cranfield finds the key to the meaning of the phrase, "For not all who descended from Israel are Israel," in the statements contained in verses seven and eight. In these verses, "Abraham's children," "God's children," and "Abraham's offspring" are distinguished from the more general categories described as "Abraham's descendants" and "natural children."[84] In other words, the more nuanced use of Israel in verse six refers to ethnic Israelites who were both natural and spiritual children of Abraham.[85]

The restriction of the title Israel to those Israelites who were spiritually attuned to God's purpose has precedents in the teaching of both Moses and Jesus, who respectively narrowed the meaning of "children of God" and "children of Abraham" to those who lived as such (Deuteronomy 32:5; John 8:39–44). Moreover, in Romans 2:28–29, Paul himself had similarly narrowed the meaning of "Jew" and "circumcision" (cf. Leviticus 26:41).

Israel is used three other times in Romans 9, always with reference to the descendants of Jacob. The first two uses (v. 27) are linked with the quotation of Isaiah 10:22–23, which refers to the salvation of only a remnant of the nation. Paul identifies this limited return to God with the limited response of his own generation to the preaching of the gospel. In verse 31, Israel is used as a collective noun with reference to the error committed by the majority of his contemporaries who sought righteousness on the basis of works rather than faith.

The first use of Israel in Romans 10 is in the rhetorical question, "Did Israel not understand?" (v. 19), with a view to demonstrating that the nation is inexcusable. Israel's guilt derived from the fact that she had not obeyed the proclamation of the gospel even though the prophecy of Deuteronomy 32:21 had been fulfilled. The name Israel is used again in verse 21 to distinguish between the Jews and other nations. In all of these cases the term Israel is used to identify the descendants of Jacob.

In Romans 11, the terms "Israelite" and "Israel" are used in two distinct ways. In the first six verses, "Israelite" is used with reference to "a remnant chosen by grace" while in the remaining verses, "Israel" is used with reference to the unbelieving majority of the nation. The chapter opens with a rhetorical question requiring a negative answer: "I ask then, Did God reject his people? By no means!" (11:1). Paul proceeds to identify himself as an Israelite and to use the seven thousand faithful Israelites of Elijah's time as an analogy. This is followed by the assertion that "in the present time there is a remnant [of Israel] chosen by grace" (v. 5), that is, those who have recognized the saving work of Jesus as the only grounds of their justification (v. 6; cf. 3:21–4:25).

Paul then addresses the problem posed by the unbelieving majority (*hoi de loipoi* . . . , v. 7b), by speaking of a hardening which will continue "until the full number of the Gentiles has come in" (v. 25). Much of Paul's argument in this section turns on the distinction between Israel and the Gentiles. This is clearly demonstrated in Paul's recurring theme of the inappropriate boasting of the Gentiles because their place in "the olive tree" is based entirely on faith and does not depend on natural rights (vv.13–14, 20–24).[86]

In his presentation of the place of Israel in God's plan, Paul uses an *a fortiori* argument (vv. 12, 15) in order to show the effects on the rest the world of both Israel's present unbelief and her future return to the Lord. Regarding their present unbelief (v. 12), Israel's "transgression" or "loss" (*hēttēma*) is producing riches for the "world" or "the [other] nations." Regarding Israel's future return to the Lord, described here as her "fullness" (*plērōma*, cf. v. 26), it is expected that it will produce even "greater riches."[87] In this whole section, Paul demonstrates that the function of Israel, as a chosen instrument of God, is constant in history and is not eclipsed by the entrance of the Gentile nations (cf. vv. 24–27).

The same kind of reasoning is repeated in verse fifteen, where he asks, "If the exclusion (*apobōlē*) of Israel from its position of privilege means the reconciliation of the world, what can be the expected effect of her re-admission (*proslēmpsis*[88]) if not life from the dead?" The eschatological nature of this statement becomes evident when the concept of rejection with which Paul characterizes the present experience of Israel is compared with his statement in verse 25 where the partial hardening of Israel is said to continue "until the full number of the Gentiles has come in." Mention of "the world" in the first part of verses twelve and fifteen suggests that the expression "life from the dead," which describes the effect of Israel's future re-admission (v. 15), also has to do with world history.

Not all interpreters agree that Paul's discussion in Romans eleven concerns two distinct periods. For example, in his treatment of verses 25–27, Luz appeals to the fact that the conversion of Israel is more important than the order of events, reaching the conclusion that it is not necessary to consider the Parousia a distinct moment in salvation history. According to Luz, a careful study of the prophecies cited in verses 26–27 shows that Paul is thinking mainly in terms of the first advent of Christ and has in mind the work of Christ viewed in its entirety.[89] This interpretation neglects the fact that the temporal references in verses 25–27 are basic elements in the revelation of the "mystery," which suggests that the apostle introduces a new stage in the history of salvation in verse 26. That Paul has in mind two different stages in salvation history is also suggested by his distinction between present and future in verse fifteen and by his statement in verse 24 that, in the future, the natural branches "will . . . be grafted into their own olive tree!"

Whereas Luz considers the mystery passage (vv. 25–27) an integral part of verses 11–32, Christoph Plag considers it an extraneous element which may have been extrapolated from another of Paul's writings. Plag reaches this conclusion on the basis of his conviction that Romans eleven presents two different ways in which Israel reaches salvation. The first of these envisages Israel returning to God by conversion (vv. 11–24, 28–32).[90] The second way, which Plag considers incompatible with the first, is prophesied in verses 25–27. This second way is thought to depend entirely upon God, both in the choice of the moment and in its realization.[91]

Plag is right when he asserts that verses 25–27 have a unique quality. In fact, in introducing them, Paul utilizes the term "mystery." However, there are numerous elements in common between these verses and the rest of the chapter, which suggest that Paul has in mind two distinct moments in Israel's return to God throughout the passage. For example, in verse eleven Paul affirms that the part of Israel which has stumbled has not fallen beyond recovery, and in verse 24 he affirms that this part will be grafted in again. Besides, nothing in verses 25–27 leads the reader to doubt that some Israelites will be saved during the present time in which God is bringing in "the full number of the Gentiles." The expression "all Israel" not only emphasizes the exceptional nature of the event described in verses 26–27, it also presupposes the conversion of some Israelites in the present.

The term "Israel" appears twice in verses 25–27. The fact that the content of these verses is described as a *mustērion* ("mystery") makes the reader aware that Paul is about to present something which could not be imagined without the help of special revelation. For the ancient Greeks, the word *mustērion* indicated that which must not or cannot be said.[92] In the New Testament the emphasis shifts to what cannot be known without divine revelation.[93] Thus grasping the meaning of the term "Israel" in these verses is particularly important because of the future reference of the passage. If the object of this special work of God is ethnic Israel, it follows that this nation still figures as the object of God's special love, despite the existence of the new people of God made up of both Jews and Gentiles.

The first part of the "mystery" clarifies the relationship between the partial hardening of Israel in the present time and world evangelism, as Paul says, "Israel has experienced a hardening in part until the full number of the Gentiles has come in" (v. 25b). This brings us to the central statement of the revelation: *kai houtōs pas Israēl sōthēsetai* ("And so all Israel will be saved," NIV). This phrase, and the passage of which it is the center piece, have provoked much thought. Refoulé lists seven ways, besides his own, in which it has been understood.[94] The first three of these have in common that they seek to define the content of the "mystery." This has been variously understood to concern the fact that "all [historical] Israel" will be saved,[95] the time sequence by which "all Israel" will be saved,[96] and the manner in which the salvation of Israel will be achieved.[97] According to the fourth view, the "mystery" teaches the mutual dependence of the salvation of pagans and Jews.[98] According to exponents of the fifth view such as Oscar Cullmann,[99] the passage teaches how the pagan nations, by becoming part of "all Israel," enter salvation history and thereby give meaning to history in general. According to the sixth view, which was held by Karl Barth, the passage has to do with the constitution of "the Israel of God."[100] As in the case of Cullmann's view, Barth understands "all Israel" to be made up of both pagan converts and Jews.[101] According to the seventh view, the object of the "mystery" is to announce the entirely different way Israel will be saved—not through faith in Christ, but through a special intervention of God.[102] Refoulé's own view[103] is that *pas Israēl* is elect Israel, which he understands to be the sum total of the remnant of Israel of each succeeding generation. In his opinion, elect Israel includes the part of Israel which has been temporarily hardened. The latter is not to be confused with historical Israel, which Refoulé believes to be under the judgment of God (1 Thessalonians 2:15–16).[104]

I have three difficulties with Refoulé's view. In the first place, the language of 1 Thessalonians 2:14–16 is no more severe than that used in Ephesians 2:3 ("objects of wrath") to describe God's former attitude toward people destined to become his "workmanship, created in Christ

Jesus" (v. 10). That there was still hope for disobedient Israelites is clear from Peter's appeal on the day of Pentecost and from the immediate inclusion in the Church of some repentant Jews who shared responsibility for the death of Jesus (Acts 2:36–42).

Romans 11:26–27 envisages a similar transformation of unbelieving Israel at the Parousia and contains my second objection, which has to do with the identification of "the others" (Romans 11:7b). Refoulé limits this group, and similarly the Israelites for whom Paul prays (10:1) to the remnant of each generation of Israelites who will eventually come to faith in Christ. This appears arbitrary because it presupposes that of every generation of Israelites, including the generation which will be alive at the time of the Parousia, God will harden only those who will later come to faith. If the others are not hardened, it is not clear why they do not come to faith in Christ, particularly those living at the moment of Christ's return in glory.

My third objection has to do with Refoulé's understanding of election. His exegesis presupposes that "election" is virtually a synonym of "salvation." But God's sovereign purpose in the election of Israel (Romans 9:7–13) has more in view than the salvation of individual Israelites.[105] In any case, in verses 7–27 Paul writes concerning the majority of Israel, who were not part of the "remnant according to the election of grace" (11:5). Following the logic that a revelation normally concerns something previously unknown, I find the second of the above views most satisfactory: that the "mystery" concerns the sequence by which "all Israel" will be saved.

Paul introduces the phrase "all Israel will be saved" with the conjunction *kai*, followed by the adverb *houtōs*. In the past, this adverb was widely understood to have temporal significance, giving *kai . . . houtōs* the sense "and then," but the presence of the temporal proposition "until the full number of the Gentiles has come in," at the end of the previous sentence (v. 25b), makes such a meaning superfluous.[106] According to Gie Vleugels, the sense of the adverb is concessive, with reference to the immediate context, "notwithstanding Israel has experienced a hardening."[107] Bruce understands the sense to be modal, implying "that 'in this way'—by the operation of the divine purpose that the gospel should be received by the Gentile first, and then also by the Jew—the salvation of 'all Israel' will come about."[108] Douglas Moo concurs, understanding the reference to be to the process outlined in verses 11–24 and summarized in verse 25b. Moo further observes that *houtōs*, "while not having a temporal meaning, has a temporal reference: for the manner in which all Israel is saved involves a process that unfolds in definite stages."[109] Bauer, who also takes *houtōs* to be an adverb of manner, understands it to be used correlatively with *kathōs*[110] with reference to the occasion and manner of the eschatological salvation of "all Israel" (vv. 26b–27). The Old Testament prophecies quoted in these verses certainly contribute to our understanding of the manner and the occasion of the salvation of "all Israel."[111] Whether it is understood to refer to what precedes or to what follows the words "all Israel will be saved," understanding *houtōs* to be an adverb of manner fits best with the flow of Paul's thought. In both cases the description of manner involves a time reference.

So far as the meaning of Israel in verse 26 is concerned, the interpreter is obliged to attribute to it the same meaning it bears in verse 25. As there is no doubt that the reference in verse 25 is to ethnic Israel, we may conclude that Paul is speaking about the salvation of ethnic Israel in verse 26.[112] The use of the proper name Jacob in verse 26 also provides further confirmation of this.

Understanding Israel to refer to ethnic Israel in verse 26 raises the question as to whether "all Israel" is to be understood in an absolute sense. Zerwick and Grosvenor render *pas Israēl* "all (the whole of) Israel."[113] But does this mean that without exception, every Israelite alive at the time of the Parousia will be saved and will enter into a new covenant relationship with God? In this regard it is helpful to note that, although the term Israel refers to historical Israel as a whole in verse 7, exception is made for Israelite believers. Similarly, we may presume that in the case of the re-admission of the nation into the olive tree (vv. 12, 15, 24, 26–27), the nation as a whole is in view even though there may be exceptions in this case as well. Murray sums up the evidence by saying, "the salvation of Israel must be conceived of on a scale that is commensurate with their trespass, their loss, their casting away, their breaking off, and their hardening."[114]

On the basis of this survey of Paul's use of Israel in Romans 9–11, we concur with Siker when he writes concerning these chapters: "[Paul] denies that Jewish rejection of Christ implies God's rejection of the Jews (Romans 11:1, 11). Although their rejection of Christ shows their current disobedience, the Jews remain included within God's promises because God is faithful" (Romans 11:28–31).[115]

Other New Testament Evidence. Romans 9–11
contains the only extended discussion of the problem
posed by unbelieving Israel and the implications of such
unbelief for the continuance of Israel as God's elect
people. However, there are other elements in the New
Testament which appear to imply the permanence of
Israel as God's special, covenant people.

Paul's own apostolic ministry reflected his conviction
that Israel continued to be unique among the nations.
Despite the obstinate unbelief of many of his own nation,
he continued to go to the Jew first (Acts 13:14, 46;
17:1–2; 18:4, 19–20; 28:16–17). That this custom was
not only dictated by good missionary strategy is clear
from the following passages of Romans: 1:16; 2:9–10;
3:1–4; 15:25–32. These passages demonstrate that Paul
was fully prepared to make the supreme sacrifice in order
to facilitate the conversion of his own race (Romans
9:1–5; 10:1). Furthermore, he described the Gentile
Mission as an "offering" which he hoped would provoke
envy amongst his own people in order to save some of
them (Romans 15:16; cf. 11:13–14).

There are other New Testament passages which
seem to envisage a distinctive future for physical Israel
as well, thus excluding the logic of replacement theology.
Two affirmations made by Jesus containing the adverb
"until" appear to be particularly significant. The first of
these concerns the relationship of the Jews and the city of
Jerusalem to what Jesus calls "the times of the Gentiles."
Jesus says, "They will fall by the sword and will be taken
as prisoners to all the nations. Jerusalem will be trampled
on by the Gentiles until the times of the Gentiles are
fulfilled" (Luke 21:24). The use of the adverb "until"
(*achri*) does not, in itself, prove that there will be a period

of historical time following "the times of the Gentiles." However, it is clear that the idea of fixed periods of time is present. I. Howard Marshall suggests that the reference is to one of the "allotted times" of prophetic scripture[116] and he links the theme with early church teaching reflected in Romans 11:25–27.[117]

In the second passage, Jesus makes the following affirmation concerning unbelieving Israel: "Look, your house is left to you desolate. For I tell you, you will not see me again until you say, 'Blessed is he who comes in the name of the Lord,'" (Matthew 23:38–39). This statement presupposes that the people of Israel will see Jesus again and will pronounce this benediction upon him. Furthermore, it implies that this occasion will coincide with the end of the prophesied state of desolation of the house of Israel.

Such statements as these may have helped to convince Jesus' disciples that the period of world mission, into which they were introduced by the coming of the Holy Spirit at Pentecost (Acts 1:5–8; 2:1–36; cf. Matthew 28:18–20; Mark 16:15–16; Luke 24:44–47; John 20:21), was to be followed by the realization of another dimension of kingdom promises. The following statement made by Peter denotes such a prospect: "[Jesus] must remain in heaven until the time comes for God to restore everything, as he promised long ago through his holy prophets" (Acts 3:21).

Assessment

According to some scholars, a number of the New Testament passages which we have examined require us to accept the logic of replacement theology. This seems to be reading too much into the text. Although several of these passages taken on their own (especially Galatians 6:16 and 1 Peter 2:4–10) may be said to be compatible with replacement theology, they do not require it. Moreover, in order for replacement theology to qualify as a biblical option, passages which allow such an interpretation are not enough. There need to be passages which clearly teach it and no passages which actually exclude it. I believe that the teaching of Romans 9–11 and the other New Testament affirmations which we have just considered do in fact exclude replacement theology.

Some might object that even if the New Testament cannot be said to teach replacement theology as such, it does display anti-Judaic attitudes, which, after all, have been one of the driving forces behind anti-Semitism. But here the issue really concerns the general presupposition of the New Testament writers, that Jesus of Nazareth is the Messiah whose coming was predicted by the Hebrew prophets. To those who do not accept this, much in the New Testament will appear anti-Judaic. Furthermore, passages in which Jews and Gentiles are said to share in something more glorious than what had been formerly entrusted to Israel (Ephesians 2:11–21; Hebrews 11:39–40), or that describe the Church as a chosen people and a royal priesthood (1 Peter 2:9), will seem to be both illegitimate and arrogant. Similarly, statements according to which Gentiles are admitted into the sphere of God's blessing on grounds other than personal faithfulness to the Torah (Acts 15:7–11; Romans 3:21–31) will almost certainly be perceived as a seed of replacement theology.

On the other hand, a Jewish reader who shares the conviction that Jesus is the Messiah would be surprised if he found no evidence in the New Testament writings

of the gospel being taken to the Gentiles (see Genesis
12:3; Isaiah 49:5–6; cf. Acts 13:46–47; Galatians 3:8).
Similarly, talk of a new covenant and of the purifying
work of the Holy Spirit will not have the appearance
of innovations to those acquainted with the prophecies
of Jeremiah, Isaiah, Ezekiel, and Joel. Moreover, when
confronted with unfulfilled elements of Old Testament
promise, perplexed readers will find reassurance when
they read of a second coming of Christ (Acts 3:20–21;
cf. Matthew 13:36–43; 23:23; Luke 19:11–27; John
14:1–3).

What we find in the New Testament is a climate of
debate within Judaism and a critical attitude toward those
Jews who did not accept Jesus as the promised Messiah.
On the other hand, even in a context of heated debate such
as that described in John 8:31–58, Israel is not repudiated
as a nation. Joel Marcus writes, "the very same New
Testament polemics against Jews could be construed
as either anti-Semitic or not, depending on the ethnic
identity and sociological setting of the narrator and his
audience."[118] According to Marcus, the polemic against
Jews in the New Testament "is mostly . . . a criticism
formulated by Jews against other Jews, and the audience
for whose benefit the criticism is enunciated also includes
a sizeable number of [Jewish Christians]."[119] Moreover,
the fact that Paul attributes the status of "elect" to Israelites
who are "enemies of the Gospel" (Romans 11:28) shows
that the continuing elect status of Israel does not depend
on her faithfulness any more than it did in the times of the
Hebrew prophets (see Jeremiah 31:35–37).

If our findings are valid, it follows that the origin of
replacement theology must be sought in the post-apostolic
period.

3

THE DEVELOPMENT OF
REPLACEMENT THEOLOGY IN
POST-APOSTOLIC TIMES

The Pattern of History

While it is dangerous to generalize the movements of history, few would dispute that the disastrous Jewish war of AD 66–70—which witnessed the destruction of Jerusalem and the Second Temple—began a process that significantly changed the face of Judaism and Jewish-Christian relations.[1] Although Jewish apocalypticism continued to be an influential rival to Pharisaic Judaism during the following decades, the failure of the Jewish revolt led by Bar-Kochba in AD 132–135 strengthened the position of Rabbinical Judaism as the only enduring form of the Jews' historical faith. Other earlier rivals, such as the parties of the Zealots, the Essenes, and the Sadducees, had been either crushed or rendered obsolete by the Roman conquest.[2] At the same time, the importance of Jewish Christianity was greatly reduced by the forced exile of the Jerusalem Christians to Transjordan in AD 66 and the loss of prestige which Jewish Christianity suffered due to the destruction of Jerusalem.[3]

During this period, both Christianity and Judaism experienced hostility because both were monotheistic and opposed to the use of images. The consequent struggle for survival produced a spirit of rivalry between these communities of faith. Georgi sees a link between this spirit of rivalry and the growing exclusivism of both monotheistic communities. He writes, "Toward the end of the first century CE, Jews and Christians began to develop their own identities; not only against each other but also against the huge range of other options available to them both. These options were suddenly considered deviant."[4]

So far as Christianity was concerned, Jaroslav Pelikan observes that "the appropriation of the Jewish Scriptures and of the heritage of Israel helped Christianity to survive the destruction of Jerusalem and to argue that with the coming of Christ, Jerusalem has served its purpose in the divine plan and could be forgotten. It also enabled Christianity to claim an affinity with the non-Jewish tradition as well as with the Jewish."[5]

The vastly decreased dependence of Christianity on its Jewish roots and the freedom with which it absorbed elements from the Greco-Roman cultural tradition is reflected in the fact that, while among the writers of the New Testament Luke alone was not a Jew, as far as we know, none of the church fathers were Jews, although both Hermas and Hegesippus may have been.[6]

With Judaism engaged in a struggle for survival, and Christianity moving more and more into the milieu of Greco-Roman culture, it is hardly surprising that these two faiths increasingly saw themselves as rivals.[7] Thus at Jamnia, where Yohanan ben Zakkai had received permission from Rome to set up a school for rabbinical study, the rabbis developed puns to distort the meaning of the word *euangelion* ("gospel").[8] Moreover the Birkath ha-Minim, a pronouncement against heretics which is part of the twelfth "benediction" in the Jewish liturgical prayer "Eighteen Benedictions," is thought to be directed against Christians.[9] There is evidence of this in Justin Martyr's Dialogue with Trypho, written about AD 150. Justin accuses the Jews of "cursing in [their] synagogues those that believe on Christ."[10] Such attitudes were not unilateral. Ignatius of Antioch, writing around AD 115, instigated his readers to oppose all things Jewish. He claimed that the Hebrew prophets had lived according to Jesus Christ and not according to the Jewish law.[11]

Lee Martin McDonald suggests that another factor contributing to "the Christians' strong negative stance against Jews and Judaism . . . around the turn of the first century . . . may have been the vast difference in the size of their religious bodies." He estimates that Christians may have numbered fewer than 100,000 while Jews numbered somewhere between six and seven million.[12] The negative stance of Christians toward Jews and Judaism eventually consolidated into an *Adversus Judaeos* tradition[13] which permeated much of the writings of the Church Fathers and contributed to the development of replacement theology.

A particular area of rivalry between Christianity and Judaism concerned the Old Testament Scriptures. For their part, the Rabbis rejected the Christian interpretation of the Hebrew Scriptures when these were used to demonstrate that Jesus was the Messiah of Israel.[14] On the other hand, Christians freely appropriated to themselves much in the Hebrew Scriptures that was originally addressed to Israel.[15] This was facilitated by the practice of allegorical interpretation.[16]

Replacement Theology in Early Christian Writings

The Epistle of Barnabas: The Disinheriting of Israel

One of the main purposes of this pseudonymous second century writing was to show that the Jews, by interpreting the Old Testament ceremonial law literally, lost sight of its true import.[17] To gain a perspective on this unknown writer's opinion concerning ethnic Israel, we may begin by observing his reasoning in chapter XIV, 3–4. Commenting on the historical data concerning the golden calf and the fact that Moses broke the original tables of stone when he became aware of the nation's transgression, the writer concludes that the Lord never did give the promised testament to unworthy Israel; instead it has been given to the Church, which, through Christ, has received the promised inheritance. "He was manifested, in order that [the Israelites] might be perfected in their iniquities, and that we, being constituted heirs through Him, might receive the testament of the Lord Jesus" (XIV, 5).[18]

This disinheriting of Israel is evident throughout Barnabas. For example, alluding to Exodus 33:1–3, the author treats God's promise of land to Abraham, Isaac, and Jacob as a parable of the Christians' inheritance through Christ and regeneration by the Spirit (Barnabas VI, 6–17). In IX, 3–4 he claims that the practice of physical circumcision was, in reality, a transgression which an evil angel misled them to do, whereas God's command concerned only spiritual circumcision. Levitical food laws are similarly discredited in chapter X.

Of particular significance for our study is the use Barnabas makes of Genesis 25:21–23. Chapter XIII begins, "But let us see if this people is the heir, or the former, and if the covenant belongs to us or to them" (XIII, 1).

The chief point in discussion is the phrase "the older will serve the younger" quoted by Paul in Romans 9:12. In Genesis the older is clearly Esau (and his descendants) while the younger is Jacob (and his descendants). Paul quotes this prophecy in Romans to show that Israel's position as the elect nation depends upon God's purpose and not upon human works. The author of Barnabas completely ignores the way the phrase is used both in Genesis and Romans and links it instead with Genesis 48:17–19, contending that in both cases the younger child refers to the Church, the true heir to the covenant.

Barnabas shows little respect for Old Testament institutions. For example, in chapter XVI, 7, a temple made with hands is likened to a habitation of demons, full of idolatry. The writing, as a whole, manifests the latent presupposition that the Church, the true heir of the promises, occupies the place that Israel had always been unworthy of occupying.

The Letter to Diognetus: Is the Old Testament Canonical?

This anonymous writing[19] is an apology for the Christian way of worshipping God. It dates from around the middle of the second century when the Christians began to feel the need to defend and explain the faith in a way that was comprehensible to pagan neighbors and philosophers. In this writing Levitical offerings are compared with idolatry (III, 5) while food laws, Sabbath keeping, circumcision, and fasting are called "superstition" and "utterly ridiculous and unworthy of notice" (IV, 1). Thus depreciation of the Jews is extended to depreciation of the Torah. Circumcision, which was particularly offensive to Greco-Roman culture,[20] is singled out for particular comment: "to glory in the circumcision of the flesh as a proof of election, and as if, on account of it, they were specially beloved by God, how is it not a subject of ridicule?" (IV, 4). [21]

By lumping together "the superstition of the Jews" with pagan idolatry (I, 1) and treating as superstition what is prescribed by the Mosaic Law (chapters III–IV), the author, besides showing contempt for the Jews, ignores the canonical status of the foundational parts of the Old Testament.

The Writings of Justin Martyr: The Church is the "True Israelitic Race"

Although our interest will focus mainly on the Dialogue of Justin with Trypho, a Jew, Justin's presentation of the concept of "logos" in his First Apology is also relevant to our purpose. His theory of the eternity of the logos is invoked to answer objections regarding the relatively recent appearance of Christ on the scene of history.[22] He writes, "We have declared above that . . . [Christ] is the Word of whom every race of men were partakers; and those who lived reasonably are Christians, even though they have been thought atheists; as, among the Greeks, Socrates and Heraclitus, and men like them; and among the barbarians, Abraham, and Ananias, and Azarias and Misael, and Elias, and many others whose actions and names we now decline to recount, because we know it would be tedious."[23]

It is noteworthy that Justin adopts a typically Greek attitude toward Abraham, Elijah, and Daniel's three friends, calling them "barbarians." It is important to follow Justin's reasoning here. By understanding Christianity to be a product of the logos, "the most ancient philosophy and father of all rational thought," he finds no reason for attaching particular importance to physical Israel.

Justin's Dialogue with Trypho[24] is more of a monologue than a dialogue. In fact while Justin freely presents his point of view, Trypho is allowed little room for voicing his. This imbalance reflects the fact that, by the time Justin was active as a Christian apologist (c. AD 150), the Jews were at a distinct disadvantage when debating with Christians. This is seen in the exchange between Justin and Trypho concerning the words "from the wood," which introduce into Psalm 96:10 the idea that Jesus reigns, as God and Lord, from the cross. Justin assures the Jew that the words, now thought to be a gloss,[25] were part of the original text of Psalm 96:10 and had been deleted by Jews who did not believe in Jesus. Trypho's comment is: "Whether [or not] the rulers of the people have erased any portion of the Scriptures, as you affirm, God knows; but it seems incredible" (LXXIII).

The tendency to Christianize the Old Testament is evident throughout the Dialogue. Christians, in fact, are described as "the true Israelitic race." For example, in commenting on Isaiah 42:1–4, Justin writes, "Christ is the Israel and the Jacob, even so we, who have been quarried out from the bowels of Christ, are the true Israelitic race" (CXXXV).[26] The people of Israel are correspondingly held in contempt, as may be seen in the following statement: "God has from of old dispersed all men according to their kindreds and tongues; and out of all kindreds has taken to Himself your kindred, a useless, disobedient, and faithless generation; and has shown that those who were selected out of every nation have obeyed His will through Christ, whom He calls also Jacob, and names Israel" (CXXXV, 3–4).

Throughout the Dialogue, Abraham is presented as an exemplary Christian believer of whom Justin idealizes the state of uncircumcision (XI, 3–4; XXIII, 3–4). So far as the sign of circumcision is concerned, Justin states its purpose as follows: "For the circumcision according to the flesh, which is from Abraham, was given for a sign; that you may be separated from the other nations, and from us; and that you alone may suffer that which you now justly suffer." (XVI, 2).[27]

This negative connotation which Justin attributes to circumcision, accompanied by contempt for the circumcised people, is further accentuated in these words which he addressed to his Jewish interlocutor:

> Noah was the beginning of our race; yet, uncircumcised, along with his children he went into the ark. Melchizedek, the priest of the Most High, was uncircumcised; to whom also Abraham, the first who received circumcision after the flesh, gave tithes, and he blessed him: after whose order God declared, by the mouth of David, that He would establish the everlasting priest. Therefore to you alone this circumcision was necessary, in order that the people may be no people, and the nation no nation; as also Hosea, one of the twelve prophets, declares. (XIX)[28]

We have seen that Justin used Scriptural terms very loosely, as when he identified Christians as "the true Israelitic race" and regarded circumcision as a sign of inferiority instead of the positive covenant sign that it was (Genesis 17:12–14). Thus it seems that the basis of his evaluation of the Jews is not so much the Scriptures of the Old and New Testaments as much as the opinions concerning the Jews which he gleaned from such sources as the Epistle of Barnabas, the Letter to Diognetus, and other sources common to all three writings. We may safely say, then, that replacement theology, as taught by Justin, arises from what Gregory Baum has termed "theological embroidery."[29] We may presume that this development represents a response to the challenge posed by Judaism, which, although it did not recognize Jesus as the promised Messiah, showed no sign of disappearing from the scene.

Irenaeus' Against Heresies:[30] *God's Promises to Israel Are for the Church*

Irenaeus, bishop of Lyons from c. 178 until his death in c. 195, was an important figure in second century Christianity who, while still a young man, had heard Polycarp speak about his conversations with the apostle John. He is probably best known for his strong defense of the orthodox faith against Gnosticism.[31] In order to defend orthodoxy, Irenaeus distinguished between the canonical writings of the New Testament—particularly the four Gospels[32]—and extra-canonical writings, so making an important contribution to the definition of the New Testament Canon.

In book 5 of his famous work, *Against Heresies*, Irenaeus applies four Old Testament prophecies to the gathering into the Church of "those that shall be saved from all the nations."[33] The first of these is Isaiah 26:19, where the prophet predicts the resurrection of the dead. Some commentators have seen in this verse a veiled reference to the restoration of Israel from captivity.[34] In the second quoted passage (Ezekiel 37:12–14), God foretells that he will miraculously resurrect the whole house of Israel, by means of his Spirit, and will resettle her in her own land. The third quotation is drawn from several passages in Ezekiel, including 36:24–25 in which the re-gathering and re-settling of Israel in her own land is said to be followed by purification. The last of the series is an abbreviated quotation of Jeremiah 23:6–7 where the future salvation of Judah is predicted and, consequently, "people will no longer say, 'As surely as the LORD lives, who brought the Israelites up out of Egypt,' but they will say, 'As surely as the LORD lives, who brought the descendants of Israel up out of the land of the north and out of all the countries where he had banished them.'"

Irenaeus finds the fulfillment of all these passages in the salvation of people from the Gentile nations. By so doing he disinherits Israel of promises which are clearly addressed to her and at the same time manifestly makes the Church the new or true Israel. In other words he bases his exegesis on the assumption that the Old Testament should be read in light of what we have called replacement theology, which he apparently considered to be a part of orthodox Christian thought.

Tertullian's Answer to the Jews:[35] *Israel Must Serve the Church*

Tertullian's contribution to Christian theology is unique in a number of ways. Living in the period c. 160–225, he was the first theologian to write extensively in Latin. Furthermore, he coined numerous theological terms which proved useful in the formulation of classical Trinitarian and Christological statements. He was also the only orthodox theologian of the early centuries to leave the official church. In his opinion, the official church had come to lack moral vigor and its episcopal structure had become overbearing, to the detriment of its essential, pneumatic nature.[36]

Considering Tertullian's capacity for original, rigorous thinking, it is reasonable to expect an original contribution to the Church's understanding of its relation to the Old Testament people of God. To some extent his contribution was original. In fact, in his work *An Answer to the Jews,* he appears more concerned about defending the Christian faith than listing the errors of the Jews. Moreover, as the "clue to the error of the Jews," he correctly presents the doctrine of the two advents of Christ—one characterized by humility and suffering and the other by honor and glory (chapter XIV). Yet some of the themes which we have found in the previous writings recur in Tertullian's *Answer*, in particular the tendency to minimize the importance of the Mosaic law and to consider physical circumcision a sign given to mark Israel out as a "contumacious people" (chapters II–III).

What is most significant for our study is Tertullian's use of Genesis 25:21–23 in the opening paragraphs of his *Answer*, where he follows the kind of allegorical exegesis which we have already met with in the Epistle of Barnabas. Here is his comment on the phrase, "the older will serve the younger": "Accordingly, since the people or nation of the Jews is anterior in time, and 'greater' through the grace of primary favor in the Law, whereas ours is understood to be 'less' in the age of times, as having in the last era of the world attained the knowledge of divine mercy: beyond doubt, through the edict of divine utterance, the prior and 'greater' people—that is, the Jewish—must necessarily serve the 'less'; and the 'less' people—that is, the Christian—overcome the 'greater.'"[37]

So, if Israel has any continuing role, it is as a servant of the Church (cf. Romans 11:11–15). Tertullian proceeds to adduce reasons for this inversion of roles, finding the main cause in Israel's idolatrous practices. He concludes, "For thus has the 'less'—that is the posterior—people overcome the 'greater people,' while it attains the grace of divine favor from which Israel has been divorced."[38]

Tertullian wrote in Latin. It is instructive that commentators of the Greek text of Romans did not follow Barnabas and Tertullian in identifying the "older" people with the Jews and the "lesser" people, that is the posterior, with the Christians. In fact, those who commented on Romans 9:12–13 during the fourth to the ninth centuries, do not make any mention of *Christianoi, hē ekklēsia* or *ethnē* ("Christians," "the Church," or "Gentile nations").[39] These commentators link the Genesis quotation strictly with Paul.[40]

Although, as we have seen, Tertullian held to the main tenets of replacement theology, he also wrote positively concerning the place of Israel in God's plan. For example, in his treatise *Against Marcion* he used Romans 10:2–4 and 11:33 to demonstrate that the God who had been known imperfectly during Old Testament times was the same God who had now revealed himself more fully in Christ.[41] In this context Tertullian makes reference to Paul's recognition of Israel's zeal for God. Furthermore, in one of his later writings entitled *On Modesty*,[42] he greatly modified the standard interpretation of the parable of the prodigal son, according to which the younger, prodigal but repentant son represents the Church while the older, unrepentant son represents Israel. According to Tertullian the older son represents the Church just as much as Israel and, following Israel's loss of the land, the younger son represents Israel as much, if not more, than the Church. He concludes as follows: "it will be fitting for the Christian to rejoice, and not to grieve, at the restoration of Israel, if it is true, (as it is), that the whole of our hope is intimately united with the remaining expectation of Israel" (VIII).[43]

It is possible that Tertullian's disenchantment with the Catholic Church, which occurred before he wrote *On Modesty*, is linked with this change of attitude. All we can say for sure is that, in his interpretation of the parable of the prodigal son, Tertullian's criticism of the official church is paralleled by a return to a more Pauline view of the future of Israel.

The Contribution of Origen: Corporeal and Spiritual Israel

The work of Origen (c. 185–c. 254),[44] Clement's successor as head of the catechetical School of Alexandria, strengthened the theoretical basis of replacement theology by grounding it in biblical exegesis.[45] However, his exegetical methodology was profoundly influenced by the intellectual climate in which he grew up. The Greeks had used allegorism to make the mythical content of ancient works, such as those written by Homer and Hesiod, acceptable to readers with a more philosophical turn of mind. Origen was also influenced by the example of Philo, a first century Alexandrian Jew who had interpreted the Old Testament Scriptures allegorically in order to make them harmonize with Platonism.[46]

Allegorism played an important part in Origen's theory of interpretation and, as he was the first biblical scholar to work out "a complete hermeneutical theory,"[47] his work was destined to exert great influence on the Christian approach to the Hebrew Scriptures for centuries to come. Allegorism allowed Origen to freely appropriate Old Testament passages where ethnic Israel is clearly intended while denigrating the Jewish people themselves. It is ironic that Origen was inspired in part by the example of a Jewish scholar in applying the allegorical method to the biblical text.

Origen is remembered for his philosophical speculation and as the allegorist *par excellence* among Biblical interpreters. To be fair, however, it must be said that allegorical interpretation was widely practiced by Christian writers before Origen's time. Moreover, part of Origen's purpose was to refute the heretical teachings of Marcion. The latter, while insisting on a literal interpretation of the Old Testament, had taught that the "god" who speaks in these Scriptures is not the God and Father of Jesus Christ.[48]

Origen offered his own rationale of allegorism in book IV, section 1 of his work *On First Principles.*[49] For him, Proverbs 22:20 authorizes interpreters to seek a three-fold meaning in each passage of Scripture: fleshly, psychic, and spiritual.[50] In practice, Origen insisted mainly on distinguishing between the literal and spiritual meaning of the Biblical text, the spiritual meaning belonging to a higher order of ideas than the literal. He motivated this view by appealing to the principle of divine inspiration and by affirming that many statements made by the biblical writers were not literally true and that many events, presented as historical, were inherently impossible.[51] Thus only simple believers could limit themselves to the literal meaning of the text.[52]

Of course, Origen recognizes that some of the events mentioned in Scripture must be considered historically true if the reader is to make any sense out of the text.[53] Thus it is the task of the interpreter to decide which events are to be taken literally and which are not. He writes, "the exact reader must, in obedience to the Savior's injunction to 'search the Scriptures,' carefully ascertain in how far the literal meaning is true, and in how far impossible; and so far as he can, trace out, by means of similar statements, the meaning everywhere scattered through Scripture of that which cannot be understood in a literal signification."[54]

The words, "in how far the literal meaning is true, and in how far impossible," reveal an inherent weakness in Origen's hermeneutical theory because they leave the door open for cultural prejudice, the limited experience of the reader to determine what God can and cannot do, and whether events or biblical prophecies described are to be taken literally or not. A good example of what cultural prejudice can do to interpretation is Origen's view that thinking of "God as he deserves to be thought" means interpreting all scriptural passages which speak of his wrath in light of his presumed impassibility.[55] From this example it is clear that once the center of the hermeneutical process shifts from the Scriptures themselves to the cultural milieu in which the interpreter operates, philosophy can justifiably influence a reader's decision regarding "that which cannot be understood in a literal signification."

Origen exemplifies his hermeneutical theory by discussing the difference between a "bodily" race of Jews and those who are "Jews inwardly." With reference to bodily Israel and Judah, he writes,

> And do not such promises as are written concerning them, in respect of their being mean in expression, and manifesting no elevation (of thought), nor anything worthy of the promise of God, need a mystical interpretation? And if the "spiritual" promises are announced by visible signs, then they to whom the promises are made are not "corporeal". . . are not the "spiritual" Israelites, of whom the "corporeal" Israelites were the type, sprung from the families, and the families from the tribes, and the tribes from some one individual whose descent is not of a "corporeal" but of a better kind—he, too, being born of Isaac, and he of Abraham—all going back to Adam, whom the apostle declares to be Christ?[56]

An attitude of contempt toward Israel had become the rule by Origen's time. The new element in his own view of Israel is his perception of them as "manifesting no elevation [of thought]." It follows that the interpreter must always posit a deeper or higher meaning for prophecies relating to Judea, Jerusalem, Israel, Judah, and Jacob which, he affirms, are "not being understood by us in a 'carnal' sense."[57] In Origen's understanding, the only positive function of physical Israel is that of being a type of spiritual Israel. The promises were not made to physical Israel because she was unworthy of them and incapable of understanding them.[58] Thus Origen effectively disinherits physical Israel.

In the continuation of the section of *On First Principles* in which Origen distinguishes between physical and spiritual, he presents a platonic concept of the Church. According to this view, every family which is related to God takes its commencement from Christ. Moreover, Adam and Eve are "types of the Church, inasmuch as in a pre-eminent sense they are . . . descended from the Church."[59] The Church itself is conceived of in non-temporal, heavenly terms. This platonic understanding of the Church implies the secondary nature of historical realities, including Israel. Thus the Church's appropriation of the Old Testament appears to be legitimate, while the importance that Scripture itself attributes to history is ignored.

Applications of Origen's hermeneutical principles to physical and spiritual Israel may be found both in his *Commentary on Matthew* and in his *Old Testament Homilies*. For example, commenting on Matthew 19:6–8, Origen likens Israel to a divorced wife in whom an unseemly thing had been found.[60] He writes, "And a sign that she has received the bill of divorce is this, that Jerusalem was destroyed along with what they called the sanctuary."[61]

The "unseemly thing" of which Origen speaks is the request that Jesus be crucified and Barabbas be released.[62] Origen pushes the analogy of divorce still further by suggesting that Israel has joined herself to another husband, "Barabbas the robber who is figuratively the devil, or some evil power," while Christ has joined himself to a new wife, the Church.[63] Furthermore, Origen takes Christ's words, "the lost sheep of Israel" (Matthew 15:24) in the narrative concerning the faith of the Canaanite woman, as referring to intelligent Gentiles who respond to the gospel, while "the wise of this world" and "the things that are" (1 Corinthians 1:27–28) are taken to refer to unbelieving Israel.[64]

The concept that the promises were not addressed to physical Israelites but rather to spiritual Israelites (the Church), is repeated in Origen's *Old Testament Homilies*. For example, in his "Homilies on Genesis," he distinguishes sharply between Jacob and Israel.[65] In his comment on Leviticus 24:10–14 he states that he who is a Catholic Christian and accepts the spiritual meaning of the Scriptures is an Israelite "by both mother and father."[66] It follows that all that Israel according to the flesh prefigured is fulfilled in the true and heavenly Israelites.[67] Thus all who see God—angels and members of the church of the firstborn (Hebrews 12:18–20)—are "children of Israel."[68]

Origen warns the Church, which he considers to be the true Israel,[69] to not take from the events the meaning that they have for Jews and heretics.[70] Jews, as a race, are viewed as obtuse and inferior to members of the Catholic Church who are able to interpret the Old Testament allegorically. True Israel is the heir of all that was promised and given to physical Israel.[71]

In light of the above, it is unclear what Origen means when he writes that after the fullness of the Gentiles comes in "the whole of Israel, whom Celsus does not know, may be saved."[72] In this he certainly depicts the Jews as more honorable than other ancient races inasmuch as the whole of their history and polity were administered by God. Moreover, by their fall salvation has come to the Gentiles (Romans 9:11–12).[73] Thus when he speaks of "the whole of Israel" attaining to salvation, either Origen intends the reader to understand a change of subject when he switches from the name "Jews" to "Israel,"—the latter indicating spiritual Israelites—or we must conclude that he did hold out the possibility of physical Israel still receiving divine blessing. The latter is possible because, in his comment on the "mystery" passage in Romans 11,[74] he takes the indications of verses 26–27 quite literally and expresses the belief that a certain "Israel" will be saved after what he calls the period of "blindness" (cf. v. 25). However, he remains unsure whether the reference is to those who have been blinded—natural Israelites—or to people from the nations not calculated in the fullness mentioned in verse 25.[75]

Even if Origen did envisage a future conversion of the Jewish people, this would not substantially modify his portrayal of ethnic Israel as an unworthy subject of Christian theology.

Major Shapers of Christian Thought and Practice

Ambrose and Augustine

Origen's contribution to replacement theology is particularly incisive because of his exegetical prowess and because he was the first Christian writer to attempt making a complete statement of the Christian faith.[76] Even though a number of Origen's speculations, such as the pre-existence of souls and the doctrine of universal salvation, were later anathematised,[77] this did not significantly lessen his influence. Thus, for churchmen who read his commentaries and homilies during subsequent centuries, the idea that true Israel had always been the Church appeared to be something taught by the Bible itself.[78]

Origen's view, that physical Israel is not a subject of theological reflection, found authoritative confirmation in the teaching of Augustine, whose influence on the development of Christian theology is without parallel. Pelikan writes, "In Augustine of Hippo Western Christianity found its most influential spokesman. . . . The role of Augustine in the evolution of Christian thought and teaching affected the history of every doctrine."[79]

So far as his understanding of Israel is concerned, we may presume that Augustine was influenced by the ideas of his spiritual mentor, Ambrose of Milan, so it is with the latter that we must begin.

Soon after Augustine's arrival at Milan toward the end of AD 384, he began listening to the preaching of Ambrose, who had been catapulted into the role of bishop ten years earlier. Near Easter, 387[80] when Augustine was baptized by Ambrose, Ambrose delivered his "Exameron"[81] in a series of nine orations. In the ninth discourse, delivered on the sixth day, the bishop applied Jeremiah's rhetorical question, "Can the Ethiopian change his skin or the leopard its spots?" (Jeremiah 13:23), to the soul of the Jewish people. In so doing, he considered the Jews to be irrevocably perverse and incapable of any good thought.[82] This tied easily into his notion that "Jews" were a type of the infidel.[83]

That the anti-Semitism of Ambrose was entrenched in his thinking is evident from the famous letter he wrote to Theodosius I (c. 346–395, Roman emperor from 379) in December 388.[84] The local bishop of Callinicum, Syria, had apparently ordered the burning of the local synagogue and the Emperor had ordered him to have it rebuilt at his own expense. Ambrose ordered the emperor to change his mind on the grounds that burning a Jewish synagogue was not a crime. It is reported that on the following Sunday, Ambrose not only pitted the Church against the Synagogue in a sermon but also publicly enjoined the Emperor to annul the sentence previously issued against the bishop of Callinicum. Ambrose refused to continue the order of service until Theodosius had given him his word![85]

There is no record that Augustine used his office to sanction anti-Jewish activity as Ambrose had done. Nevertheless, in his major apologetical work, *The City of God*, there is evidence that he shared the view of Origen and Ambrose concerning physical Israel. At the first mention of the "kingdom of the Jews" in book IV, he attributes their downfall to their "impious curiosity, which . . . drew them to strange gods and idols, and at last led them to kill Christ."[86]

Similar ideas are portrayed in Augustine's *Tract Against the Jews,* which was one of the most influential anti-Judaic writings emanating from the centuries following Origen.[87] Because of the almost canonical status enjoyed by Augustine's writings during medieval Church history, the dominant form of the anti-Jewish polemic during this period is commonly called "Augustinian." In this tradition, replacement theology and the consequent normativity of Jewish subservience to Christians, were understood to be certain. This did not exclude toleration of the Jews, however, because they preserved the original form of the Old Testament and because their eschatological conversion was envisaged.[88]

John Chrysostom (347–407)

This popular church father is important for our study because he influenced public opinion both at Antioch and later at Constantinople, where he was patriarch from 398. His fame as a preacher later merited him the name Chrysostomos or "golden mouthed." Among the hundreds of his sermons that survive, eight are directed against the Jews. [89]

Chrysostom's anti-Jewish sermons were delivered at Syrian Antioch in the year 387. Despite their virulent nature, they contain little indication of the circumstances that gave rise to them. But even allowing that there could have been some circumstantial justification for them, Chrysostom's vehemence is surprising. He accused the Jews of murdering their offspring[90] and of worshiping devils and not God.[91] Furthermore, he insisted that Jews were hated by God and, since they had murdered Jesus, they were no longer given the opportunity to repent.[92] God's purpose in concentrating all their worship in Jerusalem was only to facilitate its destruction.[93] Moreover, the suffering inflicted upon them was an expression of the wrath of God and his absolute rejection of the Jewish people.[94] Finally, since God hated them, Christians were duty bound to hate them as well.[95]

It is remarkable that neither Chrysostom nor those who accused the Jews of deicide, balanced this accusation with a recognition of the necessity of Christ's death.[96] This omission implies that the Church would have been better off had the Christ of God never taken the sinner's place on the cross. It is also indicative of a general failure to recognize that believing Jews had taken the Christian gospel to the rest of the world.[97]

The anti-Jewish attitudes evident in the preaching of Chrysostom are part of a general trend that can be traced through the *Adversus Judaeos* literature.[98] Many of these writings were motivated by the desire to prove that the Jesus of the Gospels was the Christ prophesied in the Old Testament and that the Jews were culpable in not recognizing his Messiahship. However, most of these writings also manifest a general antagonism toward all things Jewish and very often develop a theology of contempt.

The fact that Chrysostom's study of Romans 9–11[99] did not induce him to take a stand against this trend is surprising when it is remembered that he stood in the Antiochene tradition which favored the literal interpretation of Scripture.[100]

Cyril of Alexandria (c. 370–444)

Cyril is remembered as a major voice at the Council of Chalcedon but also as a bellicose ecclesiastic who was greedy for power.[101] His position as Patriarch of Alexandria from 412 till his death in 444 meant that he was able to wield considerable influence. For our purposes, it is significant that this important figure in the development of Christian orthodoxy was also anti-Jewish. On one occasion he even led Christians in pillaging the city's Jewish quarter, which resulted in the death of many Jews and the expulsion of the remainder from the city.[102]

Cyril's opposition to Jews had a theoretical basis. This is seen in the way he begins his commentary on Romans chapter 9: "In the beginning, God made Israel a chosen one and therefore he called him 'first born' (Exodus 4:22). But they have become arrogant and reckless and even worse: murderers of the Lord. Therefore they have perished, for they have become exiles and outcasts, and because they have lost their close relationship to God altogether, they have been placed behind the nations and have been alienated from the hope of the fathers."[103]

91

This was not only the opinion of Cyril; by his time it had become the official position of the Church as we shall see when we consider the development of anti-Jewish legislation.

Pope Gregory I (540–604)

Gregory I is known to history as Gregory the Great because his careful administration and astute diplomacy[104] enabled him to consolidate the Roman papacy during the years 590–604. He also reformed the Roman liturgy and, as a doctor of the Roman Catholic Church, popularized the teachings of Augustine,[105] developing what has been called "Augustinian traditionalism."[106]

Along with occasional condemnatory allusions to the Jews based on allegorical interpretation which occur throughout his writings,[107] some of his Epistles deal directly with matters affecting Jews. These letters throw light on the way that exclusion of ethnic Israel from Christian theology affected the attitudes of the clergy. In fact, Pope Gregory found it necessary to admonish the bishops of Terracina, Palermo, Cagliari, and Naples for having made threats to the Jews and for having confiscated synagogues and other goods from them. He insisted that they be granted the rights that the Theodosian Code reserved for them.[108] Gregory was in favor of Jews converting to Christianity but insisted that sincere conversions could be effected only by preaching, not by force.[109] At the same time, he was against granting the Jews more privileges than those envisaged in the Theodosian Code.

This reference to the Theodosian Code reminds us that the Church's theological understanding of the Jews found expression both in canon law and state legislation. Such regulations of the relations of Christians with Jews gave legal warrant to a growing feeling of mistrust toward the Jewish minority. This in turn facilitated the development of lists of accusations and a general attitude of contempt on the part of followers of the dominant religion. In the following survey we will only consider canon law because of its more direct link with Christian thought.

Emperor Constantine and Canon law

In AD 325, Constantine wrote a letter to those bishops who had not been present at the Council of Nicea concerning the date of Easter.[110] The following consideration contained in this letter, "We ought not, therefore, to have anything in common with the Jews," sums up one of the key ideas behind much subsequent legislation against the Jews. All things Jewish were understood to be totally incompatible with Christianity. This concept was reflected in the confessions which, in later centuries, Jewish converts to Christianity were required to make at the moment of their baptism.[111]

The theory of the total incompatibility of Christian faith and Judaism contrasts sharply with the testimony of the New Testament. The apostle Paul declared at an advanced stage of his ministry, "I am a Pharisee" (Acts 23:6) and clearly considered the practice of Jewish customs compatible with the Christian faith (1 Corinthians 9:20; Romans 14:1–8; cf. Acts 18:18; 21:20–26). The theory of the total incompatibility of Christian faith and Judaism also ignores the fact that the God of Israel is the God worshipped by Christians, while the Jewish Scriptures make up three quarters of the biblical Canon accepted by the Church.

The following samples of canon law show that the Church was not prepared to recognize the fact that Judaism and Christianity have much in common. According to Canon I of the Synod of Antioch (341), whoever observes Easter at the same time as the Jews makes himself "an alien from the Church, as one who not only heaps sins upon himself, but who is also the cause of destruction and subversion of many."[112]

The Synod of Laodicea, which met sometime between 343 and the Council of Constantinople (381), decreed: "It is not lawful to receive portions sent from the feasts of Jews or heretics, nor to feast together with them.[113] It is not lawful to receive unleavened bread from Jews, nor to be partakers of their impiety."[114]

The legal rights of Jews were also greatly restricted by "The Code of Canons of the African Church," issued by two hundred and seventeen "fathers" assembled at Carthage in AD 419. In Canon CXXIX, Jews, along with all those who have the stain of infamy, that is heretics and the heathen, are forbidden the right to bring legal accusations apart from in their own suits.[115]

The Council of Chalcedon also gave attention to relations with Jews. A new restriction was the stipulation that no Christian parent was to give his child in marriage to a Jew.[116] More complete ostracism was decreed by the Council which met at Trullo in 692: "Let no-one in the priestly order nor any layman eat the unleavened bread of the Jews, nor have any familiar intercourse with them, nor summon them in illness, nor receive medicine from them, nor bathe with them, but if anyone shall take in hand to do so, if he is a cleric, let him be deposed, but if a layman, let him be cut off."[117] Moreover, one of the so-called "Apostolic" canons also approved at

Trullo, forbade clergymen and laymen to enter a Jewish synagogue to pray, or to take oil on a feast day, on pain of excommunication.[118]

The seventh "ecumenical" council (II Nicea), which met in 787, required that, in order to be received as genuine Christians, Jewish converts must abandon all semblances of Jewish customs and ordinances.

After affirming its disapproval of forced baptism, the fourth council of Toledo (c. 631) decreed what punishments should be meted out on Jews who had accepted Christian baptism but had subsequently lapsed. Some of these were quite severe. For example, children of the lapsed, if they had been subsequently circumcised, were to be taken away from their parents. In a mixed marriage, the non-Christian partner had the choice of separation or accepting Christianity. Children of mixed marriages were to be brought up as Christians. A worse fate was in store for Jews who had never accepted baptism. Such Jews could not hold office and were to be deprived of their children.[119] It is clear, then, that by the seventh century Jews were, for all practical purposes, denied the privileges of citizenship. They were forced to live in what amounted to a social and legal ghetto long before the appearance of the material Jewish ghetto.[120]

Anti-Jewish legislation was advanced still further by the fourth Lateran Council in 1215. The Council began by sharpening previous anti-Jewish legislation, including the authorization of Crusaders to not pay their debts to Jewish money lenders. New canon laws also included: prohibiting Christians from having commerce with usurious Jews (67), requiring Jews to wear a distinctive badge or dress to mark them off from Christians, forbidding them to appear in public during Holy Week in order to avoid the risk of insult to Christians (68), and denying them any public function involving the exercise of power over Christians (69).[121]

Conclusion

The requirement to wear a distinctive badge stigmatized the Jewish community as nothing else had done. It showed that there was no safe place for the nation which had refused to accept Jesus as the promised Messiah and which doggedly awaited a different manifestation of God's kingdom.

However, it is far more significant for Christian theology that anti-Jewish canons were formulated in the context of Councils—such as the Council of Chalcedon (451)—which live in the Church's memory as occasions in which orthodoxy was defined. This reveals a parallel development of Orthodox theology on the one hand and an official anti-Judaic stance on the other. Why is this?

I believe that the clue to this unlikely association is to be found in what we have called replacement theology. Our findings have led us to conclude that this concept was not the product of careful reflection on Scripture; rather, Scripture was interpreted allegorically in such a way as to convalidate it. This is particularly evident in the way Origen sought to legitimize the categories of carnal and spiritual Israelites, to indicate historical Israel and the Church. It is even echoed in the later writings of Rupert of Deutz (c. 1070–1129). He has the following to say concerning such Old Testament passages as Zechariah 8, Isaiah 2:2–3, and Micah 4:1–2, which refer specifically to the Jews, Jerusalem, and the land of Israel: "These things which are promised are spiritual, and they are appropriate

for spiritual people and desired by them. Those however
to whom the Word came were carnal, and desired carnal
things. . . . Condescending to the carnal, therefore, like an
old man with children, lisping in order to amuse them, the
divine Word says, 'Old men and old women shall again
dwell in the streets of Jerusalem.'"[122]

Such allegorical interpretation of the Old Testament
effectively disinherits Israel of their Scriptures. James
Parkes makes this general statement concerning the
Church's reading of the Hebrew Scriptures:

> For the Gentile Church the Old Testament no longer
> meant a way of life, a conception of the relation of
> a whole community to God, but a mine from which
> proof texts could be extracted. Instead of being the
> history of a single community, and the record of its
> successes and failures, it became the record of two
> communities, the pre-Incarnation Church symbolized
> by the 'Hebrews', and the temporary and rejected
> people of the Jews. Out of this artificial separation
> of history into two parts, on the simple principle that
> what was good belonged to one group and what was
> bad to the other, grew the caricature of the Jew with
> which patristic literature is filled.[123]

Among the various effects of replacement theology,
three must be mentioned at this point. First, the Church
tended to establish its own identity in anti-Judaic terms;
the Church is what the Jews are no longer or never have
been.[124] Second, Christendom's way of interpreting the
Old Testament, based on prejudice, has made it very
difficult for Jews to take seriously the claim that Jesus
of Nazareth is the Messiah of Israel.[125] Third, Christian

writers have tended to talk about Israel in the past tense, as may be seen in the convention of terminating histories of Israel with the advent of Christianity or with the fall of the second temple in AD 70.[126]

4

REPLACEMENT THEOLOGY
AND ECCLESIOLOGY

According to Origen, corporeal Israelites were mere types of spiritual Israelites. Origen identified the latter in the Church, which he understood in transcendental terms and as already in existence at the time of Adam.[1] Clearly there is a link between Origen's concept of physical Israel and his concept of the Church. The purpose of the present chapter is to determine whether this connection is peculiar to the theology of Origen or whether there was a more general link between the pattern of Christian understanding concerning Israel and the developing pattern of ecclesiology.

The problem we face in pursuing this objective is the spontaneous nature of ecclesiastical developments in the early centuries.[2] However, as J. N. D. Kelly observes, despite the lack of "consciously formulated ecclesiology," there was, in fact, considerable development in ecclesiology in the second and third centuries, particularly in the area of the sacraments and in the concepts of catholicity and unity of the Church.[3] Apparently the question was not put as to whether New Testament teaching concerning the nature of the gospel and the Church justified these developments. However, the question remains, What caused these apparently spontaneous developments? Is it possible that, in the absence of a conscious formulation of ecclesiology, the disinheriting of Israel by the Church had repercussions on the development of the Christian ministry and church structure?

As a basis for evaluating these developments we will briefly consider the New Testament teaching concerning church structure and the nature of the Christian ministry as well as various attempts to explain subsequent developments. We will then examine the patristic writings in order to discover whether there is a discernible relationship between post-apostolic replacement theology and the developing concepts of Christian ministry and hierarchical Church structure. Our survey will extend to the time of Constantine.

New Testament Teaching Concerning Church Structure and the Nature of the Christian Ministry

Jesus prophesied that he would build a church that would withstand all opposing forces (Matthew 16:18; cf. John 10:16). On the other hand, his disciples dreamed of the restoration of the kingdom to Israel in a context of apocalyptic glory, hoping that their close relationship with Jesus would procure them positions of prestige and power in this kingdom (Mark 10:35–41; cf. Luke 19:11; Acts 1:6–8). When James and John, the sons of Zebedee, formulated a specific request in this sense, Jesus used the circumstance to affirm that such positions did not reflect the true nature of Christian discipleship: "You know that those who are regarded as rulers of the Gentiles lord it over them, and their high officials exercise authority over them. Not so with you. Instead, whoever wants to become great among you must be your servant, and whoever wants to be first must be slave of all. For even the Son of Man did not come to be served, but to serve, and to give his life as a ransom for many" (Mark 10:42–45).

The role of Jesus' disciples was to be that of special witnesses to his earthly ministry and resurrection and heralds of the gospel to the whole world (Acts 1:8, 21–22; Mark 16:15–16). Ultimately, they would even be instrumental in multiplying the number of Jesus' disciples (Matthew 28:18–20; cf. Acts 6:7; 11:26).

For a fuller idea of what Jesus envisaged for the community of his disciples, we need to consider what the Holy Spirit revealed after the ascension of Jesus (John 16:12–15). As far as church structure is concerned, the role of elders, who had been part of Israel's national life from the time of Moses (Exodus 4:29), was confirmed almost at once in the apostolic church (Acts 11:30; 15:2, 22–23). Moreover, Paul and Barnabas introduced government by a college of elders into the new Gentile churches (Acts 14:23; cf. 20:17; Titus 1:5; 1 Timothy 4:14). The same concept of leadership was later affirmed by Peter (1 Peter 5:1–3).

The function of the body of elders or "presbyters" (*presbuteroi*) is to oversee God's people, hence their office is described as that of "overseers" or "bishops" (*episkopoi*) in several New Testament passages (Acts 20:17, 28; Philippians 1:1; 1 Timothy 3:1). The New Testament also refers to the ministry of "deacons" whose function is more circumscribed than that of elders (Romans 16:1; 1 Timothy 3:8–13; cf. Acts 6:1–6).

Although the New Testament uses a variety of terms to describe church leaders (cf. Acts 13:1; Galatians 2:8–10; 1 Thessalonians 5:12), it is clear that "presbyter" refers to the same person as "bishop"[4] and that only a two-tier ministry, of bishops and deacons, was envisaged. Furthermore, the role of bishops or overseers was limited to one local church (Philippians 1:1–2; 1 Peter 5:1–4). That which appears significant, in light of subsequent developments, is the absence of a three-tier ministry consisting of a bishop as a distinct figure, a college of local elders, and deacons.

The most important ministries envisaged for church leaders were teaching and pastoral care (Acts 20:28–31; 1 Peter 5:1–4), while deacons were responsible to meet the practical needs of the congregation. However, the concept of ministry was not limited to the roles of bishops and deacons. Both Peter and Paul conceive of the Church as a society in which every member has his or her function and is called to serve according to the particular *charisma* ("gift of grace") received (1 Peter 4:10–11; Romans 12:4–8; 1 Corinthians 12:7–30). In light of later developments, it is striking that nowhere in the New Testament are elders invested with a priestly function which sets them apart from the rest of the church. Moreover, no list of spiritual gifts includes a particular *charisma* for performing priestly functions. The purpose of all the gifts was the edification of the Church, not mediation between God and other church members. Nor did the distribution of gifts entail the conferment of special prerogatives for the dispensing of divine grace. Both Peter and the writer to the Hebrews make it clear that priesthood is a prerogative of all members of the spiritual house which Christ is building and over which he presides (1 Peter 2:1–10; Hebrews 3:1–6; 4:14–16; 7:11–10:23). The only distinctive priestly function in the context of the new covenant is the high priesthood of

Christ which is described as permanent and as being "over the house of God" (Hebrews 7:23–25; 8:1–2; 10:19–22).[5] As for Peter and Paul, they understood their apostleship as involving witnessing and teaching but not in terms of a special priestly function (1 Peter 5:1; 2 Peter 1:12–13; 1 Corinthians 1:17; 1 Timothy 2:7).

When Paul elaborated on what it means to be ministers of the new covenant (2 Corinthians 3:4–11), he was careful to distinguish this ministry from what pertained to the Mosaic covenant. While both are glorious, ministry pertaining to the new covenant is more glorious, first because it is peculiarly the ministry of the Spirit and thus life-giving (vv. 6, 8), and second because it has to do with what is permanent (v. 11). The purpose of this ministry is reconciliation—"as though God were making his appeal through us." Such reconciliation is made possible by the saving work of Christ on the cross (2 Corinthians 5:18–21). It is clear from the superiority and permanency of the ministry pertaining to the new covenant that the forms of the Mosaic covenant are incompatible with it (2 Corinthians 3:7, 11; Hebrews 10:1–23). This is confirmed by the commemorative, rather than sacrificial, nature of the Lord's Supper (Luke 22:14–21; 1 Corinthians 11:23–26).

Various Opinions Concerning the Reasons for Subsequent Developments in Ecclesiology

According to two Roman Catholic scholars who write concerning ecclesiology and ecclesiastical institutions in the early church,[6] the attenuation of collegial leadership in the churches, after the close of the apostolic era, depended partly on persecution and partly on the absence of bishops on which the function of the presbyters depended.[7] They affirm that from the time of Ignatius (Smyrna VIII), "The bishop is head of the community in all of its manifestations."[8] For our purposes it is significant that, according to these scholars, certain elements in the developing Christian liturgy were patterned on aspects of Jewish liturgy.[9]

In the Cunningham Lectures of 1902,[10] Thomas Lindsay observed that by the end of the second century Ignatius' dream of church life and order being based on the office of the bishop had become a reality. By the third century "every Christian community had at its head a single president who is almost always called the bishop."[11] According to Lindsay, the causes for this, besides persecution and what he calls natural development, were the requisites for the celebration of the Lord's Supper. Already in the writings of Ignatius this celebration had been associated with an "altar" (*thusiastērion*), a concept derived from the Levitical tradition.[12]

Concerning the change in the concept of Christian ministry which occurred during the same period, Lindsay writes, "Without any apostolic sanction, in virtue of the power lying within the community and given to it by the Master, the Church of the second century effected a change in its ministry quite as radical if not more so, as that made by the Reformed Church in the sixteenth century."[13]

For the purposes of our study, it is important to understand the grounds for this radical change. Philip Schaff makes the following general statement: "Judaism, with its religion and its sacred writings, and Graeco-Roman heathenism, with its secular culture, its science, and its art, were destined to pass into Christianity to be transformed and sanctified."[14]

According to Schaff, then, Judaism, as a religion, helped to shape Christianity. Panfilo Gentile also attributes certain developments in second century Christianity to a takeover of aspects of Judaism.[15] Dunn considers this takeover a retrograde step: "Rabbinic Judaism was able to survive the loss of a cult center (the Temple), and so also the loss of the possibility and need for sacrifice and priesthood, by reorganizing itself round the Torah. In rabbinic Judaism priest was replaced by teacher. In contrast, and somewhat surprisingly, it was Christianity which found it necessary to revert to OT categories of sacrifice and priesthood, at first in a spiritual or allegorical way, as a means to expressing continuity with the ideal of OT spirituality, but then in an increasingly literal way."[16]

According to Dunn, the way Christianity appropriated some central features of Old Testament religious practice had negative effects not only upon the concept of Christian ministry but also upon the concept of the Church as the body of Christ.[17]

Replacement Theology and Developments in Concepts of Church Structure and Ministry

At the Close of the First Century

The letter known as 1 Clement,[18] written in the name of the Roman church to its sister church in Corinth (AD 90–100), contains a surprising anticipation of some future developments. In order to explain what it means to be "made partakers in the blessings of His elect," the author quotes Deuteronomy 32:8–9, where it is stated that "His people Jacob became the portion of the LORD, and Israel the lot of His inheritance."[19] Later in the letter this is followed by a definition of church order and ministry in which free use is made of Old Testament Levitical terminology. For example, the author mentions three levels of ministry—high priest, other priests, and Levites—all of which are distinguished from the role of the laity. Church members are exhorted not to go beyond the boundaries of each one's own particular ministry, that is "beyond the rule of the ministry prescribed to him."[20]

Thus a simple form of replacement theology—the Church identified as Israel—is followed by the application of the Levitical model to ecclesiastical order and the concept of Christian ministry.

In the Epistles of Ignatius

In his Epistle to the Philadelphians, Ignatius orders his readers not to listen to anyone who preaches the law (VI, 1). Moreover, he links Abraham with the Church, making his acceptance with God depend upon Jesus' role as High Priest (IX, 1–2). Other elements in this letter which point in the direction of a simple form of replacement theology are its three-tier concept of the Christian ministry and the use of the term "altar" to qualify the Eucharist.[21] When Ignatius refers to the "one Eucharist," he also speaks of "one altar; as there is one bishop, along with the presbytery and deacons" (IV, 1).

The dominant theme in these letters is solidarity with the bishop as the secret of Christian unity.[22] The passage just quoted suggests that behind the crucial role attributed to the bishop is the Levitical model of ministry now presumed to pertain to the Church. The direction in which the new concept of ecclesiastical structure would take the Church is further suggested by the way Ignatius greets the church of Rome, which is said to "preside over the region of the Romans," and even more significantly, to "preside over love" (*prokathēmenē tēs agapēs*).[23] These expressions bear witness to the beginning of the concept of the primacy of Rome, which certainly was to take root in the thought of later Church Fathers.[24]

In Pseudonymous 2 Clement

In 2 Clement we meet for the first time the idea of the Church being pre-existent[25] and essentially spiritual in nature (XIV, 1). As well as considering the Church to exist from eternity past, the writer of 2 Clement uses Old and New Testament writings indiscriminately. For instance, he makes belonging to the Church and obtaining final salvation depend upon observing the law of purity and doing works of righteousness (XV–XIX). Thus we see that disregard for the essential link between the Old Testament and Israel and a failure to consider the specificity of the Church in God's plan, leads to the neglect of the gospel of grace on which membership in the true church depends (see Acts 15:1–11).

In Justin Martyr's Dialogue with Trypho, a Jew[26]

Justin was convinced that the Church occupied the place which the Jews believed was reserved for them. After listening to the Christian apologist freely apply to the Church promises originally addressed to Israel, his Jewish interlocutor exclaimed, "What then? are you Israel? and does He [God] speak such things [Isaiah 19:24–25; Ezekiel 34:12] to you?"[27]

For Justin, the presupposition that the Church had replaced Israel meant that Old Testament concepts could be applied indiscriminately to the Church. This is evident when he speaks of the priesthood in chapter CXVI: "We are the true high priestly race of God, as even God Himself bears witness, saying that in every place among the Gentiles sacrifices are presented to Him well-pleasing and pure. Now God receives sacrifices from no one, except through His priests."

This theme is further developed in chapter CXVII where Justin builds on Malachi 1:10–12 in order to prove the unacceptable nature of the sacrifices offered by the priests of Israel.[28] According to Justin, the passage refers to the "sacrifices" of the bread and the cup of the Eucharist. He denies that there was a Jewish dispersion at the time when Malachi was written and claims that by his own time there were "Christians in all places throughout the world." He was mistaken on both counts, yet his exegesis of the Malachi passage became part of presuppositional replacement theology. For example, in his *Tract Against the Jews*, written almost three centuries later, Augustine uses Malachi 1:10–11 to show that the Jews have been dismissed while Christians offer acceptable sacrifices everywhere on earth and in heaven![29]

The most questionable aspects of Justin's exposition of the Malachi passage are, first, his complete neglect of what the prophet's words would have meant for readers of his time and, second, the definition of the memorial meal instituted by Jesus in terms analogous to the Levitical sacrifices.[30] Justin's reasoning has important implications for the concept of Christian ministry, which he understands as being essentially that of offering sacrifices which replace those offered by unworthy Jewish priests.

In Irenaeus' Against Heresies[31]

In our last chapter we saw that Irenaeus read the Old Testament in light of replacement theology. We now turn to his teaching concerning church structure and the Christian ministry.

Irenaeus appealed to an uninterrupted succession of bishops from the apostles to his own time as a guarantee of orthodoxy. Where no bishop standing in this line of succession was present, meetings were to be considered unauthorized and could be occasions for the dissemination of the perverse opinions of men.[32] According to Irenaeus, the importance of being able to trace the succession of bishops increased in the case of the church of Rome, because it was supremely this church, founded by the apostles Peter and Paul, which guaranteed the faithful transmission of the apostolic tradition. He writes, "For it is a matter of necessity that every Church should agree with this Church, on account of its preeminent authority."[33]

It is clear that Irenaeus' primary concern here is the preservation of apostolic truth. However, it is significant that a Church Father who set himself to defend orthodoxy and stressed the canonicity of certain writings also stressed the office of the episcopate, thus considering a three-tier concept of church leadership an essential part of Christian orthodoxy.

Irenaeus' treatment of sacrifices also raises the question of the nature of the Christian ministry. He uses a catena of Old Testament quotations to show that God did not desire sacrifices and holocausts for himself but instituted these for Israel even though he intended faith, obedience, and righteousness to be the mechanisms of Israel's salvation.[34] Irenaeus then proceeds to use Malachi 1:10–11 as a basis for asserting that the sacrifice that God seeks is what Jesus' disciples offer him in every place among the nations. According to Irenaeus, Malachi 1:11 indicates "in the plainest manner . . . that [the Jews] shall indeed cease to make offerings to God, but that in every place sacrifice shall be offered to Him . . . among the Gentiles."[35] The whole of chapter eighteen of book IV is dedicated to a discussion of the Eucharist which Irenaeus describes variously as "the oblation of the Church" and a "sacrifice."[36]

The parallelism which Irenaeus creates between Levitical sacrifices and what he considers the "sacrifice" consisting in the bread and wine of the Eucharist, ignores the unique and final value of Christ's sacrifice (Hebrews 10:10–18). He also neglects the specificity of Old Testament Scripture in its relationship to Israel and shows gratuitous contempt for Israelites whom he describes as slaves.[37] This neglect of the specificity of Israel and its institutions in the divine plan leads him to confuse Christ's unique sacrifice (Hebrews 9:1–10:19), of which the Lord's Supper was intended to be a commemoration (Luke 22:19), with Levitical sacrifices. Thus the Eucharist is understood to not only be similar to, but actually better than the Levitical sacrifices and having salvific value in and of itself. He says, "For as the bread, which is produced from the earth, when it receives the invocation of God, is no longer common bread, but the Eucharist, consisting of two realities, earthly and heavenly; so also our bodies, when they receive the Eucharist, are no longer corruptible, having the hope of the resurrection to eternity."[38]

In terms of the development of the Christian ministry, the most significant word here is "invocation" (*epiklēsis*). Moreover, it is noteworthy that the transformation of the

bread into a heavenly as well as earthly reality is said
to infuse incorruptibility into the bodies of those who
receive it. Ignatius had already taught that the bread,
when received in a context of obedience to the bishop
and the presbytery is "the medicine of immortality."[39]
Irenaeus adds that the transformation of the bread into
this special substance is caused by the invocation. A study
of the theme of invocation (*epiklēsis*) in early Christian
writings and liturgies[40] shows that it was understood to be
a priestly function performed by the bishop. It is possible
that the origin of this invocation is to be traced to Jewish
synagogue practice and ultimately to the concept of the
divine *Shekhina* which filled the Tabernacle (Exodus
40:34–35).[41] Irenaeus' expression "the invocation of
God" harmonizes well with this view. Eventually the
invocation would become the prayer for the coming of
the Holy Spirit and for the transformation of the bread
and wine into the body and blood of Christ.[42] According
to the *Apostolic Constitutions*, the authority to effect this
transformation is "conferred by the laying on of the hands
of the bishop."[43]

Irenaeus' teaching concerning the Eucharist marks a
significant development in the understanding of Christian
ministry. Inasmuch as the practice of the invocation of
God can be traced to Old Testament influence,[44] it is
another instance of how the Church indiscriminately
appropriated Old Testament liturgical practice. It is
striking that an ecclesiastic of the stature of Irenaeus
should develop a Christian doctrine of invocation without
regard for what the New Testament teaches concerning
the nature of authentic Christian worship and its attendant
privileges (John 4:23–24; Hebrews 10:19–23; 13:15;
1 Peter 2:4–5). The fact that his teaching on the Eucharist

was accompanied by an attitude of contempt for the Jews further illustrates the relationship between replacement theology and the tendency to confuse aspects of Levitical practice with Christian ministry.

In the Writings of Tertullian

In our last chapter we saw that Tertullian shared Justin Martyr's conviction concerning circumcision, that it was given to Israel to mark her out as a "contumacious people." Furthermore, on the basis of Genesis 25:23, he considered Israel to be the servant of the Church. Because such exegesis ignores the clear meaning of the biblical text (cf. Romans 9:11–12), it appears that Tertullian's understanding of Israel's place in the divine economy depended primarily on the *Adversus Judaeos* tradition.[45] This may also be seen in his work *An Answer to the Jews*, where he writes, "The 'less'—that is the posterior— people attains the grace of divine favor from which Israel has been divorced."[46]

We noticed in the last chapter that Tertullian coined a number of theological terms which are still in use today. One of these, which he introduced while still a member of the Catholic Church, is *domina mater ecclesia*, which characterizes the Church as the mother of Christians.[47] Moreover, in his *Prescription Against Heretics* written in the same period,[48] Tertullian claimed that faith, in order to be apostolic, must descend from the apostles, through apostolic churches.[49] At the time of making this assertion, Tertullian held to the organic unity of the catholic, apostolic church.

In this early period he also introduced the term *summus sacerdos* in his work *On Baptism*. This term defined the bishop as the priest who stood above elders and deacons.⁵⁰ At the same time, Tertullian concluded that the laity, without special authorization from the bishop, could not perform functions reserved for the latter because the bishop—and to a more limited extent the elders and deacons—was presumed to have special powers.⁵¹ This concept of special powers has much in common with the prerogatives of Levitical priests (Leviticus 1–9, 16, 21) but little in common with the New Testament teaching concerning the Christian ministry. Tertullian considered baptism to be one of the higher functions which properly belonged to the bishop (*summus sacerdos*). For Paul, on the other hand, preaching belonged to a higher order of ministry than did baptizing converts (1 Corinthians 1:14, 17), a conviction shared by Peter (cf. Acts 15:7–11 with 10:36–48).

The assimilation of Jewish titles such as "high priest" tended to give pre-eminence to Christian rites over faith and discipleship. Tertullian himself became dissatisfied with a church characterized by such religious forms, to the extent that he eventually left the official church around AD 205. Some interesting changes are discernible in the writings which follow Tertullian's disenchantment with the official church. In his work *On the Veiling of Virgins* he criticizes the idea of an hierarchical church: "[The churches founded by apostles or by apostolic men] and we have one faith, one God, the same Christ, the same hope, the same baptismal sacraments; let me say it once for all, we are one church. Thus, whatever belongs to our brethren is ours: only, the body divides us."⁵²

Tertullian no longer saw apostolic succession in terms of a human catena or of structural solidarity with the Roman hierarchy; rather, he identified it in five of the elements listed by Paul in Ephesians 4:1–6. The omission of the one Spirit and the one body (1 Corinthians 12:12–13) is not accidental. In fact Tertullian stated openly that "the body divides us." Furthermore, in a previous chapter he had spoken of the Paraclete's administrative office as including, among other things, "the direction of discipline," something he saw sadly lacking in the hierarchical church where custom was put before truth. Tertullian takes up his polemic again with what he calls the "Psychic Church" in chapter XXI of his work *On Modesty*, in which he reasons that the keys entrusted by Christ to Peter concerned entrance into the kingdom and "had nothing to do with the capital sins of believers."

When describing the kind of church which is authorized to administer discipline and the forgiveness of sins, Tertullian distances himself from the hierarchical church by asserting the concept of the gathered church: "For the very Church itself is, properly and principally, the Spirit Himself, in whom is the Trinity of the One Divinity—Father, Son, and Holy Spirit. . . . And thus, from that time forward, every number [of persons] who may have combined together into this faith is accounted 'a church,' from the Author and Consecrator [of the Church]."[53]

Although Tertullian makes a substantial move toward the New Testament concept of the Church, his concept of Christian ministry proved to be less flexible. Thus, in the chapter from which we have just quoted, he continues to use Levitical language, as when he writes of "the ministry of a priest ordained" to a sacred office.[54] Even so, it appears significant that the attenuation of the concept of replacement theology in his later writings coincided with a critical stance toward the conception of a monolithic, hierarchical church.

In the Writings of Origen

We have already seen how Origen's replacement theology went beyond that taught by Justin Martyr and Irenaeus. In fact, it is probably more appropriate to describe his theological position of the disinheriting of all "corporeal" Israelites, including those who lived before Christ, as radical. Yet his prowess as a biblical exegete helped to make this version of replacement theology a standard presupposition of Christian theology. Thus, as we have seen, churchmen such as Ambrose of Milan, Cyril of Alexandria, John Chrysostom of Antioch, Augustine of Hippo, and Pope Gregory the Great all regarded replacement theology as fact.

Immediately after presenting corporeal Israelites as mere types of spiritual Israelites in Book IV of *On First Principles*, Origen describes the Church as a transcendent reality, from which even Adam descended.[55] He thus asserts that physical Israel never occupied the place in God's plan that a literal reading of the Old Testament would suggest. The real members of God's people had always been spiritual Israelites, that is, the Church, understood to be something quite distinct from corporeal Israelites.

The question we now have to consider is whether Origen's replacement theology influenced his understanding of church structure and Christian ministry in a similar way that it influenced the ecclesiology of the Church Fathers that we have already examined. Given Origen's predilection for heavenly realities and his belief that earthly realities had merely typological or allegorical value, we might well expect that he would dispense with the literal use of Levitical categories. However, as Hanson observes, "[Origen] always intended to interpret the Bible as the Church interpreted it. He was a loyal churchman. . . . The whole life, custom and practice of the Church was very dear to him."[56]

In order to understand Origen's view of the relevance of Levitical categories to Christian ministry, we will examine some of his Homilies on Leviticus and the Song of Songs.

In the introduction to his Homilies on Leviticus, Origen establishes the principle that, as the Word of God had taken the form of flesh, so the written Word of God had taken the form of the letter. Accordingly, the interpreter's goal is to perceive the hidden, spiritual meaning contained in the "letter."[57] Later in these Homilies he teaches that the references to Christ's flesh and blood in John 6:53 and 55 are to be understood as referring to Jesus' Word.[58] Moreover, in discussing the eucharistic doctrine he allows "the more usual interpretation concerning the Eucharist" for the simpler folk, but he adds, "to those who have learnt to hear deeper things, let it be understood also according to the more divine promise about the nourishing word of truth."[59]

According to Origen, the efficacy of the eucharistic bread depends partly on the words pronounced by the one who prays over it and partly on the state of worthiness of those who receive it.[60] The importance which Origen attributes to the words pronounced over the eucharistic bread raises an important question, Did he follow others in understanding the Christian ministry in Levitical terms?

While recognizing that Christ conferred the privilege of priesthood upon all members of the Church,[61] Origen insists that the forms of the Levitical ministry are pertinent to Christian ministry. Thus Leviticus 8:13 teaches to distinguish between lesser and greater priestly ministries in the Church, while the role of "pontiff" or bishop is similar to that of Moses and Aaron.[62] Moreover, Paul's teaching concerning church leaders serves to confirm the validity of the instructions given to the priests in Leviticus 9:7; 10:8–9, and Numbers 18:20. Thus the precepts contained in 1 Timothy 3:2–3 and Titus 1:7–8 are addressed to "the priests" and "the princes of the priests."[63] Similarly, commenting on the limitations of entrance into the Jewish tabernacle, Origen divides humanity into priests who can enter the holy place, the pontiff who alone can penetrate the most holy place, the "children of Israel, that is the laymen," and the foreigners who have not yet been numbered in the Lord's Church.[64] Origen seems to have forgotten that by prescribing the divisions of the tabernacle and restrictions of entry, "the Holy Spirit was showing . . . that the way into the Most Holy Place had not yet been disclosed." (Hebrews 9:8).

The clear implication of Hebrews 9:1–8 is that the division of humanity into the categories of high priest, priests, laymen, and foreigners was temporary. Both the writer to the Hebrews and the apostle Paul teach that the finished work of Christ made it possible for those who had been excluded from covenant blessings to gain full access to God's presence (Hebrews 10:10–23; Ephesians 2:11–22).

Because of the prevalence of Origen's use of allegoricalism as his preferred hermeneutical method in his Homilies of the Song of Songs, we may consider opinions expressed there to be particularly indicative of his own thought. This is confirmed in the Prologue. The Song of Songs, writes Origen, is not to be interpreted according to its "carnal" sense; even the author of the work is to be regarded not as the son of David or the king of Israel, but as a symbolic "Solomon."[65] Yet even in this work Origen reverts to transposing Old Testament hierarchical distinctions into the context of the Church. For example, the things contemplated by the queen of Sheba in 1 Kings ten indicate the ecclesiastical order made up of the episcopate and the presbytery, while the attending servants indicate the deacons who assist the divine office.[66] Elsewhere Origen suggests that we are to understand the Levites to be superior to the twelve tribes of Israel because they were not counted in the census (Numbers 2:32–33), while the priests are to be considered superior to the Levites (Numbers 3:5); thus also the true Church is superior to the physical Israelites.[67]

Among the influences which determined Origen's use of Old Testament forms, the platonic concept of the Church propounded by Clement, his predecessor at the School of Alexandria, stands out as particularly prominent. According to Clement, "the grades here in the Church, of bishops, presbyters, deacons, are imitations of the angelic glory."[68] This three-tier concept of ministry has the following ancestry: first Israel, as God's elect people and heir of the promises, was disinherited, then the instructions which the God of Israel gave to the Levites were applied to the Church. Allegorical interpretation of the Scriptures gave the Church free rein to indiscriminately apply to herself what had pertained to Israel under the Mosaic covenant.

How far can this process be taken without losing sight of the specificity of the Church and the terms of the new covenant as taught by the apostles? It is evident from the writings of Origen that, once replacement theology becomes an axiom of Christian hermeneutics, nothing can prevent the wholesale appropriation of Old Testament cultic practice into Church life.

The Eclipse of the Old Catholic Church

Cyprian (c. 200–258)

Some four decades after Tertullian's death, another churchman of Carthage left his mark on the developing Christian tradition. Cyprian, bishop of Carthage from 248 until his death in 258, is significant for the theme of our present chapter because, as well as writing *Three Books of Testimonies* against the Jews,[69] he also made a distinctive contribution to ecclesiology.[70] This contribution has been evaluated in very different ways. On the one hand, Vatican Council II made repeated use of his writings in expounding Roman Catholic ecclesiology.[71] On the other hand D. F. Wright assesses Cyprian's contribution to ecclesiology in substantially negative terms: "His rigid correlation of Church and episcopate and his application of OT sacrificial and priestly categories to Christian ministers and sacraments constituted an unhappy legacy."[72]

Our main task will be to establish whether or not there is a relationship between Cyprian's replacement theology and the ecclesiological elements to which Wright draws attention. This will help determine the extent to which replacement theology contributed to what became standard Christian ecclesiology for more than a thousand years.

The logical place to begin this survey is with Cyprian's explicit statement of replacement theology in his introduction to his work *Three Books of Testimonies Against the Jews.* He writes, "I have endeavored to show that the Jews, according to what had before been foretold, had departed from God, and had lost God's favor, which had been given them in past time, and had been promised them for the future; while the Christians had succeeded to their place, deserving well of the Lord by faith, and coming out of all nations and from the whole world."[73]

Cyprian's replacement theology concerns both the past and the future. A sampling of chapter headings of the *Three Books of Testimonies Against the Jews* shows the extent to which his thought was impregnated with replacement theology. Moreover, it is evident that while assimilating certain Old Testament sacrificial and priestly categories into the context of the new covenant, he also projected certain Christian terms back into the Old Testament economy. Here is the sampling:

Chapter 12.   That the old baptism should cease, and a new one should begin [Isaiah 43:18–21; 48:21; Matthew 3:11; John 3:5–6].

Chapter 16.   That the ancient sacrifice should be made void, and a new one should be celebrated [Isaiah 1:11–12; Psalm 50:13–15, 23; 4:5; Malachi 1:10–11].

Chapter 19.   That two peoples were foretold, the elder and the younger; that is, the old people of the Jews, and new one which should consist of us [Genesis 25:23; Hosea 2:23; 1:10].

Chapter 20.   That the Church which before had been barren should have more children from among the Gentiles than what the synagogue had had before [Isaiah 54:1–4; 1 Samuel 2:5].

Chapter 22.   That the Jews would lose while we should receive the bread and the cup of Christ and all His grace, and that the new name of Christians should be blessed in the earth [Isaiah 65:13–15; 5:26–27; 3:1–2; Psalm 34:8–10; John 6:35; 7:37–38; 6:53].[74]

In no case does a straightforward reading of the passages mentioned above lead to the conclusions suggested in the chapter headings.

In the third book of *Testimonies*, Cyprian affirms "that the Eucharist is to be received with fear and honor."[75] The biblical passages on which this consideration is based are Leviticus 7:20 and 1 Corinthians 11:27. The first of these speaks of sacrifice, literally a "fellowship offering belonging to the Lord," which was not to be eaten in the case of it becoming ceremonially unclean, on pain of death. The second is related to the Lord's Supper which Jesus' disciples were commanded to celebrate (1 Corinthians 11:27; cf. Luke 22:19). The only logical link between the two passages is the requirement to act according to God's instructions with an accompanying warning concerning the consequences of disobedience. For the rest, the differences are profound. The reference in Leviticus is to a sacrifice which could be offered any number of times and which had to be taken to a priest who offered it to the Lord (Leviticus 7:14–19). On the other hand, the Lord's

Supper has to do with the giving of thanks (*eucharistia*) and the commemoration and proclamation of the once-for-all sacrifice which Christ offered to God, thus putting an end to all sacrifices (1 Corinthians 11:23–26; cf. Hebrews 7:27; chapters 9–10).

It is significant that the ninth, tenth, and eleventh chapters of Romans are virtually ignored in the *Three Books of Testimonies Against the Jews*. In particular, no part of these chapters is quoted in which reference is made to the present status or future prospect of unbelieving Israel.[76] The choice to ignore these passages shows that Cyprian's conviction that Israel has irretrievably lost what had been given them in past time and what had been promised them for the future was based on a selective use of Scripture.

Cyprian's contribution to ecclesiology was tied to the greater historical events of his lifetime. As bishop of Carthage he had to face the problem of how to treat baptized Christians who, after having denied their faith in Christ during the persecution decreed by Emperor Decius (250–251), repented and sought re-entry into the Church. The different positions propounded regarding the possibility of re-admitting these people caused some serious divisions in the church of Carthage. Following two Synods of African bishops, Cyprian took an intermediate position between the inflexible stance of Novatus and the more liberal attitude of those who opposed him. However, the Church remained divided and this caused Cyprian to meditate on the whole question of Christian unity. This led to the writing of his most famous treatise *On the Unity of the Church*.[77]

According to Cyprian, the unity of the Church has its origin in the apostle Peter, understood to be the source of the episcopate and the foundation of the Church.[78] He identified "the throne of Peter" in the succession of Roman bishops in terms of primacy rather than supremacy.[79] Consequently, the true church is that which maintains fellowship with the petrine bishop of Rome and submits itself to legitimately ordained bishops who replace their predecessors in the same See. Where cohesion between the local See and the legitimate bishop of Rome is lacking, the Church does not exist and all religious functions, including baptism and the Eucharist, are null and void.[80] Cyprian's ecclesiology is summed up in the memorable phrase, "He can no longer have God for his Father who has not the Church for his mother."[81] The word "Church" here refers to those parts of Christendom whose unity with Christ is mediated by the apostolic See of Rome.

A second characteristic of Cyprian's ecclesiology is his use of the term "catholic." Whereas previously this term had been used with reference to the worldwide church[82] and to those holding to orthodox doctrine,[83] Cyprian now associated it with a more limited concept of the true church,[84] according to which catholicity depends on the "sacrament of unity, this bond of a concord inseparably cohering [with the Roman See]."[85] Outside of this unity, which he calls the Catholic Church, the sacrifices offered by priestly rivals are considered invalid.[86]

A reader of the New Testament may well ask what the offering of sacrifices and priestly rivals have to do with Christianity? Such talk has much more to do with Levitical categories than anything the New Testament has to say about Christian ministry. Yet the following passage taken from Cyprian's tractate on Christian unity illustrates the extent to which his ecclesiology was organized in Levitical categories: "Does he think that he has Christ, who acts in opposition to Christ's priests, who separates himself from the company of His clergy and people? . . . An enemy of the altar, a rebel against Christ's sacrifice . . . a hostile brother, despising the bishops, and forsaking God's priests, he dares to set up another altar . . . to profane the truth of the Lord's offering by false sacrifices."[87]

Cyprian's concept of Christian unity, based on a combination of apostolic succession and priestly ordination, produced episcopal exclusivism. This new principle replaced the apostolic concept of Christian unity based on the gospel (see Acts 15:1–14; Romans 15:7). Cyprian's contribution turned out to be a watershed in the history of ecclesiology. After his life and ministry the Catholic Church ceased being the universal church and became the Roman Catholic Church, while orthodoxy came to mean obedience to the ecclesiastical institution thought to mediate God's grace through the sacraments. All of this presupposed the conviction that the Church now occupied the place which was once Israel's and that its ministers possessed the same prerogatives as the Levitical priesthood.

Emperor Constantine

Constantine's Contribution to the Development of Christian Anti–Semitism. The edict of toleration promulgated by emperor Galerio in AD 311 and the ecclesiastical politics of Constantine, which began with the publication of the edict of Milan (313), inaugurated a new era for the Church. With imperial persecution virtually a thing of the past, it was reasonable to expect that members of the Church would be free to live according to their Christian conscience. In actuality, freedom from persecution was immediately followed by interference in the affairs of the Church on the part of the secular power in the person of the emperor.[88] Constantine reorganized the Church using the administrative structures of the Roman empire as his model. This factor, wedded to the hierarchical structure inherited from the School of Alexandria and from Cyprian, radically changed the concept of the Church from that of a body whose leaders were servants, to that of "a fixed order where some were permanently set over others."[89] This must be kept in mind in order to understand the nature of Constantine's relationship with the Church. The "people" were counted as part of the Church only through their link with the bishop who incarnated the Church's true substance.[90]

Constantine believed that his religious role as *pontifex maximus* ("supreme priest") included being high priest of the Christian church as well as of all the pagan religions. Hence he felt it was his duty to maintain order in the Church, and took it upon himself to convene councils to resolve doctrinal disputes.[91] By such interference[92] and by the creation of ecclesiastical regions, he left an indelible mark on the life of the Church. In what follows, we will first examine how Constantine set in motion what was to become standard practice in Church-Israel relations. We will then consider some long term effects of his religious politics on ecclesiology itself.

The main concern of the Council of Nicea (AD 325), convened and presided over by the emperor himself, was to overthrow Arianism by defining orthodox Christology. However, a number of less important matters were also discussed. Among these was the question concerning the date of Easter. Constantine treated this in a letter he sent to those not present at Nicea. At a certain point in this letter, he writes, "It was declared to be particularly unworthy for [Easter], the holiest of all festivals, to follow the [calculation] of the Jews, who had soiled their hands with the most fearful of crimes, and whose minds were blinded. . . . We ought not therefore, to have anything in common with the Jews . . . we desire, dearest brethren, to separate ourselves from the detestable company of the Jews. . . . [Even if their deliberations were not wrong] it would still be your duty not to tarnish your soul by communications with such wicked people."[93]

For the first time in history the Church's theological understanding concerning Israel dictated official policy, albeit indirectly. It may appear paradoxical that while the Church felt free to take over cultic forms and sacrificial language from the Jewish Scriptures, she scrupulously avoided any identification of the Christian Easter with the Jewish Passover despite the fact that the New Testament establishes a close link between Jewish practice and Christian faith at this point (Luke 22:14–16; 1 Corinthians 5:7). A possible explanation is that the Church felt free to assimilate elements of Levitical cultic practice into the pattern of Christian worship because the sacrificial system and all that went with it were no longer a part of contemporary Jewish life. On the other hand, the Passover celebration did continue to occupy an important place in the Jewish religious calendar,[94] as indeed it still does today. Hence the Church, in its desire to disassociate with physical Israel, felt the need to hold its own Easter celebration on a different date from that of the Jewish Passover.

Constantine's letter established a precedent for the practice of making official statements which discriminated against the Jews.[95] James Parkes makes this general comment: "There is no other adequate foundation [for modern anti-Semitism] than the theological conceptions built up in the first three centuries. But upon these foundations an awful superstructure has been reared, and first stones of that superstructure were laid, the very moment the Church had power to do so, in the legislation of Constantine and his successors."[96]

Constantine's Influence on the Development of Ecclesiology. The link established between the Church and the secular state was to have a profound effect both on the concept and the perceived role of the Church. In the eastern part of the Roman Empire the practice of the state exercising power over the Church became normative after AD 330 when Constantine shifted his capital to Byzantium and renamed it Constantinople. Meanwhile, the West, accustomed to a powerful political head in Rome, increasingly attributed a unifying political role to its bishop. Thus the Roman bishop grew in prestige to the point of eventually gaining ascendancy over secular powers.

Constantine's religious policies had three further effects. They favored the concept of the territorial Church; they consolidated the division between clergy and laity; and they contributed to the development of medieval theocracy. Here we will consider the first and second of these aspects, leaving the development of the medieval theocracy for the next chapter.

In order to understand the importance of Constantine's policy of favoring the Christian religion throughout the

Roman Empire, it is necessary to remember that religion was generally subservient to the state in the Roman world. Thus Constantine's decision to favor Christianity over paganism turned Christianity into a state church whose dimensions corresponded to a given territory. All those living in this territory were expected to be Christians. This goal was facilitated by a sacramental understanding of baptism, which was understood to confer divine grace on those baptized and introduce them into the Church.

The sacramental understanding of baptism had developed gradually and was already well established by the time Tertullian wrote his treatise *On Baptism* (c. AD 200). There is a certain tension in Tertullian's doctrine of baptism which both affirms the sacramental value of the rite and teaches that entrance into the Church implies living a holy life. The first of these elements is present in the opening phrase of his treatise: "Happy is our sacrament of water, in that, by washing away the sins of our early blindness, we are set free *and admitted* into eternal life!"[97] Towards the end of the same work Tertullian recommends that baptism be delayed in the case of small children and the unwedded in order to lessen the probability of grave sins being committed after baptism.[98]

Half a century after Tertullian wrote his treatise, Cyprian counseled Fidus not to wait to baptize infants until the eighth day because "the mercy and grace of God is not to be refused to any one born of man."[99] It is clear from this advice that baptism had, by Cyprian's time, come to be understood as effecting forgiveness of sins and entrance into the Church. The preference to baptize infants on the eighth day as Fidus had expressed,[100] rested on the conviction that Christian baptism took the place of circumcision. However, because baptism was thought to be an efficacious means of communicating God's mercy and grace, Cyprian deemed it advisable to override the symbolism of the eighth day.

The practice of baptizing the newly-born was part of a general tendency linked with a priestly understanding of the Christian ministry. In Constantine's day this sacramental understanding of ministry facilitated the formal conversion of the Roman Empire to Christianity. But are there grounds for considering baptism analogous to the rite of circumcision and the chief means whereby lost sinners receive saving grace?

The issues of circumcision and of how God administers salvation were the two interrelated questions discussed at the Jerusalem Conference during the apostolic era. Many modern scholars regard this meeting, of which the proceedings are summarized in Acts 15:1–29, as the first Church Council.[101] It is significant that nobody at this important meeting, not even Peter (vv. 7–11), suggested that baptism had replaced physical circumcision. More significant still, in light of later teaching concerning baptismal regeneration, is the lack of any suggestion that baptism is a means whereby sin is forgiven and salvation is applied. The fact that the deliberations of the Jerusalem meeting were substantially ignored by Christian leaders in subsequent centuries, while priestly administration of both baptism and the Eucharist became the chief functions of Christian ministers, testifies to the far-reaching effects of confusing the institutions of the Church with those of Israel.

The other effect of the Constantinian revolution concerned the order of Christian worship. Justo Gonzàlez sums it up well: "the congregation came to have a less active role in worship."[102] Gonzàlez also describes some formal changes: "Incense, which was used as a sign of respect for the emperor, began appearing in Christian churches. Officiating ministers, who until then had worn everyday clothes, began dressing in more luxurious garments. Likewise, a number of gestures indicating respect, which were normally made before the emperor, now became part of Christian worship. The custom was also introduced of beginning services with a processional."[103]

Constantine's religious policies favored the building of basilicas such as the one dedicated to the Most Holy Savior, now known as St. John Lateran. The design of these buildings reflected and consolidated the ecclesiological developments which we have been considering: "In the atrium there was a fountain where the faithful could perform ritual washings, next there were naves for the people, with a pulpit on either side for the reading and exposition of Scripture. At the end of the central nave, on a higher level, there was the sanctuary with an altar at its center. There was space on this elevated area for the officiating ministers, as it was here that communion was celebrated. If it was the bishop's main church, there was a special chair or 'cathedra'[104] for the bishop."[105]

Constantine gave architectural expression to the separation of the clergy from the laity. He also rendered the idea that the main function of the clergy was the administration of the sacraments, in particular of the Eucharist, on an altar of sacrifice in the most holy place. Baptisteries were usually built separately. While proclamation was important, it was shown not to be central. From this point on the basilica with its officiating ministers was perceived as the true church while the laity, who received the ministrations offered by the hierarchical church, became subservient to the leadership. Inasmuch as the general structure and functions of the basilica are comparable to those of the Jewish tabernacle and temple, it is no exaggeration to say that such forms and functions were the practical consequence of the assimilation of Levitical cultic forms and priestly ministrations into Christianity, a practice which was facilitated by presuppositional replacement theology.

Replacement Theology in the Catechetical Lectures of Cyril of Jerusalem

The fact that Cyril (c. 310–386) was familiar with the condition of the so-called "Holy Places" before Constantine began adorning them,[106] suggests that he spent some of his early years in Jerusalem. He was ordained deacon sometime before the death of Bishop Macarius in 334 or 335 and bishop about fifteen years later.[107] His role as defender of orthodoxy, his personal concern for the poor, and the fact that he was bishop of the Apostolic See considered to be "the Mother of all the Churches," all make Cyril's pronouncements particularly significant.

In his seventeenth lecture, Cyril explains that because of the existence of "a Church of evil doers . . . [and] heretics," it was necessary to use the formula "the one Holy Catholic Church" to describe "the Church of us Christians."[108] This church replaced the former one: "But after the Jews for the plots which they made against the Savior were cast away from His grace, the Savior built out of the Gentiles a second Holy Church, the Church of us Christians, concerning which he said to Peter, 'And upon this rock I will build My Church, and the gates of hell shall not prevail against it.'"[109]

In teaching that the Churches of Christ throughout the world replace the "one Church in Judea [which] is cast off,"[110] Cyril failed to take into account the vital role that the Jewish Christian church played in apostolic times. Paul gave recognition to this role when he gathered a collection for the poor among the saints in Jerusalem from the Gentiles who "shared the Jews' spiritual blessings,"(Romans 15:25–27). Not only was the first Christian church Jewish, it was from the Jewish church in Jerusalem that the Christian gospel was taken first to Samaria, later to Syrian Antioch, and thence to the rest of the world. Cyril, on the other hand, used the expression "Church in Judea" as a synonym for unbelieving Israel which he identified as "the Congregation of evil doers" abhorred by David (Psalm 26:5). Moreover, he followed the tradition of applying God's words of displeasure in Malachi 1:10 to the Jews, while applying the prophecy of God being known and worshipped among the nations to the Holy Catholic Church (v. 11).[111]

The effects of such replacement theology are evident in the immediate context of these declarations. After linking the idea of the Church with priesthood,[112] Cyril describes the Holy Catholic Church as the sphere in which, "receiving instruction and behaving ourselves virtuously, we shall attain the kingdom of heaven, and inherit eternal life; for which also we endure all toils, that we may be made partakers thereof from the Lord."[113] Such behavior means to go "from Baptism to the Holy Altar of God, and enjoy its spiritual and heavenly mysteries."[114] Here again a sacramental understanding of Christian ministry and of the duties of Christians takes precedence over the proclamation of the gospel and the response of faith.

This brief survey of the ecclesiology of Cyril of Jerusalem gives further grounds for concluding that replacement theology favors a "Christian ministry" understood in terms of a new Levitical priesthood. Moreover, it shows that in returning to the logic of the Levitical covenant, the Church lost sight of the "better things" which spring from Christ's victorious redemptive work.

In Post-Reformation Times

The logic of presuppositional replacement theology continued to influence ecclesiology even after the eclipse of the monolithic power of the papacy in the West. This is seen in the debate on Church government which took place in Puritan England over a thousand years after the time of Cyril. In *The Answer of the Assembly of Divines to the Reasons of the dissenting Brethren*, the Presbyterians who stressed "the continuity between old and new Israel" wrote the following: "The JEWISH *subordinations*, being no *Temple Ordinances*, nor *Typicall* or *Ceremoniall*, doe in the morall equity of them concern Us, as well as Them: at least we may, with much more reason urge an Argument, *à pari ratione*, from Subordinations in the *Jewish Church* to prove a subordination *still* . . . there should be Subordinations *now* in the Christian Church, that was *then* in the *Jewish*."[115]

In other words, Israel's Levitical order is seen to constitute a model for the Church. Even in our day replacement theology can be seen to influence some protestant ecclesiology. Edmund Clowney, writing in the late twentieth century, says, "In the history of revelation, the Old Testament people of God become the Church of the Messiah."[116]

Clowney, who identifies Peter as the foundation of the new form of God's people,[117] affirms that the Church was renewed, and not founded, at Pentecost.[118] When speaking of ethnic Israel, Clowney accentuates all that was negative in her national life, and affirms that her significance ended with Christ.[119] On the other hand, the Church is "the new and true Israel in Christ and it is this which must inspire our mission in the contemporary world."[120]

While this concept of the Church may conceivably serve to inspire some aspects of the Church's mission in the contemporary world as Clowney suggests, it also creates a serious obstacle for evangelistic outreach to the Jewish people. In fact, replacement theology and its corollary—the Church's self-understanding as the true Israel—are historically linked with overt contempt for Israel. This is evident both in the *Adversus Judaeos* tradition and in the anti-Semitic thought and practice of Post-Reformation Europe.

Conclusion

Various reasons are given for the changes in church structure and for the transformation of Christian ministry in the early centuries.[121] Persecution and the influence of Greco-Roman culture are among the external influences widely recognized as significant factors. So far as internal influences are concerned, it is thought that the dearth of competent bishops and the requisites for the celebration of the Lord's Supper played a significant part. According to Philip Schaff and James Dunn this list would not be complete without mentioning the gradual assimilation and adaptation of Judaism and a return to Old Testament categories of sacrifice and priesthood.

Our purpose in examining the post-apostolic literature and later patristic writings has been to see whether this return to Levitical categories depended in some way on replacement theology. We have found considerable evidence that presuppositional replacement theology did in fact facilitate the normalization of Levitical categories in the Church. A striking case of this is the way Malachi 1:10–12 was interpreted by Justin Martyr, Irenaeus, Augustine, and Cyril of Jerusalem, all of whom understood this passage to mean that, while the Jews have been dismissed, Christians offer sacrifices which are acceptable to God. Thus, on the assumption that the Old Testament is a thoroughly Christian book, it became a standard practice for the Lord's Supper and the Christian ministry to be described in Levitical terms.

This had many ramifications for ecclesiology. In particular, it led to the virtual eclipse of the apostolic concept of the Church as a charismatic body, the abandonment of the doctrine of the priesthood of all believers, and the neglect of gospel preaching. Moreover, it facilitated the development of a new concept of Christian unity which was no longer conceived as being based on the gospel of the grace of God but rather on cohesion with the bishop of Rome. So far as liturgical developments are concerned, the use of Levitical terminology such as "sacrifice" and "altar" in the context of the Lord's Supper obscured the memorial nature of the ordinance and the unique value of Christ's once-for-all sacrifice.

What emerges from the data we have examined is that the radical transformation of the Christian ministry during the second and third centuries was, to a large extent, the result of the Church taking over Levitical practice on the assumption that such instruction was intended for the Church. This assumption is a fruit of replacement theology, according to which the Church, and not Israel, is the true subject of the Law and the Prophets.

The Roman Catholic "Jubilee" witnesses to the continuing influence of such thinking on ecclesiastical practice. The Old Testament Jubilee had in view the restitution of property to rightful owners, the emancipation of slaves, and the recognition that the people of Israel are God's servants (Leviticus 25). It was to *follow* the Day of Atonement and so was not concerned with the problem of sin. On the other hand, the central feature of the Roman Catholic "Jubilee," announced for the first time by Pope Boniface VIII on February 22, 1300, and which reached its twenty-third edition in the year 2000, is the promise of plenary indulgences. This Roman Catholic "Jubilee," which corresponds neither to the Old Testament institution nor to New Testament teaching concerning the grounds for forgiveness, illustrates both the theological and practical effects of replacement theology.

5

REPLACEMENT THEOLOGY
AND ESCHATOLOGY

*"Israel is the church's eschatological goad and
it is no accident that the church has lost the sense of
eschatological tension; this happened as the church
increasingly lost sight of the mystery of the
permanence of Israel."*[1]

The Importance of Eschatology

According to Peter Beyerhaus, failure to observe the
distinctions between the different stages in which the
redemptive economy of God is unfolded has the effect
of "changing the Kingdom of Heaven, as promised and
given to God's sons and daughters, into a Kingdom on
Earth which is to be constructed solely by the autonomous
efforts of man himself."[2] Thus in circles such as the World
Council of Churches, loss of eschatological precision has
been followed by the demise of mission.[3] This is not
the first time that a substantial change in eschatological
orientation has impinged on the way in which the
Church has perceived its role in history.[4] According to
Archibald Robertson, the eclipse of millenarianism[5] in
the early Christian centuries produced an earth-bound
"medieval theocracy."[6] My purpose in this chapter is to

determine whether there is a cause-effect relationship between replacement theology and what Robertson calls "medieval theocracy."

Before returning to the patristic writings we need to consider a fundamental issue: Is the complete assimilation of the promised messianic kingdom into the present life of the Church justified by the New Testament? If it is, there is no point in investigating the matter further; we must simply accept the verdict of the New Testament. However, if the process of assimilation alluded to above cannot be justified by the New Testament, then it is at least possible that presuppositional replacement theology contributed to the development of medieval theocracy.

There are very different opinions on this matter. For example Hans LaRondelle claims that Old Testament Kingdom promises have been completely fulfilled in Christ's saving work and in the Church.[7] He writes, "The Church, as the eschatological Israel, with its new covenant in the blood of Christ, is the fulfillment of God's plan with ancient Israel."[8] To support this position LaRondelle considers Christ and the Church as anti-types of all the institutions, as well as the people, of Israel. This analysis of type and anti-type is based on the following trajectory: "Among all the nations of the Oriental world, only Israel developed an eschatology, a hope in which God gradually unfolded His promise, corrected false, nationalistic hopes, and constantly transcended Israel's concepts of His kingdom by pointing to a future fulfillment that would exceed all Israel's earthly expectations (Isaiah 64:4; cf. 1 Corinthians 2:9)."[9]

This trajectory neglects the fact that both Jewish particularism and universal purpose are evident in God's dealings with Israel throughout the whole of the Old

Testament, from the call of Abraham (Genesis 12:1–3) to the prophetic predictions made by exilic and post-exilic prophets (Ezekiel 36–40; Zechariah 12–14).

In order to make statements such as "Jesus is Israel, and in His resurrection Israel's restoration is accomplished,"[10] LaRondelle builds on some tenuous exegesis. For example, he takes Hosea 6:2 as a veiled prediction of Christ's resurrection[11] and uses Romans 9–11 selectively.[12] Furthermore, his assimilation of the messianic kingdom into the present implies that the consummation will be limited to judgment.[13]

Jewish opinion concerning the realization of kingdom promises[14] is summarized by the Roman Catholic scholar Rosemary Ruether: "For Judaism, however, there is no possibility of talking about the Messiah having already come, much less of having come two thousand years ago, with all the evil history that has reigned from that time to this (much of it having been done in Christ's name!), when the Reign of God has not come. For Israel, the coming of the Messiah and the coming of the Messianic Age are inseparable."[15]

Pinchas Lapide, a Jewish New Testament scholar open to dialogue with Christians,[16] focuses on what he considers the false claims of realized eschatology according to which the kingdom of God is being fulfilled in the Church. He writes, "A realized eschatology, which basks in a salvation which it supposes to be already attained, produces a triumphalism which transforms the kingdom of God into the church and relegates Christ the king to the far heavens. Such eschatology is like a painting in nothing but black and white: the one indicating the obstinate Jewish people, the other the ecclesiastical people which is already redeemed."[17]

A series of essays entitled "Continuity and Discontinuity"[18] has set a new standard for debating such subjects as the relationship between Israel and the Church and the mode of realization of the Kingdom of God.[19] In his Preface, John Feinberg observes that all contributors "see both continuity and discontinuity between the Testaments" although they represent opposing sides in the debate.[20] One of the reasons for this attenuation of extreme positions is the attention given to the New Testament in these essays.

It is generally agreed that the way the New Testament writers interpret the Old Testament must set the pattern for all Christian interpretation.[21] This principle implies that we must listen to what the New Testament says concerning the present and future status of Israel in God's overall plan. H. L. Ellison, a twentieth century biblical scholar also involved in the Jewish-Christian dialogue, observed: "To ignore the New Testament picture of the Jews in our formulation of its theology is surely as foolish as to foretell the future of Israel using purely Old Testament evidence."[22]

The New Testament Evidence

General Evidence

It is convenient to begin our survey with the words spoken by the angel Gabriel concerning Jesus, the son of David: "and he will reign over the house of Jacob forever; his kingdom will never end" (Luke 1:33).

Some understand these words to apply to the inauguration of the messianic kingdom through the death and resurrection of Christ and the coming of the Holy Spirit at Pentecost.[23] On the other hand, for Walter Kaiser they relate primarily to the kingdom of God understood as "a domain and a realm."[24] In evaluating the eschatological significance of Jesus, it is helpful to remember that according to Jesus himself, two advents were necessary for the completion of his ministry (Luke 4:14–21; 19:11–27; John 14:1–3; Matthew 13:36–43). These two advents were to be divided by an unspecified period of time, hence Jesus spent much time preparing human (Jewish) instruments for their crucial role in the building of his Church (Mark 3:13–19; Matthew 9:35–10:42; 16:18–19; 28:18–20). Moreover, Jesus categorically excluded that the realization of an earthly kingdom or the judgment of the nations belonged to his first advent, insisting rather that he had come to accomplish salvation (John 6:1–21; 12:47, cf. 5:24–30).

Many Old Testament predictions related to the accomplishment of salvation were fulfilled during the Messiah's first advent. Others are fulfilled in the Church's relationship with God and in its mission to the world.[25] Many would agree with Kaiser when he affirms that what Christ accomplished in his first advent inaugurated the spiritual dimension of God's kingdom.[26] They would also agree with Robert Saucy when he recognizes that the people that God is now gathering up out of all nations have much in common with God's Old Testament people, Israel.[27] This is why the experiences of Israel contain important lessons for the Church, (1 Corinthians 10:1–13) and why Israel and the Church can figure together as a complex unity in the apocalyptic vision of the new Jerusalem (Revelation 21:12–14). These elements of continuity have led some to believe that the Old Testament teaching concerning a messianic kingdom finds expression in the Church.

However, there remain some stubborn passages across the whole spectrum of New Testament literature which envisage a futuristic realization of kingdom promises as well as a distinctive future for physical Israel. While it would be a mistake to use these passages to detract from what the Church has in common with Israel, it would be equally erroneous to ignore their witness to a futuristic manifestation of the kingdom and to Israel's distinctive hope.

Three affirmations made by Jesus are significant. The first of these is presented in the form of a parable. In an introductory statement, Luke explains that the purpose of the parable is to correct the erroneous idea that the kingdom of God was to "appear" (*anaphainesthai*) at once (Luke 19:11). The parable itself makes it plain that the visible manifestation of the kingdom will follow a long absence of the appointed king (vv. 12–27).[28]

The second affirmation concerns the relationship of the Jews and the city of Jerusalem to what Jesus calls "the times of the Gentiles." He says, "They will fall by the sword and will be taken as prisoners to all the nations. Jerusalem will be trampled on by the Gentiles until the times of the Gentiles are fulfilled" (Luke 21:24).

The use of the adverb "until" (*achri*) does not, in itself, prove that there will be a period of historical time following "the times of the Gentiles." However, it is clear that the idea of fixed periods of time is present. I. Howard Marshall suggests that the reference is to one of the "allotted times" of prophetic scripture[29] and he links Jesus' statement with early church teaching reflected in Romans 11:25–27.[30] With reference to Romans 11:25, Cranfield writes, "The temporal conjunction *achris hou* must here mean 'until': though it sometimes means 'while' (e.g. in

Hebrews 3:13), it cannot have that sense here in view of the aorist subjunctive *eiselthēi*. Paul's meaning is . . . that the hardening will last until the fullness of the Gentiles comes in."[31] In the same way "Jerusalem will be trampled on by the Gentiles until the times of the Gentiles are fulfilled" (Luke 21:24).

Jesus' third statement is also prophetic. Speaking to unbelieving Israel, he warned, "Look, your house is left to you desolate. For I tell you, you will not see me again until you say, 'Blessed is he who comes in the name of the Lord,'" (Matthew 23:38–39). This statement implies that the people of Israel will see Jesus again and will pronounce this benediction upon him. Furthermore, it reveals that this occasion will coincide with the end of the prophesied state of desolation of the house of Israel.

Such statements as these may have contributed to convincing Jesus' disciples that the period of world mission, into which they had been introduced by the coming of the Holy Spirit at Pentecost (Acts 1:5–8; 2:1–36; cf. Matthew 28:18–20; Mark 16:15–16; Luke 24:44–47; John 20:21), was to be followed by the realization of another dimension of kingdom promises. The following statement made by Peter denotes such a prospect: "[Jesus] must remain in heaven until the time comes for God to restore everything, as he promised long ago through his holy prophets" (Acts 3:21). Evidently this future prospect was felt to be compatible with the disciples' awareness that the kingdom had been inaugurated by Christ's triumph over sin and death. The growth of the kingdom in a veiled form flowed from Christ's first advent and from the coming of the Spirit at Pentecost, but Jesus had made no secret of the fact that only with his return would the devil and all who do evil be finally overthrown (Matthew 13:36–43; cf. Romans 16:20 and Revelation 19:11–20:10).

The apostle Paul sounded a similar futuristic note in some significant historical and literary contexts. When he revisited Lystra, Iconium, and Antioch, "strengthening the disciples and encouraging them to remain true to the faith," he cautioned, "We must go though many hardships to enter the kingdom of God" (Acts 14:22). We may conclude from this warning that, in his preaching concerning the kingdom of God, Paul distinguished between its present aspects—"righteousness, peace, and joy in the Holy Spirit"—and a future, universal manifestation of the kingdom (Acts 20:25–27; 28:28–31; Romans 14:17).

Paul makes his most general eschatological statement in the course of a discussion concerning resurrection (1 Corinthians 15:22–28). In this passage Paul describes a sequence of events which begin with Christ's resurrection (15:23a). The second major event listed, which is to occur at Christ's return, is the resurrection of those who belong to him (v. 23b, *epeita hoi tou Cristou en tē parousia autou*). This, in turn, will be followed by "the end," when Christ will hand over the kingdom to the father (v. 24, *eita to telos, hotan paradidō tēn basileian tō theō kai patri*) after having subdued "all dominion, authority, and power." The two Greek adverbs used in this passage, *epeita* and *eita*, refer to time sequence ("then . . . next")[32] and thus link the process of subduing "all dominion, authority, and power" with the period which proceeds from Christ's second coming until "the end." Paul then quotes Psalm 110:1 in order to emphasize the necessity of Christ reigning until he has overcome all of his enemies (1 Corinthians 15:25).[33]

Before considering the eschatological content of Romans 11:25–27, we should briefly note some further New Testament passages which support what Archibald Robertson calls a "realistic eschatology."[34] In 2 Timothy 2:12 we read, "If we endure, we will also reign with him." The same idea is repeated three times, in more explicit terms, in the book of Revelation. The first of these occurrences is in the letter to the church in Thyatira: "To him who overcomes and does my will to the end, I will give authority over the nations" (2:26). The quotation of Psalm 2:9 in conjunction with this promise suggests that although referring to the future, this promise does not have in view the eternal state. Second, in relation to those purchased by Christ from every tribe, language, people, and nation, it is said, "You have made them to be a kingdom and priests to serve our God, and they will reign on the earth" (5:10). Finally, we learn from Revelation 19:11–20:6 that following the appearance of the King of kings and Lord of lords, the judgment of the beast and the false prophet, and the confinement of Satan, those who have received authority to judge will experience resurrection and will reign with Christ for a thousand years.[35] While the term "millennium" is often associated with this prophecy, the earlier references in Revelation to the saints reigning with Christ in an earthly kingdom show that the prospect of a messianic kingdom does not depend upon a knowledge of its duration.

The Future of Israel According to Romans 11

Toward the end of his long discussion concerning the present and future relationship of Israel with the history of salvation, Paul unveils a "mystery" (*mustērion*) so that his Gentile readers "may not be conceited" (11:25; cf.

v. 13). In the parable of the olive tree he had expressed a similar concern (vv. 17–21). He now strengthens the grounds for avoiding arrogance and conceit by giving more information concerning the future of Israel (cf. vv. 15, 24). Here is the text of the mystery[36] passage: "I do not want you to be ignorant of this mystery, brothers, so that you may not be conceited: Israel has experienced a hardening in part until the full number of the Gentiles has come in. And so all Israel will be saved, as it is written, 'The deliverer will come from Zion; he will turn godlessness away from Jacob. And this is my covenant with them when I take away their sins,'" (vv. 25–27).

Readers of the Old Testament already knew that non-Israelites were to be blessed through the seed of Abraham (Genesis 12:3; Isaiah 49:5–6; cf. Romans 11:12, 15), that God, when provoked by the Israelites, would harden them (see Deuteronomy 29:4; Isaiah 29:10; Psalms 69:22–23; cf. Romans 11:8–9), that Israel would return to seek the Lord "in the last days," and that, sooner or later, she would enter into the blessing of the new covenant (Isaiah 59:20; Hosea 3:4–5; Jeremiah 31:31–37; cf. Matthew 23:39; Romans 11:11–24). What is new in this mystery passage concerns the order of the events. "All Israel will be saved" after "the full number of the Gentiles has come in" and thus after the partial hardening of Israel[37] has ended.[38] What emerges is a clear contrast between the salvation of a remnant of Israel ("at the present time," v. 5) and that of all Israel as an eschatological event (v. 26).

Paul enriches our knowledge of when and how the national conversion of Israel will take place by the quotation of some Old Testament prophetic passages. The first of these is part of a messianic prophecy tied to the Davidic covenant (Isaiah 59:20), "The deliverer

will come from Zion; he will turn godlessness away
from Jacob (Romans 11:26b–27a). Part of the following
phrase, "And this is my covenant with them," appears for
the first time in Genesis 17:4, as the introduction to the
covenant God made with Abraham. It recurs in Isaiah
59:21, immediately after the prophecy quoted in Romans
11:26, and again, in a slightly different form, in Jeremiah's
prophecy concerning the new covenant (Jeremiah 31:33).
The words in Romans 11:27b, "when I take away their
sins" make clear that Paul is thinking about Israel's
entrance into the new covenant as envisaged by Jeremiah
(31:34). This event will be marked by the forgiveness
of their sins. The possibility of this forgiveness is based
on the redemptive work of Christ and will occur, at a
national level, when the messianic deliverer reveals
himself to Israel and the nation repents (cf. Jeremiah
31:34; Luke 22:20).[39] He will "turn godlessness from
Jacob" (cf. Zechariah 12:10–13:1).[40] The repentance
of some Israelites during the period between Christ's
two advents is an anticipation of this national event,
however, the attention which Paul gives in this passage
to time sequence and in particular to the eschatological
nature of the salvation of all Israel, shows that the apostle
is thinking here of a new stage in salvation history (cf.
vv.13–15; Acts 3:19–21).[41]

According to LaRondelle, Paul's failure to mention
Israel's restoration to the land in Romans 11 implies that
with the advent of the new covenant the land of Israel
has become theologically insignificant.[42] However, there
is in fact an allusion to the land in verse 26.[43] The form
of the original prophecy, "The Redeemer will come
to Zion" (Isaiah 59:20) finds an echo in the prediction
that the Messiah will reveal himself to the inhabitants of

Jerusalem who will respond by mourning for "the one they have pierced" (Zechariah 12:10–14). The preposition "from," in Paul's phrase "the deliverer will come from Zion" (Romans 11:26), suggests that the deliverer will turn away the "wickedness" (*asebeias*) of "all Israel," beginning from Jerusalem. What is common to both forms of the prophecy is the centrality of Zion—Jerusalem—in the work of the deliverer. The temporal reference in verse 25 implies that this work will be accomplished in the context of the Messiah's second advent.[44] That being the case, the reference to Zion establishes a link between the prospect of Israel's national conversion and the ultimate fulfillment of Old Testament prophecies concerning the land (see Zechariah 14:1–21). Moreover, the *a fortiori* statements of Romans eleven, verses 12 and 15, suggest that the realization of Israel's fullness will produce great blessing for the rest of the world.

Israel and Eschatology in Early Christian Theology

Millenarianism

According to Robertson, the Church's conception of the kingdom of God includes one constant element and two variables. That which remains constant is "the perfect reign of God in heaven after the Last Judgment." The variables are the understanding of Christ's reign in the visible church between his two comings and the conviction that he will reign on earth between his second coming and the final judgment.[45] Our concern here is with the variable elements.

Because "the history of the conception of the Kingdom of God . . . in the early church is the history of the prevalence and decline of Millenarianism,"[46] it will be convenient for us to follow this trajectory. Our purpose will be to determine whether the eventual decline of millenarianism was in any way related to the Church's understanding of Israel.

During the period to be considered, millenarianism did not exclude the conviction that Christ already reigned in his Church. On the contrary, the development of doctrine in this period took for granted that the age of fulfillment had dawned and that the Church was already feasting at the eschatological banquet.[47] The early Christian philosophy of history required both the presence of the kingdom and the hope of its more general manifestation in relation to the second coming of Christ.[48]

Teaching concerning a millennial reign of Christ was, in general, closely associated with Revelation 20:1–10.[49] However, the millennial hope also had roots in Jewish eschatology.[50] In fact, millenarianism fitted naturally into the Old Testament world view which envisages a literal messianic kingdom in which unrighteousness will be banished and all nations will worship the God of Israel (Isaiah 2:1–5; Ezekiel 37:15–28; Micah 4; Zechariah 14). A sampling of second century exposition of millenarianism will illustrate the above remarks.

Papias (c. 60–130), bishop of Hierapolis, is the first post-apostolic writer whose millenarianism is documented. Knowledge of it reaches us by way of Irenaeus[51] and Eusebius. The latter, alluding to certain things which Papias is said to have gathered from unwritten traditions, writes, "To these belong his statement that there will be a period of some thousand years after the resurrection of the dead, and that the kingdom of Christ will be set up in material form on this very earth."

According to Eusebius these things "were spoken mystically in figures . . . But it was due to [Papias] that so many of the Church Fathers after him adopted a like opinion."[52] However, the evidence seems to suggest that Papias simply drew together threads from Old Testament messianic prophecies and Christ's own words, linking them with the particular contribution of Revelation 20:1–6.

In the Epistle of Barnabas the thousand year reign is taken to be the ideal Sabbath rest which corresponds to the seventh day of creation, while the beginning of the eighth day is thought to be prefigured by Christ's resurrection. The writer of Barnabas quotes Isaiah 1:13 as proof that the Jewish Sabbaths are unacceptable to God.[53] Having disqualified Israel, the writer of Barnabas transfers her hope of a messianic kingdom to the sphere of Christian eschatological hope.

Justin Martyr considers Christian millenarianism, in which the eschatological hope of Israel is fully assimilated, an essential part of orthodox faith. He writes, "But I and others, who are right-minded (*orthogōmones*) Christians on all points, are assured that there will be a resurrection of the dead, and a thousand years in Jerusalem, which will then be built, adorned, and enlarged [as] the prophets Ezekiel and Isaiah and others declare."[54]

Later in his *Dialogue with Trypho*, Justin makes explicit mention of "John, one of the apostles of Christ," as the source of this teaching[55] and affirms that "those who believed in our Christ would dwell a thousand years in Jerusalem."[56] The expression "our Christ," said in the context of Justin's dialogue with Trypho the Jew, is obviously polemical. Like Barnabas, Justin freely assimilates material taken from such Hebrew prophets as Ezekiel and Isaiah into the visions of Revelation 20:1–6.

In a similar way Irenaeus uses the Old Testament to describe what Papias is reputed to have heard from John, insisting in particular on the literal fulfillment of Isaiah 11:6–9. He quotes the beatitude of Revelation 20:6 to confirm such Old Testament kingdom prophecies.[57] However, his adherence to the literal interpretation of kingdom prophecies appears tenuous as he freely applies part of another prophecy (Jeremiah 31:10–14)— concerning the re-gathering of Israel in their own land where they will enjoy material blessings from the Lord's hand—to the Church.[58]

Christian appropriation of the Jewish hope is also apparent in Tertullian's confession of faith in a thousand year reign before the final state. In his work *Against Marcion*, Tertullian states that the Jewish hope of the restoration of Judea "is spiritually applicable to Christ and His church, and to the character and fruits thereof."[59] Tertullian informs us that he has dealt more fully with the matter in his work *De Spe Fidelium*, which is unfortunately no longer extant. However, his tract *Against Marcion*, does contain the following comment: "we do confess that a kingdom is promised to us upon the earth, although before heaven, only in another state of existence; inasmuch as it will be after the resurrection for a thousand years in the divinely-built city of Jerusalem, 'let down from heaven.'"[60]

We have seen that early Christian apologists and theologians expected a literal millennial reign of Christ following his return to earth in glory and before the beginning of the eternal state. One feature of this expectation is the transferal of Israel's hope of a messianic kingdom to the Church. In some of the writings we have examined, it is very clear that this is a fruit of replacement theology.

This transferal of Israel's kingdom hope to the Church did not immediately cause radical changes in the understanding of general eschatology. This may be due to the fact that the general eschatological vision of the New Testament strongly resembles that of the Hebrew Scriptures. Jesus himself taught that the final manifestation of the kingdom was future (Matthew 13; Luke 19:11–27) while the apostles taught that at the appointed time, God would restore everything through Christ "as he promised long ago through his holy prophets" (Acts 3:20–21; cf. 1 Corinthians 15:23–28). Moreover, the visions of Revelation 19:11–20:6 both confirmed and enriched the expectation of a future messianic kingdom.

Hippolytus, a Roman churchman who died around AD 236, is known as the first Christian scholar to have calculated the date of Easter without considering the date of the Jewish Passover.[61] By so doing Hippolytus introduced a further element of separation between the Christian faith and Judaism. However, we learn from his treatise *On Antichrist* that Hippolytus continued to teach a future reign of Christ in which the saints were destined to participate.[62] While not making specific mention of the millennium in this work, his allusion to Revelation 20:6 suggests that it was not foreign to his thought. Hippolytus does not speculate on how unfulfilled biblical prophecies are to be fulfilled; he simply affirms that they will be fulfilled.[63] This is significant in light of developments at Alexandria to which we now turn.

Origen's Eschatology

Clement of Alexandria (c. 155–c. 220)[64] was unashamedly a Christian Platonist and as such he quoted from Plato, and indeed from other philosophers, with the same ease as he quoted from the Hebrew Scriptures and the New Testament. He also interpreted the Bible in light of these Platonic concepts. This is evident in the following passage in which Clement speaks of the perfect man's relation with the world:

> But I shall pray the Spirit of Christ to wing me to my Jerusalem. For the Stoics say that heaven is properly a city, but places here on earth are not cities; for they are called so, but are not. For a city is an important thing, and the people a decorous body, and a multitude of men regulated by law as the church by the word—a city on earth impregnable—free from tyranny; a product of the divine will on earth as in heaven. Images of this city the poets create with their pen. . . . And we know Plato's city placed as a pattern in heaven.[65]

Clement quotes also from Plato's *Phaedo* when speaking of future rewards and punishments.[66] His dependence on Plato is further evident in a speculative passage in which the Jews feature as "helpers" while the Christians are considered "fit to rule."[67]

Origen continued this Alexandrian tradition of interpreting the Bible in a way which harmonized with Greek philosophy. For example, in his work *On First Principles* Origen affirms the total impassibility of God to the point of excluding the objective reality of his wrath. He applies this principle to the parable of Ten Minas (Luke 19:11–27) which refers to the future manifestation of Christ's kingdom and the judgment which will accompany it. Origen writes, "We do not take such expressions literally, but seek in them a spiritual meaning, that we may think of God as He deserves to be thought of."[68]

Origen also denies the reality of God's wrath in his *Homilies on Ezekiel* in which God's interventions are said to be dictated by necessity and not by passion. God is compared with a doctor or a father who administers chastisements in order to heal the wicked or educate them.[69] Consequently, when the Bible speaks of eternal punishment such teaching has only nominal value. It serves, as do all the manifestations of God's wrath in history, to correct the wicked,[70] but spiritual death is not to be understood as eternal.[71]

Hanson observes that, "in rationalizing and spiritualizing the biblical doctrine of God's wrath and God's punishment, Origen was obviously moving with the tide of contemporary sentiment."[72] Origen reduces the concept of eternal punishment even further when he states that the judgments of God will not require "times" but rather will happen "in the twinkling of an eye." He similarly discounts the literal meaning of such phrases as "take charge of ten cities" (Luke 19:17, 19), with which Jesus describes how his faithful servants will be rewarded.[73]

An eschatology which envisages all the wicked being eventually purified and understands divine judgment as being unrelated to time, has no place for a millennial reign of Christ since it is to be ushered in by a series of judgments and is to be followed by other judgments (see Revelation 19:11–20:15). So it is not surprising that Origen opposed millenarianism. In his opinion those who understand such a prospect in literal terms did not understand the meaning of the apostle's teaching, which is spiritual rather than literal.[74] Hanson observes, "The contrast between Justin, who regards a literal interpretation of the millennial kingdom as part of Christian orthodoxy, and Origen, who regards in precisely the same light an allegorical interpretation of the same subject, is striking."[75]

Just as Origen's concept of the heavenly church excludes ethnic Israel as a subject of theological reflection, so his mystical understanding of the kingdom of God excludes the typically Jewish hope of an earthly kingdom. It is interesting that thirteen centuries after Origen the drafters of the Augsburg Confession defined those opinions as Jewish "which are even now making an appearance and which teach that, before the resurrection of the dead, saints and godly men will possess a worldly kingdom."[76]

While some aspects of Origen's eschatology— in particular his doctrine of resurrection and his Restorationism (the teaching that all people will ultimately be saved)—were later called into question,[77] his largely mystical concept of the kingdom and his rejection of millenarianism were not similarly denounced. Why? One way of explaining this is to suggest that Justin Martyr erred when he made the millennial hope an essential point of Christian orthodoxy. Another possible explanation is a waning of interest in this doctrine as the Christian era advanced. A third possibility is that, following the general acceptance of replacement theology, the world view intrinsic to Jewish eschatology was perceived as obsolete.[78]

Millenarianism After Origen

Despite his erudition, Origen's mystical teaching concerning the kingdom of God did not convince all of his contemporaries. This is seen in the fact that Commodianus, a North-African bishop, preserved a simple form of the doctrine of the millennial reign of Christ. Concerning the beginning of this age he writes that the dead who have been devoted to Christ will experience "the first resurrection," being raised incorruptible, while those who have overcome the Antichrist "will live for the whole time, and receive blessings because they have suffered evil things. They will marry and beget children for a thousand years." For the duration of the thousand year period, God will keep all evil at bay. There will follow "the day of judgment" for the unbelievers who are destined to experience a second death.[79]

There are other witnesses besides the writings of Commodianus to Origen's failure to influence the thinking of North African bishops with regard to his realized eschatology. Even Cyprian's eschatology was essentially futurist, which may be seen in the following statement regarding the Church's prospect of reigning with Christ: "he cannot attain unto the kingdom who forsakes . . . [the Church] which shall reign there."[80]

Millenarianism also continued to have supporters elsewhere. For example, Methodius (died c. 312), bishop of Olympus and a critic of Origen, describes as "miserable men" those who "deal with figures of the future as if they were already things of the past."[81] Moreover, he speaks of a seventh thousand year period.[82] Lactantius, c. 240–c. 320, was a gifted rhetorician who, after his conversion, became a Christian apologist and an historian of the last season of imperial persecution of the Church.[83] In his major work he writes polemically of the dead who "will rise again, not after a thousand years from their death, but that, when again restored to life, they may reign with God a thousand years."[84]

The millenarianism of Lactantius is presented more systematically in an *Epitome* of his former work. In chapter seventy-one he enlarges on the statement, "When the last end shall begin to approach to the world, wickedness will increase," and treats the career of the Antichrist, in terms similar to those found in Revelation 13. In chapter seventy-two he follows the sequence of events described in Revelation 19:11–20:15, stating emphatically that Christ "will deliver all nations into subjection to the righteous who are alive, and will raise the righteous dead to eternal life, and will Himself reign with them on the earth, and will build the holy city, and this kingdom of the righteous shall be for a thousand years."[85]

Lactantius's defense of future corporeal punishment, involving a post-millennial resurrection of the unrighteous and eternal punishment, is in striking contrast to Origen's teaching on these subjects and seems to confirm that a futuristic understanding of eschatology, including millenarianism, was still widespread in the fourth century. Pelikan makes the point that even the polemical attacks against this doctrine, such as that of Victorinus, "[are] evidence more for the continuation of millenarianism than for its disappearance."[86]

A futuristic concept of the kingdom is also witnessed to in the Apostolic Constitutions, which are thought to have been compiled by an eastern Arian in the late fourth century.[87] The Constitutions contain the following prayer: "Gather us all together into Thy kingdom which Thou hast prepared. Let this Thy kingdom come."[88]

About this time there was a new development in biblical interpretation associated with Antioch. In the latter half of the fourth century, Diodore of Tarsus (d. c. 391, bishop from 378) strongly opposed the allegorism which was so prominent in the writings of Origen and upon which his eschatology depended. According to Diodore, allegorism is the ruin of the text because it destitutes it of its historical foundation; history, then, is the primary foundation on which any higher meanings must rest. Prophecy, inasmuch as it is the word of God, applies to the past, present, and future.[89]

In his prologue to Psalm 118, Diodore identifies the origin of allegorism as being pagan and its purpose as being to suppress the literal sense of what is narrated in the text.[90] Diodore was acquainted with the use which Julian the Apostate[91] and Salustius made of allegorical interpretation in their anti-Christian apologetics at Antioch in order to salvage pagan myths. For these arch-enemies of Christianity, allegorical interpretation included the negation of the historical worth of the text. Clearly the historicity of the biblical text could not be dismissed in so cavalier a manner given its infinitely greater value than the texts containing pagan myths.[92]

In light of the popularity of allegorical interpretation at Alexandria, it is not surprising that Cyril opposed Antiochene teachers who insisted on the primacy of literal interpretation of the biblical text.[93] Yet, for the moment, the increasing popularity of the allegorical method[94] was insufficient to overthrow the Christian hope of a literal thousand year reign of the saints with Christ. We may presume that Origen's attacks on millenarianism failed because he did not offer a viable alternative.[95]

In summary, millenarianism remained a normative doctrine during the first four centuries of the Christian era. It was not overthrown until Augustine brought together the concepts of the Church and the kingdom of Christ in such a way as to almost equivocate the two. However, two important factors had already set the stage for the transformation of the eschatological hope of a messianic kingdom into an ecclesiastical theocracy.[96] Since the time of Justin, the prospect of an earthly messianic kingdom had become an altogether Christian hope, to the exclusion of ethnic Israel's eschatological hope. The other factor was the widespread use made of allegorical interpretation of Scripture.

Augustine's Teaching on Israel, the Church, and the Kingdom of Christ

Augustine's Teaching Concerning Ethnic Israel

We will limit our survey of Augustine's thought concerning ethnic Israel and the kingdom of Christ to relevant parts of his famous work *The City of God*. The writing of this work spanned most of the latter period of Augustine's life (c. 413–27), therefore the ideas expressed in it can be taken as representative of his mature thought.

Two circumstances stimulated Augustine to meditate on the nature of the Church in the more general contexts of history and Christian theology. The first of these was the sack of Rome in 410, followed by the attempt to attribute this calamity to Christian influence. The second was the century-old Donatist controversy which continued to trouble the North African church and in which Augustine found himself compelled to take a position. *The City of God* was Augustine's answer to the first of these challenges.[97]

It is convenient to begin our survey by noticing Augustine's treatment of ethnic Israel in *The City of God*. In book XV he associates the people descended from Abraham through Isaac with the earthly city spoken of in Galatians 4:21–31. Of this city he writes, "It was founded not for its own sake, but to prefigure another city."[98] Thus ethnic Israel, consisting of the children of promise, features in Augustine's thought as but a type of the heavenly Jerusalem. In a similar vein he suggests in book XVI that the phrase "the older shall serve the younger" used by Paul in Romans 9:13 finds its ultimate fulfillment not in the physical descendants of Esau and Jacob but rather "in some greater thing . . . in the Jews and the Christians." Augustine thus concurs with the almost universal consensus of Christian interpreters in the early centuries, according to whom the phrase "the older shall serve the younger" means "that the elder people, the Jews, shall serve the younger people, the Christians."[99]

In book XVII Augustine characterizes the Jews in terms of the wish expressed by David in Psalm 69:22–23, as incapable of contemplating heavenly things because perennially bowed down with their faces toward the earth.[100] The Jews, as a whole, are seen by Augustine as being trapped by divine decree in a mental attitude which excludes them from the blessings reserved for those belonging to the real, heavenly Jerusalem. This theme is continued in book XVIII where Augustine meditates on the prayer and song of Habakkuk. He writes, "For when many people are troubled, he saw the threatening tribulation of the Church, and at once acknowledged himself a member of it. . . . 'That I may ascend,' he says, 'among the people of my pilgrimage,' departing quite from the wicked people of his carnal kinship, who are not pilgrims in this earth, and do not seek the country above." Habakkuk sees that the nation which was to slay Christ was going to lose the abundance of spiritual supplies, which, in prophetic fashion, he set forth by the figure of earthly plenty.[101]

There are no valid grounds for attributing the idea of the disinheriting of Israel to Habakkuk.[102] Moreover, Augustine makes this disinheriting of the nation coincide with the transformation of the Old Testament moral and material concept of the kingdom into something purely spiritual in nature. The liberty which Augustine takes with this Old Testament passage is paralleled by his approach to the *locus classicus* of millenarianism: Revelation 20:1–6.

From a Future Millennium to the Reign of Christ in the Church

Augustine actually explains why he gave up belief in a future millennial reign of Christ. Concerning the opinion that the first resurrection of Revelation 20:4–6 refers to the saints who will reign with Christ for a thousand years on earth, he writes, "this opinion would not be objectionable, if it were believed that the joys of the saints in that Sabbath shall be spiritual, and consequent on the presence of God; for I myself, too, once held this opinion.[103] But, as they assert that those who then rise again shall enjoy the leisure of immoderate carnal banquets, furnished with an amount of meat and drink such as not only to shock the feeling of the temperate, but even to surpass the measure of credulity itself, such assertions can be believed only by the carnal."[104]

Augustine proceeded to give what he believed to be the correct interpretation of Revelation 20:1–6 and by so doing circumscribed the future debate concerning a messianic reign on earth to this one New Testament passage. According to Augustine, the term "one thousand years" indicates a period which reaches to the end of time. This interpretation neglects the evidence of verses 7 and 8, according to which, after the termination of the thousand years, Satan will regain the ability to deceive those whom he was formerly incapable of deceiving.[105] Other problems with Augustine's exegesis are the presupposition that entire nations belong to Christ and that the abyss where Satan is confined refers to "the countless multitude of the wicked whose hearts are unfathomably deep in malignity against the Church of God." A further difficulty is that the ban on satanic seduction is seen to extend only to those who believe.

Augustine's change of mind rested on a threefold foundation: the conviction that the images of earthly plenty contained in Israel's eschatological hope were figurative, that this hope was now the exclusive inheritance of the Church, and his disgust at the material emphasis in the millenarianism with which he was acquainted. However, the real novelty contained in Augustine's proposal is his alternative, ecclesiastical conception of the Kingdom of Christ. In his application of Jesus' parable of the tares and the wheat (Matthew 13:36–43), he cautiously identifies the kingdom with the Church: "Must we think that in this kingdom there are no scandals? Therefore, from this [Christ's] kingdom, which here is the Church, [the zizzania] are collected out."[106] Although he allows that Christ's reign does not extend to the disobedient members of the Church whom he likens to "tares," Augustine does not hesitate to identify all who are regularly ordained to ecclesiastical positions as the "wheat" in Jesus' parable. It is through these in particular that Christ, the Head of the Church, exercises his reign.

Particularly important, in view of future developments, is Augustine's further teaching concerning those who govern the kingdom during the present age. Concerning Revelation 20:4a ("I saw thrones on which were seated those who had been given authority to judge") he writes, "It is not to be supposed that this refers to the last judgment, but to the seats of the rulers and to the rulers themselves by whom the Church is now governed."[107]

It was perhaps inevitable that the crucial role which Augustine attributes to the ecclesiastical hierarchy—as principal agents of Christ's kingdom—would be accentuated in subsequent Church history to the neglect of other elements of his teaching. But this was not the only aspect of his interpretation of Revelation 20:1–6 to influence Christian practice. His exegesis of this passage also tended to legitimize the cult of the martyrs. Beginning with the assumption that the first resurrection (v. 5) refers to regeneration, he reflects on the present status of those "who had been beheaded" and subsequently "came to life and reigned with Christ a thousand years" (v. 4). According to Augustine, "the souls of the pious dead are not separated from the Church, which even now is the kingdom of Christ." The Church, then, begins its reign with Christ now, in both the living and in the dead.[108]

The medieval church understood the part which the martyrs have in ruling the Church as a special mediatorial role. Pelikan makes this general comment on the phrase "the communion of saints" in the so-called Apostles' Creed: "The close identification between Christ and his saints made it possible, and even mandatory, for believers who prayed to God to invoke the saints also, since the saints prayed for them in turn."[109]

Some Effects of Augustine's Ecclesiastical Conception of the Kingdom of Christ

A Triumphant Medieval Theocracy

Augustine considered ethnic Israel an image of the city of God and believed that all talk of divine blessing in the Scripture was to be understood in spiritual terms. Hence he abandoned the hope of an earthly messianic kingdom as taught in both the Old and New Testaments. According to this African church father, the Church embodies the kingdom of Christ imperfectly, because the visible church contains elements which have no part in the true, invisible Body of Christ. However, those who occupy positions of government in the Church are "rulers" in Christ's kingdom.

Augustine's conviction that the hierarchical church embodied the kingdom of Christ had important implications for the future relationship of Church and State. Previously, realistic eschatology had provided the Church with a workable philosophy of history, the focal point of which was "the expectation of the imminence of the second Advent with the earthly reign of Christ in its train."[110] All of this was transferred to the present in the ecclesiastical concept of the kingdom of Christ proposed by Augustine. Augustine left no precise teaching concerning the form of the hierarchy which would make his concept of the kingdom into a workable reality. However, Leo I, elected as bishop of Rome just ten years after Augustine's death, made a decisive contribution in this regard.

An able diplomat, Leo I also made a vital contribution to orthodoxy at the Council of Chalcedon (451).[111] From this time on, the Western Church began to credit the bishop of Rome with being the arbitrator of orthodoxy. Thus it is hardly surprising that near canonical value was given to Leo's teaching concerning the unique authority of the bishop of Rome as the heir of Peter and universal pastor. His most famous pronouncements to this effect are contained in a sermon delivered on the anniversary of his elevation to the pontificate, when he declared that through him, Peter "still today . . . more fully and effectually performs what is entrusted to him." Furthermore, Leo called on his hearers to "celebrate today's festival by such methods, that in my humble person he may be recognized and honored, in who abides the care of all the shepherds, together with the charge of the sheep commended to him, and whose dignity is not abated even in so unworthy an heir."[112]

The role of the medieval popes was consolidated by Gregory the Great (590–604) who effectively laid the foundation of the temporal power of the Roman Catholic church.[113] His greatness lay primarily in his ability to administrate, but he is also remembered as popularizer of Augustine's teachings.[114] From the time of Gregory it became quite normal to speak of "the reign of the Pope," even though this regal role was not accepted in the East where the emperor maintained the Constantinian role of supremacy over the ecclesiastical patriarchs.

The claim of the Roman bishop to wield supreme authority over an omnipotent church gave tangible form to Augustine's ecclesiastical concept of the kingdom of Christ. What this claim led to, in the history of the medieval church, is well known. Nepotism and political maneuvering are only two of the negative results of a papacy which believed itself the instrument of divine rule over all secular kingdoms. Papal power reached its zenith with the reigns of Innocent III (1160–1216) and Boniface VIII (1294–1303). The latter issued a papal bull, *Unam Sanctam,* which spoke of two swords, one representative of temporal and the other of spiritual authority. The following words sum up the philosophy represented in this bull: "One sword must be under the other, and temporal authority must be subject to the spiritual. . . . Therefore, if earthly power strays from the right path it is to be judged by the spiritual. . . . But if the supreme spiritual authority strays, it can only be judged by God, and not by humans. . . . We further declare, affirm, and define that it is absolutely necessary for salvation that all human creatures be under the Roman pontiff."[115]

Augustine cannot be held responsible for the abuses of power and the repeated instances of conscious fraud used to consolidate and preserve the temporal power of the Church.[116] It is safe to say, however, that the concept of the "triumphant church" was an elaboration of Augustinian thought which presupposed the logic of replacement theology and certainly contributed to the rise of ecclesiastical authority.

There is little question that the abuses of power by the "triumphant church" damaged the cause of Christ. Of particular interest to our study are the Crusades, initiated by Pope Urban II on Christmas day 1095, which led to the massacre of many Jews in the years to follow. Equally heinous were the various inquisitions authorized by Pope Gregory IX during the years 1231–1235 and by Sixtus IV in 1478, which led to great suffering for the Jews in Europe.

The Defeat of the Iconoclasts

The claim to have completely replaced Israel in God's plan or, more often, to be the reality of which Israel had only been the type, led the Church to discriminate against all things Jewish, except those things that she herself had taken over. Among the latter were the sacred Writings which God had entrusted to Israel (Romans 3:1–2) and which contain explicit commands against iconography. We have seen that the practice of allegorical interpretation permitted the Church to neglect the clear teaching of Scripture when this did not agree with current theological opinion, which explains why the Medieval Church ignored the prohibition of icons in the books of Moses, the Hebrew prophets, and Paul's letter to the Romans.

The authorized use of images came to be so common that those who opposed the practice were thought to be guilty of grave error while those supporting them were considered orthodox! Pelikan attributes this reversal of clear Scriptural teaching to ecclesiastical prejudice against all things Jewish. He writes, "To the orthodox, therefore, an iconoclast was simply 'one with a Jewish mind [*Ioudaiophrōn*],' and an iconoclastic synod was not a church council but 'Caiphas' Sanhedrin.'[117] In light of such flagrant disobedience to God's revealed will, it would have been extremely difficult for Jewish observers to accept the claim of the medieval church to be the true Israel of God.[118]

Conclusion

The literature examined in this chapter suggests that the abandonment of the hope of a future messianic kingdom in favor of the conviction that the Church itself currently embodies the promised kingdom is a logical development stemming from replacement theology. We saw that neither Jesus nor the writers of the New Testament linked the prospect of a universal kingdom of peace and righteousness with the present age, rather they associated it with the Messiah's Second Advent. Moreover, we saw that the realized eschatology developed by Augustine, which makes the Church the normative form of the messianic kingdom, required the allegorization of both Old and New Testament teaching concerning the kingdom.

It is a fact of history that the Augustinian concept of a Christian theocracy is closely linked with the anti-Semitic attitudes of the medieval church and unbelievably harsh treatment of the Jewish people. Thus it is not surprising that the traditional claim of Christendom to embody the promised messianic kingdom is an embarrassment to Christians involved in dialogue with Jewish people. Hans Ucko, executive secretary for Christian-Jewish relations in the World Council of Churches' Office on Inter-religious Relations addressed this issue: "Christians are obliged to answer the questions of the Jews: 'Where is the messianic kingdom? Where is the redeemed world? Where is the unending peace? How can Jesus possibly be the Messiah we are waiting for?'"[119]

If the view according to which the Church incarnates the promised messianic kingdom is a corollary of replacement theology, it follows that the widespread repudiation of this view should lead Christian theologians to also re-examine the grounds for realized eschatology.

6

LESSONS FOR CHRISTIAN THEOLOGY

A Summary of our Findings

We began with a survey of Israel's uniqueness. Besides examining the evidence contained in the Old and New Testaments, we briefly considered the witness of history from AD 70 to the present. Considering the institutional uniqueness of the Jews among the nations of the world, the scant attention given to Israel by Christian theologians is puzzling.

We also saw that in the early centuries of the Christian era this neglect was linked with what has become known as replacement theology. According to this concept, all that formerly pertained to ethnic Israel now pertains to the Church. In spite of the fact that Israel's status as an elect people is confirmed by Paul in Romans 9–11, the view that the Church had completely replaced Israel in God's plan became the dominant opinion in post-apostolic Christendom. Some church fathers went further when they affirmed that the Church had always been the true Israel of which physical Israelites were but the visible sign.

The logic of replacement theology required that much of the Old Testament be allegorized. Only in this way could the Church be made the subject of passages in which the nation of Israel is addressed. This led to the virtual abandonment of the Hebrew world view and concept of God and the adoption of a framework of thought which had its roots in Greek philosophy. All of this fostered an attitude of contempt toward ethnic Israel and led to the exclusion of Israel as a subject of theological reflection.

The disinheriting of Israel did not remain an isolated element in the development of Christian thought. One area of theology that it influenced in the early Christian centuries was ecclesiology. For example, in what became the standard interpretation of Malachi 1:10–12, the idea that the Church had replaced Israel was linked with the reinterpretation of the Lord's Supper in the Levitical terms of sacrifice. Once the Hebrew Bible was thought to be a thoroughly Christian book, there developed a more general use of Levitical forms and terminology in the context of the Church. Thus instead of being called elders, local church leaders began to be called priests in order to comply with the new concept of the Christian ministry as sacrificial. At the same time important characteristics of the new covenant, such as the priesthood of all believers, the sufficiency of Christ's once-for-all sacrifice, and the crucial importance of faith in Christ for personal salvation, were neglected.

Eschatology was another area of theology that was negatively influenced by the logic of replacement theology. The presumed repudiation of Israel as an elect people permitted the Church to consider itself the normative expression of the long-awaited messianic kingdom. However, instead of promoting peace and righteousness, as might have been expected of an institution claiming to mediate the universal kingdom of Christ, the Triumphant Church of the Middle Ages proved to be arrogant and self-serving. From the time of Constantine, the disinheriting of Israel was supported by ecclesiastical legislation and violence against the Jews was common among Christians.

There were, of course, a number of other influences which contributed to the transformation of ecclesiology and eschatology in the ways just mentioned. However, the documentary evidence bears testimony to the fact that they were also the logical out-working of replacement theology. This calls for reflection.

Principles Emerging from our Study

Failure to reflect seriously on Israel in light of all the relevant biblical data has serious consequences for the entire enterprise of Christian theology. It was the neglect of the relevant biblical data concerning the place of Israel in God's plan which permitted replacement theology to develop during the early centuries of the Christian era. Once replacement theology became a presupposition of theological reflection, it required that much of the Old Testament be interpreted allegorically. This involved the loss of the Hebrew world view and influenced the direction of theological reflection in areas such as ecclesiology and eschatology. The widespread repudiation of replacement theology following the Shoah confirms that more attention should have been given to the biblical data concerning the institutional uniqueness of Israel during the early Christian centuries.

Likewise, the recent development of a new majority view according to which the Jewish people have their own covenant and are thus exonerated from the need to believe in Jesus in order to be saved, is also marked by a selective use of Scripture. For example, proponents of this view make repeated use of Romans chapter eleven while ignoring chapter ten, which addresses the question of the salvation of Jews in the present. Because of this selective use of Scripture the new majority view represents a threat to Christology, soteriology, and missiology; a threat that is no less substantial than that posed by replacement theology upon ecclesiology and eschatology.[1]

Christian theology must be based on sound hermeneutical principles which presuppose the Church's essential relationship with Israel. These include taking into account the whole of the biblical Canon, taking seriously the Jewishness of Jesus and of much of the New Testament, recognizing the institutional distinctions between Israel and the Church, avoiding gratuitous allegorization of Scripture, and giving normative value to what the New Testament teaches concerning both the first and second advents of Christ. In the early Christian centuries, neglect of these five principles favored the development of a theology of the Church and of the Christian ministry in which apostolic teaching was subordinated to Old Testament cultic practice. It also favored a medieval ecclesiastical theocracy in which the qualities of the messianic kingdom described in the Old Testament were notably absent.

Implications for the Enterprise of Christian Theology

Christian theology cannot afford to ignore the momentous events of the twentieth century, especially those which threatened the very existence of the Jewish people and subsequently secured a homeland for them. The response of Christian theology to these developments has been mixed. While there have been some proposals for a post-Holocaust theology, replacement theology and its effects continue to influence the whole of systematic theology.

Post-Holocaust theologies characterized by a selective use of Scripture are insufficient for making modern theology relevant. What is needed is greater reflection on Israel by systematic theologians and biblical exegetes. Likewise, the teaching of systematic theology, whether in schools or in local churches, should include reflection on Israel just as it includes reflection on the Church. Both the similarities and institutional distinctives of Israel and the Church need to be emphasized. Theologians also need to weed out those elements in Christian theology which are the fruit of replacement theology.

Moreover, biblical reflection on Israel's place in God's plan must inform the Christian doctrines of ecclesiology and eschatology and must in turn be informed by New Testament Christology and soteriology. When one or more of the foundational elements of Christian thought are neglected, the product of theological reflection no longer corresponds to "the whole counsel of God" but rather to the intellectual climate of the moment.

APPENDIX

ISRAEL AND CHRISTIAN THEOLOGY: SOME EFFECTS OF THE NEW MAJORITY VIEW[1]

A generation before the infamous 1894 Dreyfus trial prompted Theodor Herzl to write his Zionist manifesto *The Jewish State: An Attempt at a Modern solution to the Jewish Question* and to convene the first World Zionist Congress in Switzerland, Carlo Antonio Zanini debated with representatives of the Jewish community in the public library of Mantova, Italy. At that time the majority of Christian theologians subscribed to the view that the Church had totally replaced Israel in redemption history. Zanini did not share this view. Rather he espoused a minority evangelical view based on a literal reading of Scripture.[2] Central to the understanding of Zanini was his three-fold conviction that: Israel remains God's elect people and, as such, will return to live as a sovereign nation in the land promised to Abraham, Isaac, and Jacob; that Jesus the Nazarene is the Messiah prophesied by the Hebrew prophets; and that the salvation of both Jews and Gentiles is possible only through faith in the atoning work of Jesus.

Marco Mortara, the chief Rabbi of Mantova, dedicated his 1868 Passover discourse to the issues raised by Zanini. The Rabbi's response echoed some of the recommendations made by Jewish Rabbis who had met at Vienna earlier that same year. These included recommendations to remove from Jewish liturgy all reference to the coming of a personal Messiah and to avoid all talk of a return to the Promised Land.[3] Although Zanini's Jewish interlocutors at Mantova showed no sympathy with the idea of Israel returning to the land of her fathers, the Christian evangelist lived long enough to see a significant part of world Jewry change its mind on this point. Before the close of the nineteenth century, Zanini was also able to document the presence of five hundred Messianic Jews living in part of the territory now recognized as the state of Israel.[4] Moreover, he was himself instrumental in leading some members of the Italian Jewish community to faith in Yeshua as Messiah and Savior.[5]

Much has happened for Jews and the Zionist movement since the close of the nineteenth century. In particular, the faith of Zanini and many Evangelical Christians that Israel would regain statehood has been vindicated in spite of the insurmountable odds. On the other hand, the second and third points to which Zanini drew the attention of his Jewish interlocutors—that Yeshua was the long awaited Messiah of Israel who "must remain in heaven until the time comes for God to restore everything, as he promised long ago through his holy prophets" (Acts 3:21), and that "Salvation is found in no one else, for there is no other name under heaven given to men by which we must be saved" (Acts 4:12)—have *not* found general acceptance. On the contrary, these apostolic affirmations are being increasingly either denied or ignored by Christian theologians involved in the Jewish-Christian dialogue.

Such denial and neglect of key elements of the apostolic gospel is linked with Christendom's new majority view concerning Israel. By appealing to passages such as Romans 9–11, proponents of this view have overturned the main thesis of the old majority view, which was that Israel had lost her covenant status as an elect nation by failing to recognize Yeshua as the promised Messiah. The conviction that Israel retains her elect status has led exponents of the new majority view to make a second affirmation, namely that Judaism is as much a means of salvation for Jews as Christianity is for non-Jewish nations. This affirmation ignores key elements of the apostolic gospel such as those cited above.

The new majority view is often linked with the "two covenant" model, according to which there is one covenant for the Jewish people and another for Gentiles.[6] This position has been recently defined as a "theology of recognition" with reference to Christians' recognition of Israel's status as a covenant nation.[7] This raises serious questions concerning the Christian gospel and the Church's mission.

My purpose in the present paper is to explore ways in which the "theology of recognition" is influencing the following disciplines of Christian theology: Christology, Soteriology, and Missiology, as well as the discipline of Hermeneutics. First, however, I will trace the origins of the new majority view.

In the Wake of Tragedy

The horrors of the *Shoah* and the subsequent birth of the modern State of Israel on May 14, 1948, were decisive factors in bringing about Christendom's radical change of mind concerning the present and future status of Israel. The *Shoah* disqualified the *old* majority view by revealing its nefarious effects. The trenches and massacres of the First World War (1914–1918) shocked the civilized nations of Western Europe. But wars like it, albeit on a smaller scale, had taken place throughout the entire history of fallen man. Hitler's plan to humiliate and exterminate the Jewish people, however, was unparalleled. It was the incarnation of all that is evil in human nature.

In terms of responsibility, the tragedy of the *Shoah* cannot be attributed exclusively to the Third Reich. Most so-called "Christian" nations became accomplices in the catastrophe by refusing to accept the thousands of Jewish refugees who managed to leave the territory of the Third Reich.[8] Even in Switzerland there was widespread anti-Semitic prejudice. Not only were many Jewish refugees turned away, many of those admitted to the country were harshly treated in Work Camps.[9]

But it is even not enough to put the blame on all the nations that collaborated directly or indirectly in anti-Semitic activity with Germany. It is now generally realized that part of what made both the pogroms of Russia and the *Shoah* played out in Central Europe possible was an attitude of theological contempt toward Israel that had its foundation in "replacement theology." Such theological thinking and the contempt it produced were components of the Christian tradition as early as the second century. Jaroslav Pelikan observes that, "Virtually every major Christian writer of the first five centuries either composed a treatise in opposition to Judaism or made this issue a dominant theme in a treatise devoted to some other subject."[10]

Besides the numerous writings that propounded replacement theology and fomented contempt for the Jewish people, the Church legislated against them. For example in AD 325 Constantine wrote concerning the date of Easter to those bishops who had not been present at the Council of Nicea.[11] The following consideration contained in Constantine's letter, "We ought not, therefore, to have anything in common with the Jews," sums up one of the key ideas behind much subsequent legislation against them: *All things Jewish were understood to be contemptible and totally incompatible with Christianity.* Similarly, during subsequent centuries, the confessions which Jewish converts to Christianity were required to make at the moment of their baptism were laced with contempt for all things Jewish.[12] Even Luther, just three years before his death, wrote a strongly anti-Judaic tract[13] which included a plea that all Jews be expelled from German territories. It is now widely recognized that theological prejudice and anti-Judaic legislation paved the way for the Jewish massacres which have stained the recent history of so-called "Christian" Europe.[14]

Commenting on the old majority view in the light of the *Shoah*, Daniele Garrone has said, "We must have the courage to admit that we were wrong."[15] Courage is indeed needed to acknowledge that the Christian theological tradition contributed to this immense human tragedy. According to Henry F. Knight this recognition requires that we experience shame.[16] On a practical level it means reviewing those elements in Christian theology which contributed to the rationale of the *Shoah*. As Knight observes, "After the *Shoah*, responsible Christians can . . . [move on] only with significant revision to the form and content of their theologies."[17]

Facing the shame of the *Shoah* also requires that the Church establish a new relationship with those who have experienced contempt and displacement. Awareness of ecclesiastical and theological responsibility for the disastrous events culminating in the *Shoah,* has indeed led various sectors of Christendom to seek a new, respectful relationship with the Jewish people. First in this new field was the Council of Christians and Jews (CCJ),[18] a non-missionary and non-political organization committed to promoting understanding between Christians and Jews. Established in 1942 against the background of the *Shoah,* the CCJ pre-dated the founding of the modern State of Israel and the inauguration of the World Council of Churches (WCC) by six years. The founders of the CCJ were resolved to lead the fight against anti-Semitism and other prejudices that had warped European culture.[19] Already in 1947 a general change in attitude toward the Jewish people was evident at a CCJ Conference held at Seelisberg, Switzerland. However, the "Ten Point Appeal to the Churches" which emanated from this conference, made it clear that some profound theological rethinking was necessary in order that lasting change might come about.[20]

The birth of dialogue on a grand scale can be dated from the Inaugural Assembly of the WCC in August, 1948, just three months after the birth of the modern State of Israel. At that time the WCC produced a statement concerning the status of the Jewish people in which the old majority view was radically revised. This is seen in the following statement: "To the Jews our God has bound us in a special solidarity linking our destinies together in His design."[21]

Moreover, the tone of the document is one of great respect. For example where the term "Jews" appears, it is almost invariably preceded by the definite article, while the expression "the Jewish people" is used nine times.

Other significant expressions include "Jewish neighbors" and "Jewish State."

While the new climate of dialogue is praiseworthy, we insist that the process of rethinking the Church's relationship with Israel be more closely monitored by Scripture. If not, there is a great risk that apostolic teaching will be either distorted or neglected in the interest of peace. What is needed is not emotional reaction to the effects of the old majority view but a return to all that Scripture has to say about the place of Israel in redemption history. Specifically, Romans chapters 9–11 should not be used selectively, as is so often done, omitting the missiological challenge contained in chapter ten.

The Effects of the New Majority View on Christology

It is the presupposition of the entire New Testament that Yeshua was the Messiah of Israel. Thus Christology, the study of the person and work of Jesus the Messiah, is a constitutive element of Christian theology. This being the case, it is imperative that the Church at large be aware of how Christology is modified by the new majority view.

Christians need to remember that for almost two thousand years the Jewish people have associated "Christ" with anti-Judaic attitudes manifested by the Church. Thus it is to be expected that Jewish partners in dialogue will react negatively to the claim that the Christ preached by the Christian Church is their promised Messiah. As a remedy to this problem, Ekkehard Stegemann suggests that the Church should not call Jesus the Messiah of Israel.[22] Ironically, part of the problem is that the Church has too seldom taken this fact seriously! There are two other substantial problems with Stegemann's suggestion. In the first place the New Testament states quite explicitly that Jesus is the Messiah of Israel, linking his Jewishness with his role as the Savior of the world (John 4:25–42; Romans 9:1–5; cf. Genesis 12:1–3; Galatians 3:16). Second, whoever denies that Jesus is Israel's Messiah is in fact denying the gospel which was announced to Abraham (Galatians 3:8–16; Romans 1:1–5, 16–17).

Hans Joachim Krau makes a different but equally radical proposal for modifying the Church's concept of Christ. Instead of the traditional concept of a distinct person with supernatural attributes who came to fulfill the promises made to Israel, Krau proposes a kind of mystical Christology. According to this concept the Messiah and the people of the Messiah are inseparable.[23]

I propose that, instead of avoiding Christology, Christian partners in the Jewish-Christian dialogue would do well to distinguish between the relevant biblical data and the "theological embroidery"[24] dating from post–apostolic times. In particular they should disassociate themselves from the triumphalism of the Medieval Church. In its place they should underline the Jewishness of Jesus and make clear what both Jesus and the apostles taught concerning the fulfillment of the Old Testament Messianic hope. In particular it needs to be stressed that, according to the New Testament, the fulfillment of some aspects of the Messianic hope awaits the second advent of Christ (Matthew 13:36–43; Mark 14:60–62; Luke 19:11–27; Acts 3:19–21; 14:21–23; 17:30–31).

The Effects of the New Majority View on Soteriology and Missiology

According to Paul van Buren, a close observer of the Jewish-Christian dialogue, the dialogical process is favoring the theory that there are two peoples, Israel and the Church, to which correspond two covenants. We have already noted that, according to this view, ethnic Israel, God's elect people, are redeemed through their faithfulness to the Torah while the Church is a separate community of which the great majority are from the Gentile nations and are accepted by God on the basis of the atoning work of Jesus.[25] Using this theory as his starting point, Clark M. Williamson claims that the Letter to the Hebrews is supersessionist where it claims, "that the covenant between God and the Israel of God had been abolished."[26] Williamson's evaluation of this New Testament book confuses the Sinaitic covenant, superseded by the new covenant prophesied by Jeremiah, with the Abrahamic covenant of promise on which Israel's special identity is based.

Similar to "two covenant theology" is the inclusivistic idea according to which the Jewish people are already in the one covenant.[27] Both of these theories, if accepted, require some revision of New Testament soteriology and of the Church's missionary mandate.

Despite its importance, soteriology was not one of the theological issues discussed during the first forty years of the Jewish-Christian dialogue.[28] John T. Pawlikowski does not even include soteriology among "other areas where Christianity and Judaism each can profit from the dialogical exchange."[29] John Lyden finds this lack of attention "curious, given the central role of this doctrine in both religions."[30] However, it is conceivable that the doctrine of salvation was avoided precisely because it touches the heart of the religious life of both Jews and Christians. Another reason might be that talking about theories of atonement would have meant facing up to some irreconcilable differences in the two faiths "due to the central role of Jesus in the Christian view of atonement."[31] Yet reluctance to make soteriology a subject of dialogue is unfortunate because the question of mission, which has been a major concern of dialogue,[32] cannot be satisfactorily addressed without first addressing the issue of how salvation is accomplished and applied.

There are other reasons why soteriology should not be neglected: first, because salvation is a fundamental concern of mankind;[33] and second, because the possibility of salvation is one of the central themes of biblical revelation. The concept of atonement, with its emphasis on sacrifice and repentance, is a theme common to both the Hebrew Scriptures and the New Testament writings. Moreover, both the Jewish and Christian canons of Scripture link soteriology with monotheistic faith. For example, in the Tanakh God speaks thus: "Turn to me and be saved, all you ends of the earth; for I am God, and there is no other. By myself I have sworn, my mouth has uttered in all integrity a word that will not be revoked: Before me every knee will bow; by me every tongue will swear" (Isaiah 45:22–23; cf. 49:5–6).

The uniqueness of the God of Israel implies that all nations need to come to him in order to experience salvation. The same logic is found in Paul's first letter to Timothy, with the difference that the way of salvation is further defined as being through the atoning work of the Messiah, as identified in the person of Jesus: "God our Savior . . . wants all men to be saved and to come to a knowledge of the truth. For there is one God and one mediator between God and men, the man Christ Jesus, who gave himself as a ransom for all men" (1 Timothy 2:3–6; cf. Romans 3:29–30; Hebrews 2:2–4).

The long period of comparative neglect of soteriology in the Jewish-Christian dialogue was brought to an end by a symposium held in Rome in November 1986 on the theme: "Salvation and Redemption in Judaism and Christianity."[34] The missiological implications of the Jewish-Christian dialogue were considered three years later at a "Consultation on the Gospel and the Jewish People" organized by the World Evangelical Fellowship at Willowbank, Bermuda.[35] Subsequently both the soteriological and the missiological implications of the Jewish-Christian dialogue have become common themes of books[36] and journal articles.[37]

As in other aspects of the Jewish-Christian dialogue the Church has shown a willingness to listen to its interlocutor in discussions concerning soteriology. However, willingness to listen has not always been matched by a readiness to expound distinctive New Testament teaching on the topics being discussed. It is interesting that Terry Bookman, a Jewish partner in dialogue, deems this tendency inappropriate. According to Bookman, those engaged in dialogue must avoid "liberal attempts to either include those who do not profess their faith under their particular salvific formulation or to relativize all truth away." Rather they must "talk intelligently about the central core" of what makes them what they are.[38] Soteriology is surely part of the core of what makes any religion distinctive, thus Christian partners in dialogue are duty bound to bring to bear the essential teaching of the New Testament writings on this subject.

The Rome colloquium found a solution to the diversity of Jewish and Christian soteriologies in the concept of theological pluralism. According to this position Judaism and Christianity present different but equally valid answers to the question: What must I do to be saved? This pluralistic solution is reflected in the way Rabbi Leon Klenicki summed up the point reached by the Jewish-Christian dialogue: "Overcoming the effect of memories must be followed by a religious consideration of the meaning of Christianity, the meaning of Jesus. The consideration of Christianity does not mean a conversion to Christianity. It is a recognition of a faith and its mission to others. The consideration of Christianity emphasizes our own authenticity, our own fervor and commitment."[39]

Klenicki clearly excludes the possibility of Jewish people converting to Yeshua. So do the one hundred and seventy-two Jewish scholars who signed the document "*DABRU EMET:* Statement on Christians and Christianity" dated September 10, 2000. The authors of this statement[40] conclude their description of the "irreconcilable difference between Jews and Christians" with the words, "Neither Jew nor Christian should be pressed into affirming the teaching of the other community."

What should concern us as Christian theologians is that Christian partners in dialogue tend to negate the belief that Jews need to believe in Yeshua in order to be saved. For example, the Roman Catholic scholars who participated in the Rome symposium opted for a pluralistic solution to the question of the salvation of non-messianic

Jews. While this solution might appear attractive at first glance, it involves a selective use of the New Testament and hence is not an option for those who take seriously the canonical status of the New Testament writings in which faith in Yeshua is essential for salvation.[41]

This is not to say that all fruits of the Jewish-Christian dialogue concerning soteriology have been negative. New light has been thrown on common elements in soteriology such as the call to repentance and the doctrine of atonement. Moreover, dialogue has helped to break down the stereotype of the Jew who believes that justification is by works. On the other hand, the belief that God's continuing covenant relationship with Israel exonerates the Jews from the need to respond in faith to the gospel of Jesus Christ has put powerful constraints on the discussion concerning soteriology. Christian partners in dialogue have tended to avoid mentioning some of the essential ingredients of New Testament soteriology, in particular the crucial role of Jesus as Savior and the need to exercise faith in him in order to be saved.[42]

Peter Beyerhaus observes that, "biblical essentials of Christian faith are more and more jeopardized" by the present trend toward radical pluralism.[43] The Jewish-Christian dialogue on soteriology exemplifies this general tendency, but it does more than this. Christianity's unqualified acceptance of Jewish monotheistic faith actually fosters religious pluralism. In fact, the general opinion that Israel's own covenant with God exempts her from needing to believe in Jesus in order to be saved implies that any number of peoples may have their own special relationship with God and hence be exempted from recognizing Jesus as the only means of reconciliation.[44]

Where monotheistic faith is the common ground of dialogue, the candidates for dialogue are no longer two but three: Judaism, Christianity, *and* Islam.[45] In a significant article published in *Common Ground,* the organ of the Council of Christians and Jews, Tony Bayfield, a Jewish Rabbi, calls for mutual respect among the three monotheistic religious communities. Bayfield quotes with approval the following view expressed by Maurice Wiles:[46] "If God makes himself available to be known by way of a universal offer of divine self-communication, any knowledge of God arising from that potentiality is necessarily a saving knowledge."[47] This affirmation makes "saving knowledge" derive from general revelation. In other words, a universal gnosticism takes the place of salvation based on the efficacy of Christ's work. Such a soteriology is completely devoid of biblical foundations.

Bayfield goes on to suggest that Christians should avoid presenting a unique way of salvation. Christian mission, in his view, should be limited to sharing a particular knowledge of the goodness of God as it has been made known in Jesus Christ.[48] He writes, "The route to the day on which 'God will be One and God's name One' (Zechariah 14:9) lies not through mission as conquest or conversion but through mission as the full realization in each Jew, Christian, and Muslim of the best that each of the Abrahamic faiths can teach."[49]

This is the view of someone who denies that Yeshua is the Messiah of Israel. But true disciples of Yeshua, whether they are Jews or Gentiles, are called to obey the missionary mandate which he entrusted to his followers (Matthew 28:18–20). According to the Christian gospel there is no way back to God except through Jesus.

So far as the evangelistic mission to the Jewish people in the here and now is concerned, suffice it to say that while the eschatological salvation of "all Israel" (Romans 11:24–27) is not hastened by including the Jewish people in the Church's mission,[50] this does not diminish the relevance of the principle "to the Jew first" practiced by Paul in order to "save some" of them (Romans 1:16; 11:13–14; cf. Acts 13–19; 28:17–28). The words with which Peter addresses the Jewish people and their leaders in Acts 3:24–26 and 4:8–12 confirm that all Jews of every generation need to hear and respond to the Christian gospel, just as do Gentile peoples.

The New Majority View and Hermeneutics

In this final example of the effects of the new majority view on Christian theology we will concentrate our attention on the tendency of those involved in the dialogical process to consider Sinai, rather than the death and resurrection of Jesus, the central and unifying point of salvation history. Whereas half a century ago James Parkes considered "Sinai and Calvary" to be different but complementary revelations,[51] Pawlikowski has recently written, "Some Christian theologians working on the question of the Christian-Jewish relationship, such as Paul van Buren, would seem to make Sinai the central and unifying event. Christ becomes the entry-point for all non-Jews into this one ongoing covenant."[52]

A good example of a work which builds on this hermeneutical principle is Clark Williamson's *A Guest in the House of Israel.* Williamson redefines the terms unity, catholicity, sanctity, and apostolicity, widely recognized as the signs of the Church, in such a way as to make

Sinai feature as "the central and unifying event."[53] He writes, "The covenant between the God of Israel and the Israel of God at Sinai is the fundamental covenant of the scriptures."[54]

In order to make this hermeneutical principle work, Williamson does not hesitate to deny the historicity of the Abrahamic covenant. He writes, "But [the Sinaitic] covenant is read back into history; so the J-document tells of the covenant between the Lord and Abram (Genesis 15:17–18)."[55] The theoretical basis of Williamson's claim that the Sinaitic covenant is "the fundamental covenant of the scriptures" is thus seen to stand on a very shaky foundation; in fact, the historicity of the Abrahamic covenant is affirmed time after time throughout the Hebrew and Christian Scriptures. Moreover, according to Paul, the Abrahamic covenant, which constitutes the basis of God's continuing relationship with Israel, preceded the Sinaitic covenant by 430 years (Galatians 3:17).

There are two further difficulties with the claim that Sinai is the central and unifying event of salvation history. The first difficulty is that both the early Christians and writers of the New Testament identify the unifying element of Old Testament history in the call of Abraham, to whom God announced the gospel in advance (Acts 7:2–46; 13:26; Galatians 3:6–29; cf. Genesis 12:1–3). Salvation history reflects the covenants of promise which God gave to Abraham, Isaac, and Jacob, while the consummation of these promises is expected to come about through their progeny, in particular Jesus, the Christ (Exodus 2:24; 6:4–8; Matthew 1:1; Galatians 3:16). The second difficulty is that the centerpiece of salvation history, which the Church is called to defend, is the truth of the incarnation (1 Timothy 3:15–16).

The Sinaitic covenant, as distinct from the Old Testament covenants of promise, was neither foundational nor ongoing. In fact it has been superseded by the new covenant into which the whole people of Israel must eventually enter (Jeremiah 31:31–34; Romans 11:26–27). This covenant has constitutive value for New Testament theology (Hebrews 8:1–13; 9:15; 2 Corinthians 3:1–6). In the final analysis, making "Sinai the central and unifying event" attaches more importance to a particular kind of Judaism than to the people of Israel and God of Israel.

The inauguration of the new covenant and the accomplishment of salvation are inseparable, as both were effected by the death and resurrection of "Jesus Christ, the son of David, the son of Abraham" (Genesis 12:3; Matthew 1:1, 21; Galatians 3:8, 13–14, 29; Hebrews 9:15). Thus Christian theology would commit a grave mistake if it did not continue to recognize in Jesus' death and resurrection the central and unifying event of salvation history, for Israel as well as for Gentiles. Besides, Paul makes the point that it is through the atoning death of Jesus that Jew and Gentile coexist peacefully (Ephesians 2:11–22) and it is through him that God reconciles all things to himself (Colossians 1:19–20). The hermeneutical decision to subordinate the Christ event to the Sinai event ignores the primary importance of the Christ event which, according to the apostles, constitutes the only foundation for the hope of obtaining eternal salvation.

Conclusion

The enterprise of Christian theology must be based on sound hermeneutical principles, in particular the canonical principle. Inasmuch as the Jewish-Christian dialogue involves parties that recognize two partially different canons of Scripture, Christian partners in dialogue are obliged to bring to bear their understanding of the inter-relatedness of the Hebrew Scriptures and the New Testament writings. Where the constraints of dialogue lead to the development of views involving the suppression of apostolic teaching, the best interests of both Israel and the Church are lost because no real progress can be made at the expense of truth.

NOTES

Preface

[1] The Hebrew term *Shoah* means desolation and refers to the so-called "final solution" worked out by Hitler.

Introduction

[1] "The Commission on Faith and Order," Bristol, 1967, in *The Theology of the Churches and the Jewish People: Statements by the World Council of Churches and its member churches,* Allan Brockway, Paul van Buren, Rolf Rendtorff, and Simon Schoon, eds., (Geneva: WWC Publications, 1988), p. 21 (hereafter *TCJP*).

[2] The Hebrew term *Shoah* ("desolation") is used to describe the most notorious of the long series of atrocities perpetrated against the Jewish people. The term identifies the series of events described in German Nazi language as: *die Endlösung der Judenfrage* or "the Final Solution of the question of the Jews" which Nazi Germany planned in order "to ensure that no longer would there be a single Jew upon Planet Earth" (A. Roy Eckardt, "Salient Christian-Jewish Issues of Today: A Christian Exploration," *Jews and Christians*, James H. Charlesworth, Frank X. Blisard and Jeffrey S. Siker, eds., (New York: Crossroad, 1990), p. 157). "Holocaust" is a less suitable term to describe these events, as it carries a positive connotation for Jews (see Leviticus 1:3; 6:1–6).

[3] The birth of the modern State of Israel was described by Teddy Kollek as "perhaps the most significant event of this century" (Norman Solomon, "The Christian Churches on Israel and the Jews," in *Anti-Zionism and Anti-Semitism in the Contemporary World,* Robert S. Wistrich, ed., (London: The Macmillan Press, 1990), p. 144.

[4] Richard Harries, "Dialogo Cristiani-Ebrei," *Dizionario del Movimento Ecumenico*, Giovanni Cereti, Alfio Filippi, Luigi Sartori, eds., (Bologna: edizioni Dehoniane, 1994), p. 377.

⁵ Of sixteen works published between 1980 and 1994, which I have examined, only five make significant mention of Israel, three make marginal reference while eight omit all mention of Israel.

⁶ Gordon R. Lewis and Bruce A. Demarest, *Integrative Theology,* 3 vols., (Grand Rapids, MI: Zondervan, 1994), 3:336.

⁷ Hendrikus Berkhof, *Christian Faith,* (Grand Rapids, MI: Eerdmans, 1979), p. 221. He writes of the Church: "she seems to forget Israel almost completely and not need her at all. The latter is especially the case in the creedal statements and systematic theology handbooks."

⁸ Gabriel Fackre ("The Place of Israel in Christian Faith," in *Ecumenical Faith in Evangelical Perspective,* by Gabriel Fackre, (Grand Rapids, MI: Eerdmans, 1993), pp. 148–153) distinguishes five types of supersessionism: the "Retributive Replacement View," still espoused by the reconstructionist movement which considers Israel to have been repudiated by God on account of her obstinate unbelief; the "Non-retributive Replacement View," probably the most widely held view in historic Christian theology, which sees ethnic Israel as being simply superseded by the person and work of Christ and the community of faith based upon Christ's work; a "Modified Replacement View" which stresses "the role of the Hebrew Scriptures in Christian faith" and "the right of Messianic Jews to incorporate their heritage into their Christian faith"; the "Messianic Replacement View," which sees Christ as the fulfillment of the Jewish hope and seeks to win Jews for Jesus; and finally Karl Barth's "Christological Election View."

⁹ Henry Finch, *The Worlds Great Restauration, Or The Calling of the Iewes, and (with them) of all the Nations and Kingdomes of the earth, to the faith of Christ,* 1621; Thomas Goodwin (1600–1680), *An Exposition of the First, and part of the Second chapter, of the Epistle to the Ephesians,* Works, 5 vols. (1682–1704). In his survey of anti-supersessionist perspectives, Fackre begins with the dispensationalism developed by John Nelson Darby (1800–1882). In reality the historic turning point in attitudes towards Israel, within Protestantism, began with the pre-millennial views of the Reformed German Theologian Johann Heinrich Alsted (1588–1638) and was consolidated by English Puritans (Robert G. Clouse, "The Rebirth of Millenarianism," in Peter Toon [ed.], *Puritan Eschatology 1600–1660,* (Cambridge: James Clarke, 1970), pp. 42–65); cf. Bryan W. A. Ball, *A Great Expectation: Eschatological thought in English Protestantism to 1660.* (Leiden: E. J. Brill, 1975).

¹⁰ Two of the most influential works were: *The Premillennial Advent of Christ demonstrated from the Scripture,* by the Anglican scholar William Cuninghame, London, 1815, and *Venida del Mesìas en Gloria y Majestad,* by a Jesuit, Manuel de Lacunza y Diaz and published in 1811. The English translation of the 11th ed. of this work, with Introduction by Edward Irving, was published in 1827, (*The*

Coming of the Messiah in Glory and Majesty, 2 vols., (London: L.B. Seeley and Sons, 1827)).

[11] Jaroslav Pelikan considers the Christian effort to come to terms with the unique and abiding place of the covenant with the people of Israel in the economy of divine revelation "a key to the nature of the Christian message" (Jaroslav Pelikan, *The Christian Tradition,* 5 vols., (Chicago: University of Chicago Press, 1971–1989), 5:334); cf. Willem VanGemeren (*The Progress of Redemption,* (Grand Rapids, MI: Zondervan, 1988), p. 442), who speaks of the importance of "discussions between church and synagogue that have been suspended since the II century AD."

[12] This shift in world views and its effect on the whole enterprise of Christian theology is traced by the liberal scholar, Adolf Harnack (*Lehrbuch der Dogmengeschichte,* 4th ed., 1909; It. trans., *Manuale di Storia del Dogma,* 7 vols., (Mendrisio: Casa Editrice Cultura Moderna, 1912–1914), 1:51–162; 2:175–321; 3:5–144) who affirms that everywhere the arsenal of Greek culture passed its weapons and baggage to the Church, so that philosophical theological speculation and the Greek mysteries became the principal factors in the formative process that shaped the Christian church. Harnack adds that significant elements also have their origin in Roman customs, among these the episcopal constitution of the Church. I will argue that this process was also influenced by an indiscriminate takeover of Levitical cultic practice by the Church. Harnack concludes, "Therefore, also in the church perfectly developed in all of its essential structures, we find that the philosophic schools and the Roman empire had chosen to make their home," (1:47). This assessment reflects Harnack's view that metaphysics was an alien intrusion in early Christian thought (Colin Brown, "Harnack," *NIDCC*), however it also accurately reflects the phenomenon of Greco-Roman culture replacing the biblical Hebrew world view in the development of the Christian tradition; cf. W.H.C. Frend, *The Rise of Christianity,* (Philadelphia, PA: Fortress Press, 1984), pp. 367–395.

[13] Pelikan, *Tradition,* 1:22.

[14] According to the church of Rome, "an iconoclast was simply 'one with a Jewish mind [*Ioudaiophroōn*],'" (ibid., p. 201).

[15] For a brief presentation of the effects of the new majority view, see pp. 175–192 of the present work.

Chapter 1

[1] We will not consider here possible exceptions to this rule because the nation of Israel, to which the biblical uses of the name normally refer, still exists and it is the nature of this existence we are considering. See pp. 54–64 for an examination of the meaning of "Israel" in Romans 9–11.

[2] At the conclusion of a detailed study of the uses of the terms Jews, Hebrews, and Israel in antiquity, Graham Harvey writes concerning

the latter: "Israel is primarily the name of a people. It is linked to an eponymous ancestor, also named "Jacob" whose actions and character (good and bad) are those of the people. Although it is linked with God in the phrase "the God of Israel" (and is distinct from "Jews" in this way also) "Israel" is never a totally pure community: it can be either commended or condemned. "Israel" is an audience for this God and for the authors of the literature discussed (Graham Harvey, *The True Israel*, (Leiden: E.J. Brill, 1996), p. 272).

³ *Yisra-êl*, "contender," "soldier of God," from *saràh* "to fight" and *el* "God" (William Gesenius, *Gesenius' Hebrew and Chaldee Lexicon to the Old Testament Scriptures,* trans. S. P. Tregelles, (Samuel Bagster and Sons, 1847; Reprint, Grand Rapids, MI: Baker Book House, 1979), p. 370).

⁴ *Yisra-êl*, "*Êl* persisteth or persevereth" or "Let *Êl* persist" or "Let *Êl* contend," *A Hebrew and English Lexicon of the Old Testament,* Francis Brown, S.R. Driver, Charles A. Briggs (eds.), (Oxford: Clarendon Press, 1975), p. 975.

⁵ See John Feinberg, "Systems of Discontinuity," in *Continuity and Discontinuity,* John Feinberg (ed.), (Westfield, IL: Crossway Books, Good News Publishers, 1988), p. 79.

⁶ For a discussion concerning the distinctiveness of the promissory covenants, see Thomas Edward McComisky, *The Covenants of Promise: A Theology of the Old Testament Covenants,* (Grand Rapids, MI: Baker Book House, 1985), pp. 133–142.

⁷ Particular theories concerning Old Testament chronology, such as the date of the Exodus, are not relevant to the purpose of the present work.

⁸ The Davidic covenant features as the foundation of many prophecies concerning a future Messiah and a messianic age. See: Psalm 2; 45:1–7 [cf. Hebrews 1:8–9]; Psalm 110 [cf. Hebrews 1:3; 5:6;]; Psalm 118:21–22 [cf. Matthew 21:42–45]; Micah 5:1–5; Isaiah 2:1–4; 4:2–6; 9:1–7; 11:1–12; 42:1; 49:5–6; 52:13–53:12; 55:3–5; 59:16–20; 61:1–62:4; Jeremiah 23:5–8; Daniel 7:13–18 [cf. Mark 14:61–62]; Daniel 9:26–27; Hosea 3:4–5; Amos 9:8–15; Zechariah 2:8–10; 9:9–10; 12:1–13:9. In these passages, the promise theme already present in Genesis (3:15; 12:3; 28:14; 49:9–10) is elaborated with specific reference to the nature of future fulfillment.

⁹ This prophecy establishes a basic unity between the Old and New Testaments which allows for both continuity and discontinuity.

¹⁰ An obvious example of this is the covenant that God made with the zealous priest Phinehas (Numbers 25:10–13).

¹¹ Raphael Jospe, "The Concept of the Chosen People: An Interpretation," *Judaism* 43 (1994): 130–135.

¹² For example, Refoulé claims that the reference to the irrevocable call of God in 11:29 is evidence that even in this case salvation is in view; when Paul speaks of election in verse 28b, the apparent

paradox being limited to disparity of time. Thus, the elect who are now enemies of the Gospel in the future will respond to God's call, showing themselves to be members of true Israel (François Refoulé, ". . . *Et ainsi tout Israël sera sauvé*," (Paris: Les Éditions du Cerf, 1984), pp.191–215). According to the fifth century commentator Severian of Gabala, Paul's purpose in writing verses 28–29 was to reprimand the unbelieving Jews, while the phrase "loved on account of the patriarchs" means "loved because of the fathers, in honor of whom [God] acts benevolently with their descendants and will consider loved those who will believe and will have shown the right of citizenship, whom he will save" (in *Pauluskommentare aus der Griechischen Kirche*, Karl Staab (ed.), 1933; Reprint (Münster, Westfalen: Aschendorff, 1984), p. 223).

[13] Robert L. Saucy, "Israel and the Church: A Case for Discontinuity," in *Continuity and Discontinuity*, p. 245.

[14] This movement of minorities from the northern tribes is reflected in the genealogies of 1 Chronicles 1–9; 36:22–23.

[15] Ellison (H.L. Ellison, *The Mystery of Israel*, (Exeter: Paternoster, 1966), pp. 41–56) makes a strong case for understanding the election of Israel in this way. He writes, "Here [in Romans 9–11] Paul is concerned with election (national as well as personal, in history rather than in the setting of eternity) as the means whereby He accomplishes His purposes for the world" (ibid., p. 49).

[16] The Book of Jonah was written as an incentive to Israel to fulfill her missionary task.

[17] For example, John Calvin (*Romans*, Calvin's Commentaries, John Owen [trans. and ed.], (Grand Rapids, MI: Eerdmans, 1947); *Epistles of Paul the Apostle, to the Romans and to the Thessalonians*, Calvin's Commentaries, Reprint, (Edinburgh: The Saint Andrew Press, 1961), pp. 190, 238) speaks of the "destruction" and the "rejection" of the Jews.

[18] The particle *mē* in the construction *mē apōsato ho theos ton laon autou* (11:1) has the force of excluding the idea that God has rejected his people.

[19] According to Kevin Giles (*What on Earth is the Church?* (Downer's Grove, IL: InterVarsity Press, 1995), p.185), this statement (and what follows it in Romans 11) is not fully representative of Paul's thought, much less of that of other NT writers. Giles writes: "Right from the beginning [Paul] designates the Christian community with titles once the sole preserve of Israel, but in the epistle to the Romans he shows himself to be reluctant to concede that God has completely abandoned Israel as his people. He solves his dilemma by predicating a future salvation of 'all Israel'. Later writers were bolder." Such reasoning neglects both the importance of chapters 9–11 in the structure of Romans and the fact that only here in the NT is the question of Israel's present status as an elect people discussed.

[20] Refoulé, op. cit., pp. 142–161.

[21] C.E.B. Cranfield, *The Epistle to the Romans,* 2 vols., ICC, J.A. Emerton (ed.), (Edinburgh: T. & T. Clark, 1975–1979), 2:576–577. Cranfield writes, "The references to *plērōma autōn* in v. 12, to *hē proslēmpsis* in v. 15, and to the grafting in again of the broken-off branches in vv. 23 and 24, point unmistakably to something more than what would simply amount to the salvation of the elect remnants of Israel of all the generations," (ibid., p. 577).

[22] Refoulé, ". . . *Et ainsi,*" pp. 163–165.

[23] Cranfield, *Romans,* p. 548; Calvin (*Romans,* p. 414) is also convinced that the election spoken of here is unto salvation.

[24] F. F. Bruce, commenting on those who at the time of the fall of the temple could have thought that the national life of Israel had come to an end, writes, "But the event proved them wrong. The disappearance of the temple order marked the beginning of a new and glorious chapter in Israel's story, which does not come within the scope of this book" Bruce quotes an historical fragment preserved by Sulpicius Severus, c. AD 400. (F.F. Bruce, *Romans,* Tyndale New Testament Commentaries, (Leicester, England: InterVarsity Press, 2nd ed., 1985), pp. 224–225).

[25] See James Parkes, *The Conflict of the Church and the Synagogue,* (New York: Hermon Press, 1934).

[26] Chrysostom, serm. VI, 1 (*PG* 48:903–905).

[27] Sir Walter Scott, *Ivanhoe,* Nelson Classics, (T. Nelson and Sons, 1830), p. 68.

[28] "Sussidi per una corretta presentazione degli ebrei e dell'ebraismo nella catechesi della Chiesa cattolica," *L'osservatore Romano,* (June 24–25, 1985): pp. 6–7, quoted by Enzo Bianchi, "Israele e la chiesa," *Storia cristiana* 10 (1989): 95.

[29] The term "anti-Semitism" does not imply discrimination against people who speak Semitic languages (cf. "anti-Semitism"), but rather "hatred and persecution of the Jewish people" (cf. Allan Brockway, *TCJP,* p. 139).

[30] David S. Katz, "The Abendana Brothers and the Christian Hebraists of Seventeenth-Century England," *JEH* 40/1 (1989): 28–52.

[31] Norman Bentwich, *The Jews in our Time,* Penguin Books, 1960, It. trans. by Lia Moggi, *Gli Ebrei nel nostro tempo,* (Florence: Sansoni, 1963), pp. 25–26.

[32] Nobel prizes have been awarded yearly since 1901 in accordance with the testament of Alfred Bernhard Nobel (1833–1896), "to those who, during the preceding year, shall have conferred the greatest benefit on mankind" in the fields of physics, chemistry, physiology/ medicine, literature and peace (*Encyclopedia Britannica* [1994], 8: 738).

[33] Bentwich, *The Jews,* pp. 141–146.

³⁴ Ibid., p. 147.

³⁵ Ibid.

³⁶ "Person of the Century," Elbert Einstein, cover of *Time*, December 31, 1999.

³⁷ Ibid., p. 31; Cecil Roth, *A Short History of the Jewish People*, (London: Horovitz Publishing Co., 5th ed., 1969), p. 425. Norman Bentwich shows that it was common for Jewish scholars and research scientists to encounter anti-Semitic prejudice (Bentwich, *The Jews*, pp. 142–143).

³⁸ During the first three Crusades, in 1096, 1147 and c. 1190, Jews as well as Muslims were considered infidels and massacred in great numbers (see Justo L. Gonzàlez, *The Story of Christianity*, 2 vols., (San Francisco, CA: Harper, 1984–1985), 1:293–296). James Parkes, *A History of the Jewish People*, Penguin Books, (Middlesex: Harmondsworth, 1964), pp. 72–73.

³⁹ See Roth, *A Short History*, pp. 297–311.

⁴⁰ *Encyclopaedia Judaica*, 16 vols., Jerusalem: *Encyclopaedia Judaica*, (1971), 5:538–539.

⁴¹ Roth, *A Short History*, pp. 221–235.

⁴² Ibid., p. 339. Among these were some of his own children. Mendelssohn's grandson, Felix, baptized in infancy, devoted his genius to enriching the music of the Christian church.

⁴³ Ibid., pp. 343–345.

⁴⁴ "Sorgente di Vita," RAI Due, (September 30, 1995).

⁴⁵ The movement was effectively launched by Theodor Herzl (1869–1904) when he wrote and published what was tantamount to the Zionist manifesto, "Judenstaat," after witnessing the blatant injustice meted out to Alfred Dreyfus in Paris in 1894. Zionism attracted international attention with the convening of the first Zionist Congress at Basel in 1897. See Howard M. Sachar, *A History of Israel: from the rise of Zionism to our Time*, (New York: Alfred A. Knopf, 1993).

⁴⁶ The aim of Zionism was thus formulated at the first Zionist Congress, 1897 (Roth, *A Short History*, p. 410). A reflection on the Zionist movement was published by *Judaica*, March–June 1997, for the Centenary of the first Zionist Congress.

⁴⁷ Doc. 1, para. 2, The First Assembly of the World council of Churches, Amsterdam, (August 22–September 4, 1948), *TCJP*, p. 6.

⁴⁸ Cf. R. Kendall Soulen, *The God of Israel and Christian Theology*, (Minneapolis, MN: Fortress Press, 1996), p. 156: "In the context of God's crowning Sabbath blessing, God's economy is irrevocably embodied in the carnal election of the Jewish people and in the consequent distinction between Jew and Gentile, between Israel and the nations."

Chapter 2

[1] For a helpful survey of the complex phenomenon of anti-Semitism, see Gavin I. Langmuir, *History, Religion, and Anti-Semitism*, (Los Angeles: Center for Medieval and Renaissance Studies, 1990).

[2] See Hans Ucko, *Common Roots New Horizons*, (Geneva: WCC Publications, 1994), pp. 28–29. The term "replacement theology" (cf. "Christian supersessionism") is a relatively new term in Christian theology.

[3] This is summed up in Justin Martyr's description of the Church as "the true Israelitic race" (*Dialogue with Trypho,* cxxxv [*PG* 6: 788]).

[4] See *TCJP*, pp. 5–9. Part of this statement is reproduced at the end of chapter 1.

[5] Ecclesiastical groups which have produced such statements include: The Synod of the Evangelical Church in Germany (April 1950), the Netherlands Reformed Church (May 1951), the General Synod of the Netherlands Reformed Church (June 1970), the General Conference of the United Methodist Church in the USA (1972), the General Convention of the American Lutheran Church (October 1974), the Council of the Evangelical Church in Germany (May 1975), the Central Board of the Swiss Protestant Federation (May 1977), the Norwegian Bishops' Conference (November 1977), the Synod of the Evangelical Church of the Rhineland, Germany (January 1980), the Texas Conference of Churches (January 1982), the Synod of the Evangelical Church of West Berlin (May 1984), and the General Assembly of the Presbyterian Church in the USA (June 1987). All of these declarations may be found in *TCJP*, 47–120. Moreover, a statement of "principles" for the Jewish-Christian dialogue, elaborated by the Main Assembly of the Reformed Alliance in May 1990 was published in *Kirche und Israel* 5 (1990): 88–91, while a Consultation on the Church and the Jewish People of the WCC (November 4, 1988) elaborated a statement entitled: "The Churches and the Jewish People: Towards a New Understanding," adopted at Sigtuna, Sweden (*IBMR* 13/4 [1989]: 152–154).

[6] "Nostra Aetate" para. 4, in *Tutti i documenti del Concilio,* (Roma: U.C.I.I.M., 1972), pp. 534–537.

[7] Pelikan, *Tradition,* 5:334.

[8] Rosemary R. Ruether, *Faith and Fratricide: The Theological Roots of Anti-Semitism,* (New York: Seabury Press, 1974), especially pp. 64–116.

[9] Ruether writes, "In the synoptic tradition, messianic and anti-Judaic midrashim arose as two sides of the same development" (*Fratricide,* p. 64).

[10] Gregory Baum O.S.A., *Is the New Testament Anti-Semitic?* (Glen Rock, N.J.: Paulist Press, 1960; Revised ed. 1965), p. 17.

[11] *Anti-Semitism and the Foundations of Christianity,* Alan T. Davies (ed.), (New York: Paulist Press, 1979), presented to James Parkes, on the occasion of his eightieth birthday.

[12] Ibid., "Preface," p. x.

[13] John C. Meagher, "As the Twig was Bent: Anti-Semitism in Greco-Roman and Earliest Christian Times" (ibid., p. 23). David P. Efraymson, "The Patristic connection," (ibid., pp. 98–117), comes to the opposite conclusion: "The fathers were 'carriers' to be sure, and 'aggravators' of something that had come into existence earlier."

[14] Monika K. Hellwig, "From the Jesus of Story to the Christ of Dogma" (ibid., pp. 118–136).

[15] Ibid., p. 132.

[16] Jeffrey S. Siker, *Disinheriting the Jews; Abraham in Early Christian Controversy,* (Louisville, KY: Westminster/John Knox Press, 1991).

[17] Ibid., pp. 185–198.

[18] James D.G. Dunn, *The Partings of the Ways,* (London: SCM, 1991).

[19] For example Edmund Clowney writes, "In the history of revelation, the Old Testament people of God become the Church of the Messiah" (Edmund P. Clowney, *The Church, Contours of Christian Theology,* Gerald Bray [ed.], (Downers Grove, IL: InterVarsity Press, 1995), p. 29). Thus the Church, which is said not to have begun but rather to have been renewed at Pentecost (ibid., p. 53), is "the new and true Israel in Christ" (ibid., p. 163). Similarly Colin Chapman writes: "The one and only fulfillment of all the promises and prophecies was already there before [the eyes of the New Testament writers] in the person of Jesus" (Colin Chapman, *Whose Promised Land?* (Berkhamsted, Herts: Lion Publishing, 1983), p.153). Wayne Grudem, in a brief section on the Church and Israel, makes the following statement: "the church has now become the true Israel of God and will receive all the blessings promised to Israel in the Old Testament" (Wayne Grudem, *Systematic Theology: An Introduction to Biblical Doctrine,* (Leicester: InterVarsity Press, 1994), pp. 859–862).

[20] See chapters 4 and 5.

[21] Lee Martin McDonald surveys the phenomenon of anti-Judaism in the patristics in "Anti-Judaism in the Early Church Fathers," in *Anti-Semitism and Early Christianity,* Craig A. Evans and Donald A. Hagner (eds.), (Minneapolis, MN: Fortress Press, 1993), pp. 215–252.

[22] Jeffrey Siker, *Disinheriting the Jews,* p.136; cf. D.A. Carson: "In short, Jesus resorts to a moral and ethical notion of descent as being of far more importance than merely physical descent, and as being already supported by Scripture," (*The Gospel According to John,* (Grand Rapids, MI: Eerdmans, 1991), p. 351).

[23] Siker, *Disinheriting the Jews,* pp. 136–191.

[24] Ibid., pp. 142–143.

[25] Ibid., p. 139.

[26] The same distinction between *sperma Abraam* and *tekna Abraam* found in John 8:37–39 is made by Paul in Romans 9:7.

[27] Cf. Siker's discussion (*Disinheriting the Jews,* pp. 136–143). Rosemary Ruether also uses John 8:43–47 (*Fratricide,* pp. 113–114) to argue that the NT teaches the rejection of the Jews.

[28] In the longer version of Ignatius' "Epistle to the Philadelphians" there is the following allusion to John 8:44: "If anyone preaches the one God of the law and the prophets, but denies Christ to be the Son of God, he is a liar, even as also is his father the devil, and is a Jew falsely so called, being possessed of mere carnal circumcision (*ANF,* 1:82)." Cyprian understands this verse to teach that the Jews "cannot now call God their Father," *On the Lord's Prayer,* 10 (5:450). The verse is used in support of anti-Judaic sentiment in the *Constitutions of the Holy Apostles* I, 21 (7:405) where Jews, as a class, are linked with the heathen and atheistic heretics and described as "not men, but wild beasts in the shape of men . . . destroying wolves." In general John 8:44 is used with reference to the Jewish people. This is always the case in the writings of Augustine except when he identifies in those who took Jesus to be the subject of Psalm 17:11 (*NPNF* fs 8:50) and where he identifies the subject of the phrase "You are of your father the devil" and the "strange children" of Psalm 18:46 with those who reject the NT, choosing rather to follow their own traditions (*NPNF* fs 8:54).

[29] Chrysostom, *Homilies on the Gospel of Matthew,* 68 (*PG* 58:631–634).

[30] Scot McKnight, "A Loyal Critic," in *Anti-Semitism and Early Christianity,* p. 77. McKnight observes: "It is a fact that the traditions of Israel consistently explain destructions of cities in Israel and deportations as God's judgment" (p. 75). He concludes, "Matthew . . . is no more anti-Semitic than Amos or Jeremiah" (p. 77).

[31] David Hill, *The Gospel of Matthew,* The New Century Bible commentary, Matthew Black (ed.), (Grand Rapids, MI: Eerdmans, 1972), p. 301.

[32] Ibid.

[33] D. A. Carson, *Matthew,* The Expositor's Bible Commentary, Frank E. Gaebelein (ed.), 12 vols., (Grand Rapids, MI: Zondervan, 1984), 8:454.

[34] Kevin Giles, *What on earth is the Church?* (Downers Grove: InterVarsity Press, 1992), p. 88.

[35] Thus the choice of twelve apostles shows that "Jesus had come to reconstitute Israel" (Giles, *Church,* p. 32); the Church, as "restored Israel" is understood to be "the heart of Luke's unique ecclesiology"

(p. 51; following J. Jervell, *Luke and the People of God* (Minneapolis, MN: Augsbury, 1972), p. 95), and "the Christian community, the church, in Colossians is the eschatological people of God, the new Israel" (p. 132). "The quoting of Leviticus 19:2 [in 1 Peter 1:16] . . . illustrates how completely the church has supplanted historic Israel" (p. 167), while the negative references in Revelation to Jews (2:9; 3:9) and Jerusalem (11:8), are understood to prove that "the church completely supplants the old entity" (p. 175).

[36] Strathmann, *TDNT*, 4:54.

[37] Ibid.

[38] Cf. my discussion below on Ephesians 2:11–3:6.

[39] J. A. de Waard has shown that while the rendering of Amos 9:11–12 in Acts 15:16–17 differs somewhat from the MT in meaning and from the LXX in form, it agrees, both in meaning and form, with the Hebrew of the Qumran scroll, 4QFlor 1:12 (J. A. de Waard, *Comparative Study of the Old Testament Text in the Dead Sea Scrolls and the New Testament*, (Leiden: E. J. Brill, 1965), pp. 24–26, 47, 78–79). Moreover the pesher type exegesis seen here is paralleled in 4QFlor, where parts of the same text from Amos are applied to the situation of the Qumran community (I. Howard Marshall, *The Acts of the Apostles*, Tyndale N. T. Commentaries, R. V. G. Tasker [ed.], (Grand Rapids, MI: Eerdmans, 1980), pp. 252–253). However, the basis of James' use of Amos is his conviction that God has already acted (not that he was about to act) in a way that is eschatologically significant.

[40] H. D. Betz, *Galatians*, (Philadelphia, PA: Fortress Press, 1979), pp. 116, 142, 146, 250–251.

[41] Siker, *Disinheriting the Jews*, p. 48.

[42] Dieter Georgi, "The Early Church: Internal Jewish Migration or New Religion?" *Harvard Theological Review* 88/1 (1995): 35–68.

[43] An analogous polemic is witnessed to in Ezra 4, an apocalyptic work. The writer of this work contests the restoration program of the Pharisaic rabbis following the AD 66–70 Jewish war.

[44] Dunn, "Echoes of Intra-Jewish Polemic in Paul's Letter to the Galatians," *Journal of Biblical Literature* 112/3 (1993): 459–477. Dunn concludes: "Our findings above do indicate a movement still in process of coming to terms with itself regarding its identity as heirs of the promises to Abraham, where the differences between Christian Jews were of a piece with the extension of polemical disputes elsewhere among the factions of Second Temple Judaism," (ibid., p. 477).

[45] F. F. Bruce, *Commentary on Galatians*, New International Greek Testament Commentary, I. Howard Marshall and W. Ward Gasque (eds.), (Grand Rapids, MI: Eerdmans, 1982), p. 172.

[46] E. D. Burton, *The Epistle to the Galatians,* I C C, S. R. Driver, A. Plummer, C. A. Briggs (eds.), (Edinburgh: T. & T. Clark, 1921; reprint, 1957), pp. 357–358.

[47] Bruce, *Galatians,* pp. 273–275.

[48] Ibid., p. 275.

[49] J. B. Lightfoot, *The Epistle of St. Paul to the Galatians,* 1865; 20th reprint, (Grand Rapids, MI: Zondervan, 1982), p. 225.

[50] Harvey Graham, *The True Israel,* (Leiden: E.J. Brill, 1996), p. 236.

[51] Dunn, "Echoes of Intra-Jewish Polemic," p. 477.

[52] Gutrod, *TDNT,* 3:387–388.

[53] Giles, *Church,* p. 109.

[54] T. K. Abbott, *The Epistles to the Ephesians and to the Colossians,* ICC, S.R. Driver, A. Plummer, C.A. Briggs (eds.), (Edinburgh: T. & T. Clark, 1897; 5th reprint, 1956), p. 69.

[55] Markus Barth, *Ephesians 1–3,* The Anchor Bible, (New York: Doubleday and Co, 1974), p. 314.

[56] Howard Taylor, "The Continuity of the People of God in Old and New Testaments," *The Scottish Bulletin of Evangelical Theology* 3/2 (1985): 13.

[57] James D. G. Dunn, "Anti-Semitism in the Deutero-Pauline Literature," in *Anti-Semitism,* Evans/Hagner, p. 158.

[58] While the opinion that Hebrews was addressed to Jews continues to enjoy widespread support, it is not universal. James Moffatt, *Epistle to the Hebrews,* ICC (1924; 3rd reprint 1957) xv–xvii, believes that the first readers were mainly Gentile Christians. More common is the view espoused by F. F. Bruce that the first readers were Hellenistic Jews. F. F. Bruce, *The Epistle to the Hebrews,* The New International commentary on the New Testament, F. F. Bruce (ed.), (Grand Rapids, MI: Eerdmans, 1964; Reprint, 1981), pp. xxiii–xxx.

[59] Siker, *Disinheriting the Jews,* p. 97.

[60] Robert W. Wall and William L. Lane, "Polemic in Hebrews and the Catholic Epistles," in *Anti-Semitism,* Evans/Hagner, pp. 184–185.

[61] Clark M. Williamson, *A Guest in the House of Israel,* (Louisville, KY: Westminster/John Knox Press, 1993), pp. 109–110.

[62] Wall and Lane, "Polemic," in *Anti-Semitism,* Evans/Hagner, p. 181.

[63] Willliamson, *Guest,* p. 108.

[64] F. F. Bruce, *Hebrews,* p. 177.

[65] Wayne Grudem, *1 Peter,* Tyndale New Testament Commentaries, (Downers Grove, MI: InterVarsity Press, 1988; reprint, 1992), p. 113.

[66] Peter H. Davids, *The First Epistle of Peter,* The New International Commentary on the New Testament, F. F. Bruce (ed.), (Grand Rapids, MI: Eerdmans, 1990), p. 93.

[67] Translation mine.

[68] Grudem, *1 Peter,* pp. 37–38. Grudem agrees that the first readers included Christian Jews.

[69] Georgi, "Early Church," p. 41.

[70] His readers were: *genos eklekton, basileion ierateuma, ethnos hagion, laos eis peripoiēsin . . . laos theou.* (1 Peter 2:9–10).

[71] See Ernst Käsemann, "Paul and Israel," in *Ernst Käsemann, New Testament Questions of Today,* (Philadelphia, PA: Fortress Press, 1969), pp. 183–187.

[72] Giancarlo Rinaldi, "Osservazioni sull'epistola ai Romani," *EmmanuEL,* 3 (1997):10; cf. the love of Paul for his own people (Romans 9:1–5; 10:1).

[73] Williamson, *Guest,* p. 79.

[74] See Ruether, *Fratricide,* pp. 246–251. The centrality of the historical figure of Jesus in the Jesus movement was not a unique phenomenon in first century Judaism: "The Qumran sect also put a historical figure—the Teacher of Righteousness—into a comparable central hermeneutical position" (Georgi, "Early Church," p. 43).

[75] This section of Romans is invoked repeatedly in support of the new majority view. For example, Romans 11:25–29 is cited in the statement made by the First Assembly of the WCC (August 1948) in support of the assertion that "For many the continued existence of a Jewish people which does not acknowledge Christ is a divine mystery which finds its only sufficient explanation in the purpose of God's unchanging faithfulness and mercy" (*TCJP,* p. 6). These chapters are also alluded to five times in paragraph 4 of "Nostra Aetate" promulgated by the Vatican II Council on 28 October 1963.

[76] In Romans 9:4 "the people of Israel" are those to whom belong the adoption (cf. Hosea 11:1; Amos 3:1–2), to whom God has made known his glory (cf. Exodus 16:15–18; 38:34–38), with whom he has stipulated the biblical covenants (Genesis 12:1–3; 15:7–18; 35:10–11; Exodus 24:1–8; 2 Samuel 7:12–16; 23:5; Jeremiah 31:31–34), to whom God has given a legislation (Exodus 34:28, Deuteronomy), a ritual which allowed them to have access to his presence (Exodus 19–40; Leviticus 1–16) and the promises regarding messianic times (Isaiah 11:1–12:6; 49:5–23; 52:13–55:5; Jeremiah 31:31–37; 32:37–44; Ezekiel 36:24–28 etc.). In all this, Israel is distinguished from other peoples (cf. Ephesians 2:11–12).

[77] Ulrich Luz, *Das Geschichtsverständnis des Paulus,* Beiträge zur evangelischen Theologie, Theologisch Abhandlungen, Herausgegeben von E. Wolf, vol. 49, (München: Chr. Kaiser Verlag, 1968), pp. 269–274.

[78] *mēdeis horōn tēn tōn ethnōn eisagōgēn oiesthō ton tou theou logon diapesein* . . . Arethas of Caesarea, in Staab, *Pauluskommentare,* p. 657.

[79] Gutbrod, *TDNT* 3:387.

[80] Refoulé, ". . . *Et ainsi,"* p. 181.

[81] *NIDNTT* 2:304–316. Mayer mentions the Sadducees, the baptizers, the apocalyptic movement, the Pharisees, the Zealots and quotes from the literature of Qumran.

[82] Ibid., p. 312.

[83] Contra Refoulé (". . . *Et ainsi,"* pp. 142-161) according to whom *"pas Israël"* in 11:26 corresponds to the whole of the "elect remnant."

[84] Cranfield, *Romans,* p. 305.

[85] According to Bruce W. Longenecker, it is the "faithful remnant" of the nation that is indicated. "Different Answers to Different Issues: Israel, the Gentiles and Salvation History in Romans 9–11," *Journal for the Study of the New Testament* 36 (1989): 96.

[86] Refoulé finds Paul's description of the salvation of the Gentiles and the salvation of "all Israel" parallel but distinct (". . . *Et ainsi,"* pp. 142–143).

[87] The concept suggested by the terms "fullness" and "whole bunch" (vv. 12, 16) finds an echo both in the final part of the parable of the olive tree: *posō mallon houtoi hoi kata phusin egkentristhēsontai tē idia elaia* (v. 24) and in the words *pas Israēl* in v. 25.

[88] *proslēmpsis* is a NT hapaxlegomena, thus to determine its meaning particular attention must be given to the immediate context.

[89] Luz, *Paulus,* pp. 288–295.

[90] Christoph Plag, *Israels Wege zum Heil, Eine Untersuchung zu Römer 9 bis 11,* (Stuttgart: Calwer Verlag, 1969), pp. 49–54, 61.

[91] Ibid., pp. 56–61.

[92] Colin Brown, "Secret," *NIDNTT,* 3:501.

[93] Ibid., 3:504. This is particularly evident in the following passages: Mark 4:11; 1 Corinthians 15:51 and Ephesians 3:4–6. In all *mustērion* is used 28 times in the NT.

[94] Refoulé, ". . . *Et ainsi,"* pp. 25-30, 179-182.

[95] This is the most common view and was already held by Gennadius of Constantinople in the fifth century (Staab, *Pauluskommentare,* p. 401).

[96] Thus Douglas J. Moo, *The Epistle to the Romans,* The New International Commentary on the New Testament, Gordon Fee (ed.), (Grand Rapids, MI: Eerdmans, 1996), p. 716.

⁹⁷ So Luz (*Paulus*, p. 295), according to whom Israel will be saved suddenly by divine grace after the period of her hardening which was used as a time to favor the salvation of the pagan nations.

⁹⁸ This is taught by B. Mayer, *UnterGottes Heilsratschluss, Prädestinationsaussagen bei Paulus*, (Würsbourg, 1874); quoted by Refoulé (". . . *Et ainsi*," p. 29).

⁹⁹ Oscar Cullmann, *Le Salut dans l'Histoire*, (Neuchâtel, 1966), p. 162; quoted by Refoulé (ibid).

¹⁰⁰ Karl Barth, *Der Römerbrief*, (Zürich: Evangelischer Verlag Zollikon, 1954; It. trans. L'epistola ai Romani, Giovanni Miegge (ed.), Milano: Feltrinelli, 1962), pp. 397–399.

¹⁰¹ This was the conviction of Theodor of Mopsuestia (Staab, *Pauluskommentare*, p. 159) who speaks of Israel consisting of "not only those who are naturally related to Israel . . . but also those who by means of this faith have shown themselves to be worthy of the title . . . whose provenience is from the Gentiles."

¹⁰² So Plag (see above) and W.D. Davies, "Paul and the People of Israel," *New Testament Studies* 24 (1977–1978): 4–39.

¹⁰³ Refoulé, ". . . *Et ainsi*," pp. 79–82.

¹⁰⁴ Ibid., pp. 26–27. Refoulé writes: "It is the remnant that will be saved and all Israel will be saved are not at all contradictory: it is indeed the remnant alone which will be saved, but the whole remnant, those who are already in the church and those who remain hardened in the present time. Such is the mystery announced by Paul" (ibid., p. 181). Appollinaris of Laodicea held a similar view, as may be seen in his comment on Romans 11:25: "Up until the exodus of all the peoples that have been foreknown, an insensitivity hinders Israel, but after this, the remnant of the nation, which follows that which is called Israel, will be saved" (Staab, *Pauluskommentare*, p. 75).

¹⁰⁵ Cf. Isaiah 44:28–45:3.

¹⁰⁶ Henry George Liddell and Robert Scott, *A Greek-English Lexicon*, 1897; 8th revised ed., (Oxford: Clarendon Press, 1901), p. 1098.

¹⁰⁷ Gie Vleugels, "*Houtōs*," unpublished notes, Evangelische Theologische Faculteit, Heverlee (Louvain), Belgium, n.d., p. 2.

¹⁰⁸ Bruce, *Romans*, p. 209.

¹⁰⁹ Moo, *Romans*, p. 720.

¹¹⁰ *A Greek-English Lexicon of the New Testament and Other Early Christian Literature*, W. Baur, W. F. Arndt and F. W. Gingrich (eds.); Revised ed.; F. W. Gingrich and F. W. Danker (eds.), (Chicago: The University of Chicago Press, 1979), s.v. "*Houtōs*," 2., p. 602.

¹¹¹ The same correlative of manner, *houtōs . . . kathōs*, appears in Philippians 3:17.

[112] John Murray, *The Epistle to the Romans,* The International Commentary on the New Testament, 2 vols., F.F. Bruce (ed.), (Grand Rapids, MI: Eerdmans, 1959), 2:96, writes: "It is exegetically impossible to give to 'Israel' in . . . verse [26] any other denotation than that which belongs to the term throughout this chapter. It is of ethnic Israel Paul is speaking and Israel could not possibly include Gentiles." Bruce *(Galatians,* p. 209) agrees: "It is impossible to entertain an exegesis which understands 'Israel' here in a different sense from 'Israel' in verse 25 ('a hardening has come upon part of Israel')"; so Cranfield *(Romans,* p. 576) and Hodge *(Romans,* p. 372).

[113] Max Zerwick and Mary Grosvenor, *An Analysis of the Greek New Testament,* (Rome: Biblical Institute Press, 1981), p. 485.

[114] John Murray, *Romans,* p. 98; cf. Moo *(Romans,* p. 723): "Paul is probably using the phrase all Israel to denote the corporate entity of the nation of Israel as it exists at a particular point in time." Bruce *(Galatians,* p. 209), writes: "All Israel is a recurring expression in Jewish literature, where it need not mean every Jew without a single exception, but Israel as a whole. Thus all Israel has a portion in the age to come, says the Mishnah tractate Sanhedrin (10.1), and proceeds immediately to name certain Israelites who have no portion therein." According to William L. Osborne, "all Israel" must be understood as a technical term, indicating a group representative of the whole, "The Old Testament Background of Paul's all Israel in Romans 11:26a," *Asia Journal of Theology* 2 (1988/2): 282–293. Hodge *(Romans,* p. 374) writes, "*Pas Israēl* should not be understood here to mean all the true people of God, as Augustine, Calvin and many others explain; nor as all the elect Jews but rather as the entire nation, as a nation."

[115] Siker, *Disinheriting the Jews,* p. 187.

[116] See the juxtaposition of *achri chronōn* . . . in Acts 3:21 where a distinction between present and future time is clearly intended.

[117] I. Howard Marshall, *The Gospel of Luke,* The New International Greek Testament Commentary, I. Howard Marshall and W. Ward Gasque (eds.), (Exeter: The Paternoster Press, 1978), pp. 773–774; cf. Hodge *(Romans,* pp. 372–373) who compares the use of *achris hou* in Romans 11:25 with its use in Revelation 15:8 and 17:17.

[118] Joel Marcus, "Epilogue," in *Anti-Semitism,* Evans/Hagner, p. 292.

[119] Ibid.

Chapter 3

[1] Dunn *(Partings,* pp. 230–259) shows that, in the complex pattern of relationships following the events of AD 66–70, Jewish Christianity was more of a force than has generally been thought.

[2] See F.F. Bruce, *The Spreading Flame,* The Paternoster Church History, vol. 1, (Exeter: The Paternoster Press, 1958), pp. 261–267.

[3] Inasmuch as the Romans forbade Jewish Christians to live in Jerusalem after AD 135, the church there was purely Gentile in nature (Bruce, ibid., p. 272).

[4] Dieter Georgi, "Early Church," p. 65.

[5] Pelikan, *Tradition,* 1:26.

[6] Ibid., 1:12; cf. Gillian R. Evans, "The Beginning of Christian Philosophy," in *The Science of Theology,* Gillian R. Evans, Alister E. McGrath, Allan D. Galloway, vol. 1 of *The History of Christian Theology,* Paul Avis (ed.), (Basingstoke: Marshall Pickering, 1986), pp. 26–40.

[7] Frend, *Rise of Christianity,* pp. 135–136.

[8] George F. Moore, *Judaism in the First Three Centuries of the Christian Era. The Age of the Tannaim,* 2 vols., 1927; 3rd ed. (New York: Schocken Books, 1971), 1:244.

[9] Bruce, *Spreading Flame,* p. 267; Lee Martin McDonald, "Anti-Judaism in the early Church Fathers," in *Anti-Semitism,* Evans/Hagner, p. 246.

[10] *katarōmenoi en tais sunagōgais humōn tous pisteuontas epi ton Christon, Tryph. Jud.*. 16, 4; *PG* 6:512.

[11] *To the Magnesians,* VIII, 10.

[12] McDonald, "Anti-Judaism," in *Anti-Semitism,* Evans/Hagner, p. 242.

[13] The *Adversus Judaeos* writings include *Dialogues, Books of Testimonies,* and *Homilies.* Ferdinandus Cavallera (*PG* 162:128–129) lists 22 such works written in Greek, beginning with the II century work, Epistle of Barnabas, and ending with a XIII century work by Euthymius Zigabemus, *Panoply of Dogmatics,* ch. 8 (*PG* 162: 128–129). Moreover 11 of the "Scripta Polemica" in Latin (*PL* 218: 1059–1064) belong to this tradition and bear such titles as *An Answer to the Jews,* Tertullian's seminal work dating from c. 200 (*PL* 2: 595–642) and *A Tract against the Jews,* an anonymous work written in the XII century (*PL* 213:747–808).

The following are some of the more important contributions to the *Adversus Judaeos* tradition, listed in chronological order: Justin Martyr, *Dialogue with Trypho* (*PG* 6:471–799); Tertullian, *An Answer to the Jews* (*PL* 2:595–642); Hippolytus, *Expository Treatise Against the Jews* (*PG* 10:787–794); Novatian, "On Jewish Meats" (*ANF* 5: 645–650); Cyprian, *Three Books of Testimonies Against the Jews* (*PL* 4:703–810); Ephraem of Syria, *Rhythm Against the Jews* (*Library of the Fathers,* J.B. Morris (ed.), (Oxford, 1847), pp. 61–83; Aphrahat of Persia, *Demonstrations Against the Jews,* (see J. Neusner, *Aphrahat and Judaism,* (Leiden: Brill, 1971)); John Chrysostom, *Demonstrations to the Jews and Gentiles that Christ is God* (*PG* 48:811–838) and *Eight Orations Against the Jews* (ibid., cols 839–942); Augustine, *Tract Against the Jews* (*PL* 42:51–64); Maximus the Confessor, *Treatise Against the Jews* (Edited text by C.H. Turner, *Journal of Theological*

Studies 20 (1919): 289–310); Isidore of Seville, *Against the Jews* (*PL* 83:449–538); John Damascene, *On the Orthodox Faith,* 4:23 "On the Sabbath, Against the Jews," (*PG* 94:1201–1206); Martin Luther, *The Jews and their Lies* (1543).

Around the eighth century many pseudo dialogues were composed, following the general pattern of Justin Martyr's *Dialogue with Trypho,* in which the Jewish interlocutors were figments of the imagination of the Christian writer. Despite the unilateral nature of these dialogues, they not only represented but also influenced medieval Christian thought concerning the Jews.

[14] Bruce, *Spreading Flame,* pp. 263–267.

[15] Pelikan, *Tradition,* 1:14–27.

[16] See also the section "The Christian Synagogue," in Frend, *Rise of Christianity,* pp. 120–160.

[17] Bruce, *Spreading Flame,* p. 236. According to Bruce, The Epistle of Barnabas was written between 70 and 135.

[18] The Latin text reads, "Apparuit vero, ut tum illi [Judaei] in peccatis consumarentur, tum nos per ipsum haeredes facti Domini Jesu testamentum acciperemus, qui destinatus erat, ut per adventum suum praecordia nostra, iam a morte assumpta et tradita erroris iniquitati, redimens e tenebris verbo [suo] disponat in nobis testamentum" (*PG* 1:1221).

[19] *ANF* 1:25–30/*PG* 2:1167–1186.

[20] Bruce (*Spreading Flame,* pp. 14, 270) informs us that circumcision hindered many men from becoming Jewish proselytes and featured among the bodily mutilations that were prohibited by law under Emperor Hadrian. Josephus, himself from the ranks of the Pharisees, recounts how he withstood his fellow Jews when they tried to force two men from the region of Trachonitis to be circumcised (*The Life of Flavius Josephus,* in *Works of Josephus,* 4 vols., trans. William Whiston, (Grand Rapids, MI: Baker Book House, 1974), vol. II, sec. 23). Martin Hengel (*Judentum und Hellenismus,* (Tübingen: J.C.B. Mohr [Paul Siebeck], 1973); Eng. ed. *Judaism and Hellenism,* trans. John Bowden, 2 vols., (London: SCM Press, 1974), 1:74, 278, 289; 2:96) draws attention to the attempts of Jewish ephebes to remove the signs of their circumcision in the period preceding the Maccabean revolt (1 Maccabees 1:15).

[21] The Greek text reads, *to de kai meiōsin tēs sarkos marturion eklogēs alazoneuesthai, hōs dia touto exairetōs ēgapēmenous hupo theou, pōs ou kleuēs axion* (*PG* 2:1172–1173).

[22] According to Arthur J. Droge, the logos theory is introduced by Justin "primarily to refute the charge of novelty and at the same time to appropriate the Jewish scriptures as a Christian book" (Arthur J. Droge, "Justin Martyr and the Restoration of Philosophy," *CH* 56 (1987): 315).

[23] Justin Martyr, *First Apology*, 46:3, *ANF* 1:178 (*PG* 6:334) cf. 63: 10, 16 (*PG* 6:378–379).

[24] *ANF* 1:194–270/*PG* 6:471–799.

[25] The Hebrew text of Psalm 96:10 reads: *imeru baggôyim YHWH malak, 'ap-tikkôn tebel bal-timmot yadîn Jammîm bemêsharîm* ("Say among the nations: Yahweh reigns. Certainly the world will be established firmly, it will not be moved; He will judge the people righteously"); neither does the LXX contain anything which corresponds to the words "from the wood": *eipate en tois ethnesin O kurios ebasileusen kai gar katōrthōsen tēn oikoumenēn, ētis su saleuthēsetai, krinei laous en euthutēti* (Psalm 95:10).

[26] The Greek reads, *Hōs oun Israēl ton Criston kai Iakōb houtōs legei, kai hēmeis en tēs koilias tou Cristou latomēthentes, Israēlitikōn to alēthinon esmen genos* (*PG* 6:788). Graham Harvey comments as follows on the first surviving occurrence of the association of "Israel" with "true" here and in chapter CXXIV of Justin's work: "This clearly exemplifies Christianity's separation of itself from Judaism whilst claiming the entire inheritance of the earlier Israelite tradition" (Harvey, *True Israel*, p. 1). Harvey makes this further insightful statement: "The fact that at this stage they begin to use the phrase true Israel of themselves strongly suggests that [Christians] suspect that God remains interested in some sort of dialogue with a Jewish (non-Christian) Israel," (pp. 272–273).

[27] *Ē gar apo Abraam kata sarka peritomē ei sēmeion edothē hina ēte apo tōn allōn ethnōn kai hēmōn aphōrismenoi kai hina monoi pathēte a nun en dikēi paschete . . .* (*PG* 6:509, cf. p. 516).

[28] *ANF* 1:204/*PG* 6:516–517.

[29] Gregory Baum, O.S.A., *Is the New Testament Anti-Semitic?* (Glen Rock, NJ: Paulist Press, 1960), p. 17.

[30] *PG* 7:433–1224.

[31] *Against Heresies*, bks I–II (*PG* 7:433–842).

[32] Ibid., bk III (*PG* 7:843–972).

[33] Ibid., bk V, 34 (*PG* 7:1221–1224).

[34] Franz Delitzsch, *Isaiah*, in the series Commentary on the Old Testament, C. F. Keil and F. Delitzsch, 10 vols.; Reprint, (Grand Rapids, MI: Eerdmans, 1980), 8:452.

[35] *PL* 2:595–640.

[36] *NIDCC*, s.v. "Tertullian."

[37] Tertullian, *ANF* 3:151/*PL* 2:598.

[38] Ibid., p. 152/ibid.

[39] Akazius of Caesarea (d. 366), on Romans 9:11–14, in Staab, *Pauluskommentare*, p. 54; Theodor of Mopsuestia (350–428), on Romans 9:9–13, ibid., pp. 143–144; Gennadius of Constantinople

(d. ca. 471), on Romans 9:10–13, ibid., pp. 389–390; Photius of Constantinople (c. 820–891), on Romans 9:10–13, ibid., pp. 516–517.

[40] Akazius held the view that the divine choice was related to foreknowledge of the good and bad works which Jacob and Esau would have performed: *dia to proginōskein amphoterōn ta erga, hōsper autos ho Paulos phēsin anōterō hoti hous proegnō kai proōrisen kai ta hezēs* (Akazius, in Staab, *Pauluskommentare,* p.54). For the other three commentators, the election of Jacob and his descendants was to be understood in terms of divine purpose.

[41] *PL* 2:503–508.

[42] *PL* 2:979–1030.

[43] *ANF*, 4:82/*PL* 2:996 "Christianum enim de restitutione Iudaei gaudere, et non dolere conveniet; sequidem tota spes nostra cum religua Israelis exspectatione coniuneta est (Romans.xi)." A. Cleveland Coxe assumes that Tertullian alludes here to the teaching of Romans 11:11–36 (*ANF*, 4:82, n. 9).

[44] For a good introduction to the nature of Origen's scholarship and a critical appraisal of his allegorism, see R.P.C. Hanson, *Allegory and Event, A study of the sources and significance of Origen's Interpretation of Scripture,* (Richmond, VA: John Knox Press, 1959).

[45] Ibid., pp. 160–161. As an exegete, Origen owed much to the Gnostic, Heracleon.

[46] Daniel P. Fuller, "Interpretation, History of," in *The International Standard Bible Encyclopedia, fully rev.,* Geoffrey W. Bromiley (gen. ed.) 4 vols., (1982), 2:865; cf. Hanson, *Allegory and Event,* pp. 217–218.

[47] Fuller, "Interpretation," 2:864. The allusion is to bk IV of Origen's work *On First Principles.* It is significant that Fuller begins his survey of the history of biblical interpretation with Origen (ibid., 2: 864–874).

[48] See Hanson, *Allegory and Event,* pp. 133–142.

[49] For a critical text of this work, see *Die griechischen Christlichen Schriftsteller der ersten drei Jahrhunderte,* (Berlin, 1927–), vol. 22.

[50] *On First Principles,* bk IV, ch. I, sec. 2, (*ANF* 4:359–360); cf. Hanson, *Allegory and Event,* pp. 235–258.

[51] Origen, *Princ.,* bk IV, I, 1–9, 15–21 (*ANF* 4:349–358, 364–369). An example of when Origen discounts the literal nature of an event is the story of Adam, as reported in the book of Genesis (ibid., sec. 16 [*ANF* 4:365]).

[52] Ibid., sec. 12 (*ANF* 4:360).

[53] Ibid., sec. 20 (*ANF* 4:369).

[54] Ibid., sec. 19 (*ANF* 4:369).

[55] Ibid., II, IV, 4 (*ANF* 4:277–280).

[56] Ibid. sec. 22 (*ANF* 4:370).

⁵⁷ Ibid.

⁵⁸ Ibid., but see Romans 9:3–4; Ephesians 2:12.

⁵⁹ Origen, ibid., sec. 21 (*ANF* 4:370–371).

⁶⁰ Origen, *Commentary on Matthew, ANF* 9, Allan Menzies (ed.), pp. 507–508 (*PG* 13:830–1600 contains bks 10–17 and fragments of bks 1, 2 and 7).

⁶¹ *ANF* 9:507–508.

⁶² Ibid.

⁶³ Ibid., p. 508. Origen's analogy presupposes the normativity of remarriage, following divorce, an aspect of the question not addressed by Christ in Matthew 19:1–12.

⁶⁴ Ibid., pp. 445–447.

⁶⁵ For example, commenting on Genesis 50:3, the act of burying "Israel" is taken to symbolize the detestation of all good and of all heavenly intelligence (*PG* 12:242–244).

⁶⁶ *PG* 12:553–554.

⁶⁷ "Hom. on Numbers" XI, 4 (*PG* 12:647–648; cf. *Hom.* XV, 3 (*PG* 686–688) e. XVI, 3 (*PG* 12:695). In *Hom.* XVIII (*PG* 12:718), "Israel" becomes a synonym of "soul."

⁶⁸ "Hom. on Joshua" IX, 4 (*PG* 12:874).

⁶⁹ "Hom. on Ezekiel" II, 2 . . . vero Israel, id est Ecclesia . . . (*PG* 13:682).

⁷⁰ Ibid., *Hom.* XV, 1 (*PG* 12:897).

⁷¹ Ibid., *Hom.* XXVI, 3 (*PG* 12:948).

⁷² In *Cels.* VI, 80 (*PG* 11:1120).

⁷³ Ibid.

⁷⁴ Origen, *Commento alla Lettera ai Romani,* Introduction, trans. and notes by Francesca Cocchini, 2 vols., (Genoa: Marietti, 1986), 2: 79–84. Some fragments of this commentary are preserved in *PG* 14: 1195–1202.

⁷⁵ Ibid., pp. 82–83/*PG* 14:1195–1198.

⁷⁶ The best expression of this attempt is Origen's seminal work *On First Principles* (*ANF* 4:239–384).

⁷⁷ An edict, issued by the Synod at Constantinople (543), put into effect the anathemas pronounced against Origen in a letter written by emperor Justinian to Mennas of Constantinople, moreover the V general council at Constantinople (553) listed Origen among ancient heretics (*NIDCC* s.v. "Origenism").

⁷⁸ Cf. Soulen (*The God of Israel and Christian Theology,* pp. x, 1–5, 12–13, 16–19, 29, 31–34, 48–50, 54–58, 77–79, 82–84) who makes the point that replacement theology became the unexamined presupposition of much of Christian theology. According to Soulen, the standard model provides a narrative construal of the Christian

Bible that gives powerful expression to the church's central confession "in a manner that is profoundly supersessionist in both doctrinal and structural ways," (p. 109).

Pelikan, *Tradition,* 1:292–293.

[80] D.F. Wright, *NIDCC,* s.v. "Augustine of Hippo."

[81] Giovanni Coppa calculates it being during the same holy week (*Opere di Sant'Ambrogio,* Giovanni Coppa (ed.), Classici delle religioni, (Turin: U.T.E.T., 1969; Reprint 1979), p. 49). The term "Exameron" refers to the "six days" of creation.

[82] *Six Days of Work,* Serm. IX, 15 (*PL* 14:247).

[83] Ibid., bk II, 3, 11; 3;16 (*PL* 14:149, 153) et passim.

[84] Ep. XL (*PL* 16:1102–1113).

[85] Parkes, *Conflict,* pp. 166–167.

[86] Augustine, *Civ.* bk IV, xxxiv (*NPNF* fs, 2:83/*PL* 41:140). In *The City of God,* Augustine's greatest work, he reviews world history from a theological, and thus eschatological, stand-point.

[87] *PL* 42:51–64.

[88] D.E. Timmer, "Biblical Exegesis and the Jewish-Christian Controversy in the Early Twelfth Century." *CH* 58 (1989): 310–311.

[89] *PG* 48:843–942.

[90] *Serm.* I, 6 (*PG* 48:852).

[91] *Serm.* I, 3 (*PG* 48:847).

[92] *Serm.* VI, 1 (*PG* 48:903–905): Such reasoning ignores Peter's appeals to Jews in Acts 2:36–38 and 3:17–19. Paul's strongest statement concerning Jewish guilt is found in 1 Thessalonians 2:14–16, which includes the words "the Jews, who also killed the Lord, even Jesus, and the prophets." H.L. Ellison (*The Mystery of Israel,* (Exeter: The Paternoster Press, 1966), p. 18) notes, "Paul is affirming that the actions of the Jewish leaders were merely the continuation of those of their ancestors . . . Paul is not accusing them of killing Jesus in particular."

[93] *Serm.* IV, 6 (*PG* 48:879–881).

[94] *Serm.* VI, 3 (*PG* 48:907–908).

[95] *Serm.* VI, 1 (*PG* 48:904–905).

[96] This omission was corrected by the Vatican II Council in the document "Nostra Aetate" which received formal approval on October 28, 1965. After deploring all kinds of persecution and manifestations of anti-Semitism directed against the Hebrews in all epochs and whatever their origin, the document draws attention to the fact that Christ submitted himself voluntarily to suffering and death in view of making salvation possible for sinful mankind (*Tutti i documenti del Concilio,* (Roma: U.C.I.I.M.; 5th ed., 1972), p. 536).

⁹⁷ The statement which perhaps comes closest to an exception to this rule is found in Augustine's *On Christian Doctrine,* III, 6 (*NPNF* fs, 2:559): "But those [Jews] who did believe, from among whom the first church at Jerusalem was formed . . . because they were very near spiritual things . . . were filled with such a measure of the Holy Spirit that they sold all their goods, and laid their price at the apostles' feet to be distributed among the needy, and consecrated themselves wholly to God as a new temple. . . . Now it is not recorded that any of the Gentile churches did this, because men who had for their gods idols made with hands had not been so near to spiritual things."

⁹⁸ See note 13.

⁹⁹ See his "Hom. on Romans" (*PG* 60:547–596).

¹⁰⁰ *NIDCC* s.v. "Chrysostom, John."

¹⁰¹ *NIDCC* s.v. "Cyril."

¹⁰² James Parkes, *Conflict,* pp. 234–235.

¹⁰³ "Cyril of Alexandria," *PG* 74:820.

¹⁰⁴ 708 of Gregory the Great's letters are listed in "Epistolarum ordo antea vulgatus ad novum reductus" (*PL* 77:1379–1390) and published elsewhere in the same volume (cols 431–1352).

¹⁰⁵ Robert G. Clouse, *NIDCC*, s.v. "Gregory The Great."

¹⁰⁶ Pelikan, *Tradition,* 1:350–351. This is particularly true of Gregory's *Four Books of Dialogues on the Life and Miracles of the Italian Fathers* and on the *Immortality of Souls* (593–594), which contain a simplification of many themes found in Augustine's *The City of God.*

¹⁰⁷ Such allegorical interpretation is particularly evident throughout his "Homilies on Ezekiel" where everywhere Jerusalem is assumed to be heavenly and God's people the Church (*PL* 76:785–1072). For condemnatory statements and the concept that the Church has replaced physical Israel in the divine plan, see in particular: bk I, *Hom.* 12, 18 (*PL* 76:926–927); bk II, *Hom.* 5, 2 (*PL* 76:985–986); *Hom* 6, 23 (*PL* 76:1011); *Hom.* 8, 13 (*PL* 76:1035–1036).

¹⁰⁸ *Ep.* VII, bk XIII (*PL* 77:1262–1265).

¹⁰⁹ *Ep.* XII, bk. XIII (*PL* 77:1267–1268).

¹¹⁰ *PG* 20:1074–1080.

¹¹¹ Parkes (*Conflict,* pp. 394–400) gives a sampling of such confessions.

¹¹² "The Seven Ecumenical Councils," in *NPNF*, ss, 4:108.

¹¹³ Canon XXXVII, ibid., p. 151.

¹¹⁴ Canon XXXVIII, ibid.

¹¹⁵ *NPNF* ss 14: 504.

¹¹⁶ Canon XIV, ibid., p. 278.

¹¹⁷ Canon XI, ibid., p. 370.

[118] Canons LXIV and LXXI, ibid., p. 598.

[119] Parkes, *Conflict,* pp. 356–357.

[120] A more direct foundation for the Jewish ghetto was laid in 1179 by the III Lateran Council, which forbade true believers to lodge amongst infidels. The Venetian Republic was one of the first civil governments to order (in 1516) the segregation of the Jews in a special quarter. This example would soon be followed elsewhere in Italy, in southern France, Germany, and Poland (Roth, *A short History,* pp. 210–211, 297).

[121] *New Catholic Encyclopedia,* 15 vols., (New York: McGraw Hill Book Company, 1967), 8:409.

[122] Rupert of Deutz, *Commentary on the Twelve Minor Prophets, PL* 168:756–757. David E. Timmer ("Biblical Exegesis and the Jewish-Christian Controversy in the Early Twelfth Century," *CH* 58 (1989): 319) notes that Rupert also invokes the Christological principle of interpretation. Accordingly, with reference to Jewish, literal interpretation of these passages, this Benedictine Abbot wrote, "Once this carnal and puerile interpretation was permitted; now, however, it has been emptied of meaning by Christ, and the error is inexcusable," (*PL* 168:811).

[123] Parkes, *Conflict,* p. 374.

[124] See Williamson, *Guest,* pp. 112–114.

[125] Cf. Parkes, *Conflict,* p. 373.

[126] The following works, though not in themselves anti-Judaic, follow this convention: John Bright, *A History of Israel,* (London: SCM Press, 1960); F.F. Bruce, *Israel and the Nations,* (Exeter: The Paternoster Press, 1963).

Chapter 4

[1]   Origen, *Princ.* bk IV, 1:21. (*ANF* 4:370–371).

[2]   Cf. Alister McGrath (*Christian Theology: An Introduction,* (London: Blackwell, 1994), p. 405): "Ecclesiology was not a major issue in the early church." McGrath comments further, "The eastern church showed no awareness of the potential importance of the issue. Most Greek patristic writers contented themselves with describing the church using recognizably scriptural images, without choosing to probe further."

[3]   J.N.D. Kelly, *Early Christian Doctrines,* 3rd ed., (London: Adam and Charles Black, 1965), pp. 189–220.

[4]   This is recognized by Jerome in his commentary on Titus (quoted by Eric G. Jay, *The Church: Its Changing Image through Twenty Centuries,* (Atlanta, GA: John Knox Press, 1978), p. 93). Jerome affirms that initially each church was governed by a council of presbyters and that the election of one of the presbyters to the office of Bishop was an expedient used to overcome the kind of problem

mentioned in 1 Corinthians 1:12. However, it should be noted that the most systematic presentations of the two-tier concept of the Christian ministry—elders/bishops and deacons—are found in New Testament writings which date from after Paul wrote 1 Corinthians (see Acts 20:17–31; Philippians 1:1; 1 Timothy 2:1–13; Titus 1:5–9).

⁵ Nothing in the New Testament writings contradicts what is taught explicitly in 1 Peter and Hebrews (cf. John 14:6; 1 Timothy 2:5–6), rather the opposite (John 4:19–24; Acts 11:19–23; 15:7–11; Romans 12:1–2; Hebrews 13:15); cf. Dunn (*Partings*, p. 92), "In all the references to Christian worship and Christian community within the NT *there is simply no allusion to any order of priesthood within the Christian congregations*," (emphasis his).

⁶ Vittorino Grossi and Angelo Di Berardino, *La Chiesa Antica: Ecclesioogia e Istituzioni*, (Roma: Borla, 1984).

⁷ Ibid., p. 102.

⁸ Ibid., p. 100.

⁹ Ibid., "Le matrici giudaiche" (pp. 257–263), where mention is made of the liturgy of the synagogue, the sanctification of the Sabbath and the Passover.

¹⁰ Thomas M. Lindsay, *The Church and the Ministry in the Early Centuries, The 18th series of the Cunningham Lectures, 1902*, (London: Hodder and Stoughton, 1973).

¹¹ Ibid., p. 204.

¹² Ibid., p. 208.

¹³ Ibid., p. 210.

¹⁴ Philip Schaff, *History of the Christian Church*, 2:428.

¹⁵ Panfilo Gentile, *Il Cristianesimo Dalle Origini a Costantino, Collana di Studi storici e Filosofici*, Carlo Antoni (ed.), (Firenze: Le Monnier, 1946), p. 193. According to Gentile, Christianity began to consider itself exactly as the Jews considered themselves, with the only difference that Christianity dispensed with nationalistic requisites, conceding to anyone the rights of citizenship in the new and true Israel.

¹⁶ Dunn, *Partings*, pp. 254–255.

¹⁷ Ibid., pp. 257–258.

¹⁸ *PG* 1:122–178.

¹⁹ "1 Clement," 29 (*ANF* 1:12–13/*PG* 1:151).

²⁰ Ibid., 40–41 (*ANF* 1:16/*PG* 1:158–160).

²¹ Cf. the pattern of thought observed in 1 Clement where a simple form of replacement theology is followed by the use of priestly categories in relation to a three-tier concept of the Christian ministry.

²² The errors combated by Ignatius of Antioch have been variously understood as one composite Judaeo-Christian-Docetic error or as two distinct errors: those of the Docetists and the Judaizers. Christine

Trevett suggests that Ignatius might have been combating three errors, the third being the opposition of those gifted as prophets to office bearers who lacked this charisma (Christine Trevett, "Prophecy and Anti-Episcopal Activity: a Third Error Combated by Ignatius?" *JEH* 34/1 (1983):1–18). Whatever the analysis of the errors which Ignatius set himself to combat, there is little doubt that he saw the key to its/ their solution in the general acceptance of monarchical episcopacy, perhaps a relatively novel institution.

²³ These expressions appear in both the shorter and longer forms of Ignatius' "Epistle to the Romans" (*ANF* 1:73/*PG* 5:801).

²⁴ J.N.D. Kelly, *Early Christian Doctrines,* p. 191.

²⁵ Cf. the figure of an old woman by which the Church is represented in Hermas (*Visions,* 2, 4, 1/*PG* 1:1317–1318).

²⁶ *PG* 6:471–800.

²⁷ *Tryph. Jud.* CXXIII (*ANF* 1:261/*PG* 6:764).

²⁸ The same use is made of Mal. 1:10–12 in *Tryph. Jud.* XLI (*PG* 6: 564).

²⁹ *PL* 42:60–63.

³⁰ This understanding of the Lord's Supper is already evident in the Didache, XIV, 1–3.

³¹ *PG* 7:433–1224.

³² *Haer.* III, 3, 1–2 (*PG* 7:848–849).

³³ Ibid. III, 3, 2, (*ANF* 1:415–416/*PG* 7:849).

³⁴ *Haer.* IV, 17, 1–4 (*PG* 7:1019–1023).

³⁵ Ibid., 7, 5 (*ANF* 1:484/*PG* 7:1024).

³⁶ Ibid., IV, 18, 2 (*ANF* 1:484–485/*PG* 7:1025).

³⁷ Cf. the following statement: "Inasmuch, then, as the Church offers with single-mindedness, her gift is justly reckoned a pure sacrifice with God. . . . But the Jews do not offer thus: for their hands are full of blood." *Haer* IV, 18, 4 (*ANF* 1:485–486/*PG* 7:1026).

³⁸ Ibid., 18, 5 (*ANF* 1:486/*PG* 7:1028–1029).

³⁹ Ignatius, Eph, XX, *pharmakēn athanasias, antidotos tou mē apothanein* (*PG* 5:661).

⁴⁰ Cf. "Development of epiclesis in the liturgy," by Zechariah Schariah, an unpublished paper presented at the Evangelische Theologische Faculteit, Heverlee (Louvain), Belgium, September 1992.

⁴¹ Ibid., pp. 17–22.

⁴² See the following fourth century witnesses: *Apostolic Constitutions* bk VIII, 2 (*PG* 1:553–555); Cyril of Jerusalem, *Catechetical Lectures* XIX, "Mystagogica I," 7 (*PG* 33:1072).

⁴³ *Apostolic Constitutions* III, 10. "Neither do we permit the laity to perform any of the offices belonging to the priesthood; as, for

instance, neither the sacrifice, nor baptism, nor the laying on of hands, nor the blessing, whether the smaller or the greater: for 'no one taketh this honor to himself, but he that is called of God' [Hebrews 5:4]. for such sacred offices are conferred by the laying on of the hands of the bishop," (*ANF* 7:429/*PG* 1:432). Only Bishops are allowed to ordain new ministers of the Church (*ANF* 7:430./*PG* 1:433).

44 Schariah, "Development of Epiclesis," p. 22.

45 The most important of these works are listed in chapter 3, note 13.

46 Tertullian, *Adv. Jud.* I (*ANF* 3:152/*PL* 2:598).

47 *On Martyrs,* I (*ANF* 3:693/*PL* 1:619). D. F. Wright considers this one of Tertullian's first writings, dating from 197 (*NIDCC*, s.v. "Tertullian").

48 *NIDCC*, s.v. "Tertullian"

49 *Prescription against Heretics, XX.*

50 Bap. XVII, *PL* 1:1218 "Dandi quidem habit jus summus sacerdos, qui est episcopus. Deinde presbyteri et diaconi, non tamen sine episcopi auctoritate, propter Ecclesiae honorem.

51 Ibid.

52 *On the Veiling of Virgins,* 2.

53 *ANF* 4:99–100/*PL* 2:1026 "Nam et Ecclesia proprie et principaliter ipse est Spiritus in quo est trinitas unius divinitatis, Pater et filius et Spiritus Sanctus. Illam Ecclesiam congregat, quam Dominus in tribus posuit. Atque ita eximde etiam numerus omnis qui in hanc fidum conspiraverint, Ecclesia ad autore et consacratore censetur."

54 *Exhortation to Chastity,* XI (*ANF* 4:56/*PL* 2:926–927).

55 Origen, *Princ.* bk IV, 1, 21.

56 Hanson, *Allegory and Event,* pp. 371–372.

57 *Hom. on Lev.* 1 (*PG* 12:405–411).

58 *Hom. on Lev.* VII, 5" (*PG* 12:486–489).

59 *Comm. on John* XXXII, 24, cited by Hanson (*Allegory and Event,* p. 325).

60 *Comm. on Matthew* XI, 14 (*PG* 13:952).

61 *Hom. on Lev.* (*PG* 12:440, 451, 489, 508–509, 521–523).

62 *PG* 12:450–453.

63 *PG* 12:475–478.

64 *PG* 12:452.

65 Origen, *Cant.,* Prologue (*PG* 13:81).

66 *Cant.,* bk II (*PG* 13:104).

67 Ibid. (*PG* 13:81).

68 Clement, *Strom.* VI, 13 (*ANF* 2:504/*PG* 9:328–329).

⁶⁹ Cyprian, *Testimonies* (*PL* 4:703–802).

⁷⁰ According to Eric Jay (*The Church*, p. 72), Cyprian's concept of the Church "prevailed in the West throughout the middle ages."

⁷¹ I refer to the first three chapters of Lumen Gentium (Nov. 21, 1964): I. The mystery of the Church, II. The People of God, and III. The hierarchical constitution of the Church and in particular of the episcopate. Eleven references to Cyprian's writings are to his Epistles: Ep. 11, 48, 55, 56, 63, 64, 66, 69 (twice), one general reference is to his Epistles with regard to the role of bishops, as priests and governors of the Church, and one is to his *On the Lord's Prayer*, 23 (*Tutti i documenti del Concilio*, pp. 1–41).

⁷² *NIDCC*, s.v. "Cyprian."

⁷³ *ANF* 5:507/*PL* 4:704.

⁷⁴ *ANF* 5:512–514/*PL* 4:723–724.

⁷⁵ *ANF* 5:554/*PL* 4:804.

⁷⁶ The only passages quoted in Cyprian's *Testimonies* from Romans 9–11 are 9:3–5, 11:20–21 and 11:33–36.

⁷⁷ Cyprian, *Unit. eccl.* (*PL* 4:509–536).

⁷⁸ Ibid., 4–5 (*PL* 4:512–518); cf. Ep. LIV, 7; (*ANF* 5:341/*PL* 4:358).

⁷⁹ Ep. LIV, 14; LXXIV, 15–17 (*ANF* 5:344, 394–395/*PL* 4:358, 425–426).

⁸⁰ *Unit. eccl.*, para. 4–6 (*ANF* 5:422–423/*PL* 4:512–520).

⁸¹ "Habere jam non potest Deum patrem qui Ecclesiam non habet matrem" (*PL* 4:519).

⁸² See the greeting in "The Encyclical Epistle of the Church at Smyrna concerning the Martyrdom of the Holy Polycarp" (*PG* 5: 1023).

⁸³ Irenaeus, *Haer.*, III, 4 (*PG* 7:855–857).

⁸⁴ Ep. LXIX, 1 (*PL* 4:413).

⁸⁵ *Unit. eccl.* 7 (*ANF* 5:423/*PL* 4:521).

⁸⁶ Ibid., 13 (*ANF* 5:425/*PL* 4:525–526; cf. Ep. LXIX (*ANF* 5:375/ *PL* 4:413–420).

⁸⁷ *Unit. eccl.* 17 (*ANF* 5:427/*PL* 4:529), italics mine.

⁸⁸ This came to be known as Cesare-papism, a term used to define the situation in which the Church is effectively conditioned or controlled by the secular power.

⁸⁹ See Giles, *Church*, pp. 214–215.

⁹⁰ This had been the teaching of Cyprian (Ep. LXIX, 8/*PL* 4:418– 419); cf. Joseph Ratzinger, *Popolo e casa di Dio in Sant'Agostino, Già e non ancora, n. 36*, (Milano: Cooperativa Edizioni Jaca Books, 1978), pp. 99–100. Eusebius' account of how Constantine was able to inquire quickly concerning the meaning of his famous vision of a cross of light

suggests that when Constantine moved with his Gallic army to impose his dominion over Italy, some bishops traveled with him (*The Life of Constantine*, I, 32 (*PG* 20:948).

[91] For a good introduction to this period, see Frend, "The Constantinian Revolution 305–30," *Rise of Christianity*, pp. 474–517.

[92] The Church historian, Eusebius, a contemporary of Constantine, did not consider Constantine's involvement in ecclesiastical affairs as interference, but rather as being the fruit of providence (Eusebius Pamphilus, *Oration in Praise of the Emperor Constantine* [*NPNF* ss 1: 581–610]).

[93] Eusebius, *The Life of Constantine*, III, 18–20 (*PG* 20:1074–1080).

[94] For almost nineteen centuries the Passover celebration was the occasion in which the Jews dispersed throughout the world expressed the wish: "Next year in Jerusalem!"

[95] See Parkes, *Conflict*, pp. 381–391. A recurring theme in the long list of ecclesiastical sanctions against the Jews was the contempt in which Christians were to hold all Jewish customs and practices.

[96] Ibid., p. 375; see pp. 93–96, in the present work.

[97] Bap. I, emphasis his (*ANF* 3:669/*PL* 1:1197).

[98] Bap. XIX (*ANF* 3:678/*PL* 1:1222).

[99] Cyprian, *Ep.* LVIII, 3, 6 (*ANF* 5:353–354, not in *PL*).

[100] Ibid.

[101] For a guide to the vast literature on Acts chapter 15, see Ernst Haenchen, *The Acts of the Apostles*, 14th ed., trans. from the German by Basil Backwell, (Philadelphia, PA: Westminster Press, 1971), pp. 441–442; for a helpful treatment of the "Council" which treats Acts 15 as a factual account, see Gregory Dix, *Jew and Greek*, (Glasgow: University Press, 1963), pp. 39–60. If the Jerusalem meeting can be regarded as a Church Council, it is the only such gathering during the early Christian centuries in which soteriology was the main subject of discussion.

[102] Justo L. Gonzàlez, *The Story of Christianity*, 2 vols., (New York: HarperCollins, 1984), 1:125.

[103] Ibid.

[104] "Cathedral," that is to say, the "seat" of the bishop, derives from the latin *cathedra*.

[105] Gonzàlez, *Story of Christianity*, I:125–128.

[106] Cat. XIV, 9 (*NPNF* ss 7:96/*PG* 33:929).

[107] This can be deduced from a letter written to emperor Constantius on May 7, 351 in which he refers to his consecration as bishop as a recent event (See Edwin Hamilton Gifford, "The Life of Cyril," (*NPNF* ss 7, pp. i–xi) and *NIDCC* s.v. "Cyril of Jerusalem").

[108] Cyril of Jerusalem, *Cat.*, XVIII, 25 (*NPNF* ss 7:140/*PG* 33:1043, 1045).

[109] Ibid., *PG* 33:1045.

[110] Ibid.

[111] Ibid.

[112] Ibid., 24 (*NPNF* ss 7:141/*PG* 33:1044–1050).

[113] Ibid., 28 (*NPNF* ss 7:141/*PG* 33:1050).

[114] Ibid., 32 (*NPNF* ss 7:141–142/*PG* 33:1054).

[115] *The Answer of the Assembly of Divines to the Reasons of the dissenting Brethren,* (London, 1648), p. 147, quoted by David Walker, "Thomas Goodwin and the Debate on Church Government," *JEH* 34/1 (1983): p. 94, emphases theirs.

[116] Edmund P. Clowney, *The Church, Contours of Christian Theology,* Gerald Bray (ed.), (Downers Grove, IL: InterVarsity Press, 1995), p. 29.

[117] Ibid.

[118] Ibid., p. 53; cf. Christ's statement in Matthew 16:18: "I will build my church."

[119] Ibid., p. 35.

[120] Ibid., p. 163.

[121] See "Various Opinions Concerning the Reasons for Subsequent Developments in Ecclesiology," p. 103.

Chapter 5

[1] This statement was made on Nov. 28, 1987 by the Roman Catholic scholar, Enzo Bianchi, at a seminar on the theme: "Twenty years after Nostra Aetate," Bologna (Enzo Bianchi, "Israele e la Chiesa," *Storia Cristiana,* 10 [1989]: 93).

[2] Peter P. J. Beyerhaus, *God's Kingdom and the Utopian Error,* (Wheaton, IL: Good News Publishers, 1992), p. ix.

[3] Ibid.

[4] See Archibald Robertson, *Regnum Dei,* Eight Lectures on the Kingdom of God in the History of Christian Thought, The Bampton Lectures 1901, (London: Methuen and Co., 1901).

[5] The term *millenarianism* is used as a synonym of premillennialism, while a similar term, *millennialism* is a synonym of postmillennilism. (See Grant Underwood, "Early Mormon Millenarianism: Another Look," *CH* 54 (1985): 216).

[6] Robertson, *Regnum Dei,* pp. 119–240. The "medieval theocracy" included the illusion of a Christian empire and the concept of the Kingdom of God as an omnipotent church.

⁷ Hans K. LaRondelle, *The Israel of God in Prophecy,* (Berrien Springs, MI: The Seventh-Day Adventist Andrews University Press, 1983).

⁸ LaRondelle, *The Israel of God,* p. 40. LaRondelle does not consider the possibility of the relation between Israel and the Church being characterized by partial continuity and partial discontinuity.

⁹ Ibid., p. 35.

¹⁰ Ibid., p. 68.

¹¹ Ibid.

¹² Ibid., 124–134. LaRondelle fails to take into consideration the *a fortiori* statements of Romans 11:12, 15, the temporal references in verses 24–25 and Paul's statement in verse 28 regarding unbelieving Israel's present status as an elect nation.

¹³ Ibid., p. 44.

¹⁴ There are also leading Christian scholars, such as Peter Beyerhaus, who reject the position propounded by LaRondelle. Beyerhaus asks "Why do I believe that the millennium is an intervening period between the return of Christ and the creation of a new heaven and a new earth? It is because of the specific role which the OT has assigned to the people of Israel within the messianic Kingdom. These prophecies have not yet been fulfilled, nor have they been nullified by the creation of the Church as the new spiritual Israel (Acts 1:6). Paul in Romans 11:29 very definitely states that the gifts and the call of God to Israel are irrevocable," (Beyerhaus, *God's Kingdom,* p. 35).

¹⁵ Rosemary Ruether, *Fratricide,* pp. 246–247.

¹⁶ Lapide's openness to dialogue was shown by his willingness to participate in a series of discussions on the Messianic prophecies with Walter C. Kaiser Jr., in the John Ankerberg Show in 1984.

¹⁷ Pinchas Lapide and Jürgen Moltmann, "Israele e Chiesa: Camminare Insieme? In dialogo," *Giornale di teologia,* 140, Rosino Gibellini (ed.), (Brescia: Queriniana, 1982), p. 63.

¹⁸ John S. Feinberg (ed.), *Continuity and Discontinuity, Essays in Honor of S. Lewis Johnson, Jr.,* (Westchester: Crossway books/Good News Publishers, 1988).

¹⁹ Other topics discussed in this volume are: The Hermeneutics of Continuity and Discontinuity, The Biblical Method of Salvation, The Law of Moses and the Law of Christ, and The Kingdom Promises as Spiritual/The Kingdom Promises as Spiritual and National.

²⁰ John Feinberg, *Continuity and Discontinuity,* p. 12; cf. Robert Saucy ("Israel and the Church: A Case for Discontinuity," ibid., pp. 239–259) who writes, "In our understanding, the scriptural concept of the people of God supports both a certain continuity and discontinuity," (p. 240).

²¹ S. Lewis Johnson, Jr., *The Old Testament in the New,* (Grand Rapids, MI: Zondervan, 1980), p. 23.

²² Ellison, *The Mystery of Israel*, p. 13. Ellison was first a member of the International Missionary Council's Committee on the Christian Approach to the Jews and later of the WCC Committee on the Church and the Jewish People.

²³ Fred H. Klooster, "The Biblical Method of Salvation: A Case for Continuity," Feinberg, *Continuity and Discontinuity,* pp. 156–157.

²⁴ Walter C. Kaiser, Jr., "Kingdom Promises as Spiritual and National," Feinberg, *Continuity and Discontinuity,* p. 304. Kaiser associates the words of the angel Gabriel with Daniel 2:44; 7:13–14.

²⁵ Matthew 5:17–18; Luke 24:25–27, 44–47; Hebrews 8:1–13 [cf. Luke 22:19]; 11:39–40; Isaiah 49:5–6; Mark 16:15–16; Acts 13:46–48; 15:14–18.

²⁶ Kaiser, "Kingdom Promises," in Feinberg, *Continuity and Discontinuity,* pp. 303, 306–307; cf. Acts 2:14–21; Matthew 13:1–52; 28:18; Mark 9:1; Acts 28:28–31; Romans 14:17.

²⁷ Saucy ("Israel and the Church: A Case for Discontinuity," Feinberg, *Continuity and Discontinuity,* p. 241) observes that a number of references used in the OT for Israel as the people of God are now applied to the Church which includes both Jews and Gentiles. He cites the following examples: Titus 2:14; Romans 9:25–26; 2 Corinthians 6:16; 1 Peter 2:9–10.

²⁸ Cf. the following observation: "Both Hebrew and Christian thought have their specificity in the expectation of a future redemption through the full manifestation of the majesty of God," (Daniele Garrone, "Il regno di Dio nell'antico e nel nuovo testamento," *Certezze,* n. 150, (Feb. 1996): p. 7).

²⁹ See the juxtaposition of *achri chronōn* . . . in Acts 3:21 where a distinction between present and future time is clearly intended.

³⁰ I. Howard Marshall, *The Gospel of Luke,* The New International Greek Testament Commentary, I. Howard Marshall and W. Ward Gasque (eds.), (Exeter: The Paternoster Press, 1978), pp.773–774; cf. Hodge (*Romans,* pp. 372–373) who compares the use of *achris ou* in Romans 11:25 with its use in Revelation 15: 8 and 17:17.

³¹ Cranfield, *Romans,* 2:575.

³² See Zerwick and Grosvenor, *Analysis of the Greek NT,* pp. 528–529. According to Garrone ("Il regno di Dio," p. 5), 1 Corinthians 15:24–26 offers an outline of intermediate time between the coming of Christ and the full establishment of the Lordship of God over the world.

³³ In light of this sequence of events described by Paul, I disagree with Archibald Robertson (*Regnum Dei,* p. 120) when he states that "[Paul's] belief as to the kingdom of Christ is so formulated as to positively exclude the supposition that a millennium of any kind was part of it." On the contrary, elements in his teaching, such as those reviewed above, appear to require it.

[34] With this expression Robertson intends some form of "millenarianism" (*Regnum Dei*, pp. 119–120).

[35] The formula *kai eidon* recurs in Revelation 19:11, 17; 20:1, 4, 11; 21:1. The fact that the final judgment of the beast and the false prophet is assumed in 20:10, and the binding and loosing of Satan are taught in 20:1–3, 7, strongly suggest that the events referred to here are sequential.

[36] According to G. Bornkamm (*TDNT* 4:822), "everywhere in the NT *mustērion* has an eschatological sense." Concerning the use of the term in Romans 11:25, he writes: "Paul unfolds the final destiny of Israel as a specific mystery. In so doing Paul disclaims personal cleverness (*hina mē ēte en heautois phronimoi*). To his own intelligence the hardening of Israel would be either a pure enigma or a temptation to arbitrary rational conclusions."

[37] Steve Motyer (*Israel in the Plan of God* (Leicester: InterVarsity Press, 1989), p. 55) understands this hardening to mean "doing nothing, or rather nothing beyond issuing appeals for repentance which fall on deaf ears, and simply produce an ever greater unwillingness to hear God speak. Romans 2:4–5 sums it up perfectly."

[38] According to C. F. D. Moule (*An Idiom Book of New Testament Greek*, (Cambridge: Cambridge University Press, 2nd ed., 1959, 7th reprint), p. 82), the meaning of *achris hou*, in Romans 11:25 as elsewhere, is to be considered strictly prepositional = *achris ekeinou chronou en hō*. Thus Hodge (*Romans*, pp. 372–373); Cranfield (*Romans*, 2:575); cf. the NIV "until." Contra Calvin, who asserts (*Romans*, p. 255) that *achris* does not suggest the course or order of time but rather expresses purpose with reference to the full number of the Gentiles. The way *achris* is used elsewhere in the NT (see Romans 1:13; 5:13; 8:22) favors a temporal sense. It may be significant that Calvin avoids commenting on verse 24, where the re-admission into their own "olive tree" of the branches that have been broken off, is presented in the future indicative tense.

[39] Johnson (*The OT in the New*, pp. 215–216) notes that the blend of texts quoted by Paul relate to all the unconditional covenants which God has made with Israel; moreover, "The same passages that declare a future for ethnic Israel also speak of Israel's preeminence among the nations in the kingdom of God."

[40] In light of the temporal references contained in these passages and the fact that "the deliverer" is indicated as the cause of Israel's repentance, we cannot accept Munck's suggestion that Paul conceived of his own apostleship as the determining factor in all Israel entering into the new covenant (see Munck, *Paul and the Salvation of Mankind*, pp. 40–41). Munck's thesis presupposes that *to katechon* (2 Thessalonians 2:5–6) refers to Paul's apostolic ministry. Paul clearly distinguishes between his hope that some of his own people would be saved as a result of his own ministry (Romans 11:14) and the salvation of all Israel, (v. 26).

[41] Contra Luz, *Paulus,* pp. 288–295. According to Luz, Paul attached more importance to how Israel will be converted than to the order of events.

[42] LaRondelle, *The Israel of God,* p. 132.

[43] There is no doubt that Paul's primary purpose in Romans 9–11 is to define the relationship of Israel to the "gospel of God" which has been expounded in the first eight chapters of the letter. For the OT prophets also, the question of Israel's relationship to God is more important than her relationship to the land.

[44] LaRondelle (*The Israel of God*) follows R.C.H. Lenski (*The Interpretation of St. Paul's Epistle to the Romans,* (Columbus, Ohio: Wartburg Press, 1945), p. 729) in taking the phrase "Out of Zion" to refer to Christ's first advent.

[45] Robertson, *Regnum Dei,* p. 119.

[46] Ibid., p. 169.

[47] J. N. D. Kelly, *Early Christian Doctrines,* pp. 461–462.

[48] Robertson, *Regnum Dei,* p.119

[49] See Justin, *Tryph. Jud.,* LXXXI (*PG* 6:669); Irenaeus, *Haer.,* V, 33, 4; 34, 2 (*PG* 3:1214, 1216).

[50] Pelikan, *Tradition,* 1:124.

[51] *ANF* 1:563/*PG* 6:1214. The material to which Papias bears witness is said to have derived from the teaching of the Lord himself and to have been communicated to Papias by John. The passage quoted by Irenaeus begins, "The days will come, in which vines shall grow, each having ten thousand branches, and in each branch ten thousand twigs, and in each true twig ten thousand shoots, and in each one of the shoots ten thousand clusters, and on every one of the clusters ten thousand grapes, and every grape when pressed will give five and twenty metretes of wine" (ibid.). This quotation was taken from a work entitled *Exposition of Dominical Oracles,* in 5 books written by Papias around AD 110 of which only fragments survive (*NIDCC,* s.v. "Papias").

[52] Eusebius, *Hist. eccl.* II, 39, 12–13 (*NPNF* ss, 1:172).

[53] *Barn.* XV, (*PG* 1:1224).

[54] *Tryph. Jud.* LXXX (*PG* 6:668).

[55] The reference is evidently to Revelation 20:1–5.

[56] Justin, *Tryph. Jud.,* LXXXI (*PG* 6:669).

[57] *Haer,* V, 33, 3–4; 34, 2 (*PG* 7:1213–1217).

[58] *Haer,* V, 34, 3–4 (*PG* 7:1217). The literal nature of the messianic reign is further stressed by citing Isaiah 31:9; 32:1.

[59] Tertullian, *Marc.* III, 25 (*ANF,* 3:342–343; in *PL* 2 Marc. bk III concludes with ch. 24).

[60] *Marc.* III, 25.

[61] *NIDCC*, s.v. "Hippolytus."

[62] Hippolytus, *Antichr.* V (*PG* 10:735) cf. XXIX (*PG* 10:749).

[63] Ibid., passim. In treating the Antichrist, the great harlot of Revelation 17–18, and the overthrow of earthly kingdoms by Christ, Hippolytus makes repeated reference to Daniel and Revelation and mentions the predictions of other OT prophets, Christ, and other NT writers.

[64] Clement succeeded Pantaenus as head of the Catechetical School at Alexandria in 190. Although he saw faith to be the means by which mankind arrives at true *gnōsis*, he understood that it is *gnōsis* which leads them to freedom from sin and to immortality and righteousness (*NIDCC*, s.v. "Clement of Alexandria").

[65] *Strom.* IV, 24 (*ANF*, 2:441/*PG* 8:1382).

[66] *Strom.* IV, 22 (*PG* 8:1353).

[67] *Strom.* V, 14 (*ANF* 2:467/*PG* 9:141, 144–145).

[68] *Princ.* II, 4 (*ANF*, 4:277–278); cf. *Cels.* IV, 72 (*PG* 11:1141 "Rursus iram non esse Dei affectum, sed cam in se quemque peccatis derivare").

[69] *Hom. Eze.* (*PG* 13:667–669). For further examples, see Origen's *Comm. on Matthew.* XIV, 9 *PG* 13:202–203).

[70] Origen, *Cels.,* IV, 13 (*PG* 11:1043).

[71] *Comm. on Romans* V, 2 (*PG* 14:1021–1026).

[72] For a useful introduction to the complex theme of divine punishment in Origen, see Hanson, *Allegory and Event,* p. 341.

[73] *Comm. on Matthew* XIV, 9 (*PG* 13:1205).

[74] *Comm. on Matthew* XVII, 35 (*PG* 13:1593) and *Comm. on Romans* X, 1 (*PG* 14:1249–1251).

[75] Hanson, *Allegory and Event,* p. 345.

[76] *The Augsburg Confession,* Art. XVII, in Mark A. Noll (ed.), (Grand Rapids, MI: Baker Book House, 1991), p. 93. Moreover, in the first edition of the Anglican Articles drawn up by Thomas Cranmer in 1553, the second to last of the Forty-Two Articles describes millenarianism as "a fable of Jewish dotage" (Philip Schaff, *History of the Christian Church,* 8 vols., (Charles Schribner's Sons, 1910; Reprint, Grand Rapids: Eerdmans, 1967), 2:619).

[77] *NIDCC*, s.v. "Origenism." Following a letter written by emperor Justinian 1 (483–565), a synod at Constantinople issued an edict in 543 anathematizing Origen's errors concerning the pre-existence of souls, the Incarnation, the resurrection body, and Restorationism.

[78] The overthrow of "chiliasm," a term based on the Greek term *chilias* ("one thousand"), was also facilitated by the widespread assimilation of Greek philosophical categories into Christian theology. It is significant in this regard that Tertullian, a supporter of chiliasm,

is also author of the rhetorical question, "What has Athens to do with Jerusalem?" *Prescription of Heretics* VII, 9 (*PL* 2:20).

[79] *Instructions of Commodianus,* 43–45 (*ANF,* 4:211/*PL* 5:254–256). Little is known concerning Commodianus, save what we learn from the fragments of his writings which remain. He is thought to have been a North-African bishop who was active around AD 240 (*ANF,* 4: 201).

[80] Cyprian, *Unit. eccl.* 14 (*ANF,* 5:425–426/*PL* 4:526).

[81] *The Banquet of the Ten Virgins,* IX, 1 (*PG* 18:177).

[82] Ibid. Methodius differs from Commodianus in some details, as when he excludes begetting in the thousand years. However, he has in common with Commodianus that he envisages the millennium being a part of history.

[83] *NIDCC,* s.v. "Lactantius." A. Cleveland Coxe writes, "Lactantius was doubtless the instrument of Providence in bearing the testimony of Jesus, 'even before kings', in language which promised to Roman letters the new and commanding development imparted to its language by Christianity, which has made it imperishable, and more truly 'eternal' than Rome itself," (*ANF,* 7:5).

[84] *The Divine Institutes,* VII, 22 (*ANF,* 7:218/*PL* 6:804).

[85] *The Epitome of the Divine Institutes,* 72 (*ANF,* 7:255/*PL* 6: 1091).

[86] Pelikan, *Tradition,* 1:125. Pelikan refers to a commentary on the Apocalypse (20:1–3) written by Victorinus in which he states that the "thousand years" is a mode of speaking, signifying the whole.

[87] *NIDCC,* s.v. "Apostolic Constitutions."

[88] *Apostolic Constitutions* VII.26.5 (*ANF,* 7:470); cf. Pelikan, *Tradition,* 1:126.

[89] This criterion of interpretation is expounded by Diodore in his Preface to his *Commentary on the Psalms* (Giancarlo Rinaldi, "Diodoro di Tarso, Antiochia e le ragioni della polemica antiallegorista," *Augustinianum* 33 (1993): pp. 416–430).

[90] Rinaldi, "Diodore," p. 418. Rinaldi writes: "Renouncing the historicity of the facts narrated in the myths was for Salustius, and indeed for all neo-platonists who sought to defend paganism, the only way to confer philosophical validity to the myths, to find justification for ancient feasts and cultic practices, to defend themselves from the attacks of Christians and to develop a theology which could be presented as a substitute to Christian theology," (p. 426).

[91] Julian, who had earlier apostatized from Christianity while studying under the philosopher Libanius, sought to restore the old religions during his brief reign as sole ruler of the Roman empire (AD 361–363).

[92] Rinaldi, "Diodore," pp. 426–429. Opposition to allegorism was consolidated by Theodore of Mopsuestia (c. 350–428), one of

Diodore's disciples and a leading exponent of the Antiochene School of biblical interpretation. In his work *Against the Allegorists,* of which an almost integral copy is preserved in the Cambridge University library, Or. 1318, F 17v–21Or., Theodore distinguishes between the biblical use of allegory and pagan allegorism which was developed in order to rid myths of all historical foundation (Rinaldi, *Diodore,* p. 429).

[93] *NIDCC,* s.v. "Antiochene theology," and "Ephesus, council of (431)."

[94] Augustine wrote in his treatise concerning biblical interpretation, "Now it is surely a miserable slavery of the soul to take signs for things, and to be unable to lift the eye of the mind above what is corporeal and created, that it may drink in eternal light," (*On Christian Doctrine,* III, 5 (*NPNF* fs, 2:559/*PL* 34:69); cf. *On Christian Doctrine,* III, 5–8 (*PL* 34:69–70).

[95] According to Robertson (*Regnum Dei,* p. 174), the disappearance of chiliasm "left unsatisfied a genuine Christian instinct, the demand for a tangible interpretation of the Kingdom of GOD as an object of present effort and as a now living fact."

[96] Ibid., p. 178.

[97] The occasion which led Augustine to embark on his major work, *The City of God,* is well known. Augustine himself writes of it: "Rome having been stormed and sacked by the Goths under Alaric their king, the worshippers of false gods, or pagans, as we commonly call them, made an attempt to attribute this calamity to the Christian religion, and began to blaspheme the true God with even more than their wonted bitterness and acerbity. It was this which kindled my zeal for the house of God, and prompted me to undertake the defense of the city of God against the charges and misrepresentations of its assailants," (*Retractations,* II, 43, cited by Marcus Dods, *NPNF* fs 2: xi/*PL* 32: 647–648).

[98] *Civ.,* XV, 2 (*NPNF* fs 2:285/*PL* 41:438–439).

[99] *Civ.,* XVI, 35 (*NPNF* fs 2:331/*PL* 41:514).

[100] *Civ.,* XVII, 19 (*NPNF* fs 2:356–357/*PL* 41:553–554). Augustine comments on the Jews' failure to accept the evidence of Psalm 68:20 which he quotes as: "Our God is the God of salvation: even of the Lord the exit was by death." Cf. the Hebrew: *Adonay weleYHWH lemoshaot ellanu hael tosaot lemmawet,* meaning: "The LORD YHWH is the God of our salvation; [to him belong] the exits of death."

[101] *Civ.,* XVIII, 32 (*NPNF* fs 2:379/*PL* 41:591). The passage continues, "And because that nation was to suffer such wrath of God, because, being ignorant of the righteousness of God, it wished to establish its own, he immediately says, 'Yet will I rejoice in the LORD.'" In chapter xix of the same book (*NPNF* fs 2:379–380) Augustine affirms that only the believing remnant of the nation will inherit the promises made through such prophets as Isaiah and

Jeremiah, including the prophecy of the new covenant (Jeremiah 31:31, but cf. vv. 35–37).

[102] Cf. Habakkuk 3:12–13.

[103] *Serm.* 259, (*PL* 38:1197).

[104] *Civ.*, XX, 7 (*NPNF* fs 2:426/*PL* 41:666–667).

[105] *Civ.*, XX, 7–8 (*NPNF* fs 2:426–429/*PL* 41:666–672).

[106] "Numquid de regno illo, ubi nulla sunt scandala? De isto ergo regno eius, quod est hic Ecclesia, colligentur" (*Civ.*, XX, 9/*PL* 41: 672).

[107] *Civ.*, XX, 9 (*NPNF* fs 2:430/*PL* 41:675). Augustine links this interpretation with Matthew 18:18 (ibid.).

[108] *Civ.*, XX, 9 (*NPNF* fs 2:430–431/*PL* 41:676).

[109] Pelikan, *Tradition,* 3:176. Pelikan cites in particular Peter the Venerable (c. 1092–1156), *Against the Hardness of the Jews,* 2, (*PL* 189:521) and Alain of Lille (1125–c. 1203), *On the Catholic Faith against the Heretics of His Time* 1.73 (*PL* 210:374).

[110] Robertson, *Regnum Dei,* pp. 225–226.

[111] See Leo I's Letter XXVII, addressed to Flavian, commonly called "The Tome of Leo." Bishop Dioscurus of Alexandria refused to have this letter read at the so-called "Robber's Council" (Ephesus, 449). However, at the Council of Chalcedon two years later, section four of the letter, in which Leo treats "the properties of the twofold nativity and nature of Christ," became the basis of the Symbol of Chalcedon (*NPNF* ss, 12:38–43/*PL* 54:751–756).

[112] Leo I, *serm.* III (*NPNF* ss, 12:117/*PL* 54:147).

[113] James Barmby, "Prolegomena" (*NPNF* ss, 12: vi–xvii).

[114] Many are of the opinion that, in popularizing Augustine's thought, Gregory lost sight of its original meaning. R. R. Atwell cites Reinhold Seeberg's phrase: "Almost everything in him has its roots in Augustine and yet almost nothing is genuinely Augustinian" and B. J. Kidd's summary statement: "Gregory 'erected speculation into a certainty'" (R. R. Atwell, "From Augustine to Gregory the Great: an Evaluation of the Emergence of the Doctrine of Purgatory," *JEH* 38/2 (1987): 173). Atwell shows that these evaluations are particularly apt when applied to Gregory's elaboration of Augustine's ideas about purification in the afterlife (pp. 173–186).

[115] *Corpus of Canon Law* 2.1245, quoted by Justo L. Gonzàlez, *Story of Christianity,* 1:311.

[116] Robertson (op. cit., p. 238) lists nine conscious frauds, of which the most famous are: the (false) Donation of Constantine, probably written in the VIII century (*NIDCC*, s.v. "Donation of Constantine"), and the False Decretals, which originated in the mid-ninth century and were interpolated into an earlier genuine collection of Conciliar Acts (*NIDCC*, s.v. "False Decretals"). Both of these forgeries were used to increase the temporal possessions and power of the papacy until they

were proved false by Lorenzo Valla and Nicholas of Cusa in the period of the Renaissance.

[117] Pelikan, *Tradition,* 2:201. Pelikan alludes to John V of Jerusalem, *Against Constantinus Cabalinus on the Images,* 3 (*PG* 95:313) and Nicephorous of Constantinople, *Greater Apology for the Holy Images,* 7 (*PG* 100:549).

[118] Peter Toon ("Iconoclastic Controversy," *NIDCC,* p. 498), calls attention to three elements of theological significance in this controversy and its outcome: "it caused a development of thinking about the use of icons and of sacramental theology; it emphasized the importance of tradition in the church; and (in the West) it strengthened the papacy."

[119] Hans Ucko, *Common Roots New Horizons,* (Geneva: WCC Publications, 1994), p. 8. Charlotte Klein, of "The Sisters of Sion," makes the same point: "According to the Jewish religious experience there is no sign that the Messiah has already come. Jews have continued to suffer oppression and persecution in the centuries since Jesus Christ; the messianic prophecies of the Bible still await fulfillment," (Charlotte Klein, "From conversion to dialogue—The Sisters of Sion and the Jews: A paradigm of Catholic-Jewish Relations?" *JES* 18/3, Summer (1981): pp. 398–399).

Chapter 6

[1] See the appendix to the present volume which traces the development and effects of the new majority view. See also my article: "Jewish-Christian Dialogue and Soteriology," *Trinity Journal* 20 NS (1999): 23–37.

Appendix

[1] This is the text of a lecture which Ronald E. Diprose presented at the Evangelical Theological Society's Meeting held in Nashville, Tennessee in November 2000.

[2] Zanini based his convictions on biblical predictions, 32 from the Hebrew Scriptures and 11 from the part of the Christian Bible commonly called "the New Testament" (*La Vedetta Cristiana,* II/14, 15 (July 1871): p. 109).

[3] Mortara's Passover speech was later published in *La Vedetta Cristiana,* II/10, 15 (May, 1871): pp. 105–108, following an article written by Carlo Antonio Zanini (ibid., pp. 73–75).

[4] Letter written by Carlo Zanini to Prof. Giuseppe Jarè (*L'Italia Evangelica* XVI, 42 (1897): 331–333).

[5] Domenico Maselli, *Tra Risveglio e Millennio,* (Torino Claudiana, 1974), p. 264.

[6] James Parkes was probably the first to espouse a two-covenant model in his *Judaism and Christianity,* (London: Chicago: University

of Chicago Press, 1948). For a survey of scholars using this model, see Michael G. Vanlaningham, "Christ, the Savior of Israel: The 'Sonderweg' and Bi-covenantal Controversies in relation to the Epistles of Paul," un-published PhD dissertation, submitted to the faculty of Trinity Evangelical Divinity School, Deerfield, Illinois, June 1997, pp: 8–10.

[7] Joann Spillman, "The Image of Covenant in Christian Understandings of Judaism," *Journal of Ecumenical Studies* [hereafter *JES*], 35/1 (1998): 63–87.

[8] Ezer Weizman, president of the State of Israel, recalled this fact with sadness in a message sent to the Centenary of the first Zionist Congress of Basel. Weizman writes, "If our State had been founded a decade before the II World War, we could have saved our brothers and our sisters in Europe destined to extinction because no country was willing to give them refuge," (Herzl Centennial 1897–1997, Commemorating the 1st Zionist Congress, Basel, Programme, p. 6). On the anniversary of the heroic revolt of the Jewish community of Warsaw against Nazism, Elio Toaff, Chief Rabbi of Rome, was interviewed in Jerusalem on April 23, 1998, by a journalist of RAI 1. When asked whether he still finds some aspect of the *Shoah* enigmatic, Toaff cited the refusal of the great western democracies to give refuge to the Jews or to hinder the known massacres perpetrated by the Third Reich. Ideological anti-Semitism is still a force to be reckoned with. It is calculated that there are 200,000 anti-Semitic extremists in the USA alone who are in contact with similar armed groups throughout the whole of Europe ("Insight," CNN, April 26, 1998).

[9] Simon Reeve has shown that those Jews who were not turned back at the Swiss border were treated, as one survivor of the Swiss work camps puts it, "as third-class citizens" (Simon Reeve, "Heartless Haven," *Time*, (Jan. 26, 1998): pp. 24–27).

[10] Jaroslav Pelikan, *The Christian Tradition*, 5 vols., (Chicago: University of Chicago Press, 1871–1989), 1:15.

[11] *Patrologia Graeca*, 162 vols., (Paris: J.P. Migne, 1856–1866), 20:1074–1080.

[12] James Parkes, *The Conflict of the Church and the Synagogue* (New York: Hermon Press, 1934), pp. 394–400, gives a sampling of such confessions.

[13] Martin Luther, *The Jews and their Lies* (*Luther's Works*, vols. 1–30, Jaroslav Pelikan (ed.), (Saint Louis: Concordia 1958–1967), vols. 31–55, Helmut T. Lehmann (ed.), (Philadelphia: Fortress, 1957–1986), vol. 47.) This work was written in 1543, toward the end of Luther's life.

[14] Richard Harries, "Dialogo Cristiani-Ebrei" in *Dizionario del Movemento Ecumenico* (Bologna: Edizioni Dehoniane, 1994), p. 376.

[15] Daniele Garrone, Prof. of OT at the Waldensian Faculty, Rome, made this statement at a Conference of Brethren, Methodists, and

Waldensians, on the theme "La Chiesa di fronte a Israele" ["The Church considers Israel"], held at Poggio Ubertini, Tuscany, on September 24–26, 1993.

[16] Henry F. Knight, "From Shame to Responsibility and Christian Identity: the Dynamics of Shame and Confession regarding the Shoah," *JES* 35/1 (1998): 41–62:

[17] Ibid., p. 52.

[18] The Council of Christians and Jews continues to operate in several countries, including England, Scotland, and New Zealand.

[19] See *Common Ground* (hereafter *CG*) (1993/2): 4–5; cf. Sr. Margaret Shepherd, "Christian-Jewish Relations," *Joppa Group Bulletin*, (April 1994): p. 5.

[20] For the text of the "Ten Points of Seelisberg," see L. Sestieri e G. Cereti (ed.), *Le Chiese Cristiane e L'ebraismo*, 1947–1982, (Casale Monferrato: Marietti, 1983), pp. 1–4.

[21] Ibid., p. 5.

[22] Ekkehard Stegemann, "Welchen Sinn hat es, von Jesus als Messias zu reden?," in Ekkehard Stegemann (ed.), *Messiasvorstellungen bei Juden und Christen* (Stuttgart: Verlag W. Kohlhammer, 1993), pp. 81–102.

[23] Hans Joachim Krau, "Dei Geist-Christologie im christlich-judischen Dialog," ibid., pp. 103–110.

[24] The expression "theological embroidery" was coined by Gregory Baum with reference to how the Church Fathers modified biblical teaching concerning the mystery of Israel (Gregory Baum O.S.A., *Is the New Testament Anti-Semitic?* (Glen rock, N.J., Paulist Press, 1960, Rev. ed., 1965), p. 17).

[25] Paul M. van Buren, "On Reading Someone Else's Mail: The Church and Israel's Scriptures," in Erhard Blum, Christian Macholz and Ekkehard W. Stegemann (eds.), *Dei Hebräische Bibel und ihre zweifache Nachgeschichte* (Heukirchen, Vluyn: Neukirchen Verlag, 1990), p. 595.

[26] Clark M. Williamson, *A Guest in the House of Israel* (Louisville, KY: Westminster/John Knox Press, 1993), pp. 109–110.

[27] Cf. Vanlaningham, "The 'Sonderweg' and Bi-convenantal Controversies," pp. 10–13. For a helpful survey of the various theories, see Gavin D'Costa, "One Covenant or many Covenants? Toward a Theology of Christian-Jewish relations," *JES* 27/3 (1990): 441–452. D'Costa opts for an inclusivist solution: "one normative covenant, within which there are many further legitimate covenants" in which the work of Christ is decisive but conversion to Christ is not always essential.

[28] See *TCJP*, pp. 147–179. The issues listed are: covenant and election, the scriptures, Torah and law, Jesus, anti-Semitism

and the *Shoah*, the State of Israel, mission to the Jews, common responsibility.

²⁹ John T. Pawlikowski, "Contemporary Jewish-Christian Theological Dialogue Agenda," *JES* 11/4 (1974): 615.

³⁰ John C. Lyden, "Atonement in Judaism and Christianity: Toward a Rapprochement," *JES* 29/1 (1992): 47. Rabbi Gordon Tucker ("Contemporary Jewish Thought on the Messianic Idea," *Face to Face* 14 (1988): 23) speaks for Jews when he says: "'Salvation' and 'redemption' are not among the most common entries in the Jewish lexicon even at those times when Jewish theology is being discussed. 'Creation' and 'revelation,' for example, are much more often the subjects of inquiry, perhaps in part because they are less unsettling topics."

³¹ Lyden, ibid.

³² While the WCC began by affirming the appropriateness of Christian mission to the Jewish People, more recent statements emanating from WCC circles oppose it (*TCJP*, pp. 8, 23, 77, 93, 97, 113–14). According to Sister Margaret Shepherd ("Christian-Jewish Relations," *Joppa Group Bulletin* (April, 1994): 5), Christian mission is an obstacle of far greater importance to establishing amicable relations between Christians and Jews than are memories of the Holocaust and the issue of images in some Christian churches (cf. Charlotte Klein, "From conversion to dialogue—The Sisters of Sion and the Jews: A paradigm of Catholic-Jewish Relations?" *JES* 18 (1981): 388–400).

³³ This is made clear in Lesslie Newbigin's chapter "No Other Name," in his book *The Gospel in a Pluralist Society*; Reprint; (Grand Rapids, MI: Eerdmans, 1991).

³⁴ This symposium was organized by the Anti-Defamation League of B'Nai B'rith, in collaboration with the School of Philosophy of the Pontifical University, SIDIC, Angelicum and the Centro Pro Unione. The papers presented were published in a special issue of *Face to Face*: "Salvation and Redemption in Judaism and Christianity," *Face to Face* 14 (1988); cf. Ronald E. Diprose, "Jewish-Christian Dialogue and Soteriology," *Trinity Journal* NS 20 (1999): 23–37.

³⁵ This consultation was held in April 1989; see "The Willowbank Declaration on the Christian Gospel and the Jewish People," *International Bulletin of Missionary Research* 13/4 (1989): 161–63.

³⁶ See, for example: "*La Salvezza viene dagli Ebrei*," ed. Annie Cagiati, (Roma: Carucci editore, 1987); Clark M. Williamson, *A Guest in the House of Israel* (Louisville, KY: Westminster/John Knox Press, 1993): 77–106, pp. 233–65; R. Kendall Soulen, *The God of Israel and Christian Theology* (Minneapolis, MN: Fortress Press, 1996), pp. 156–77. Among more general works which have a bearing on our theme, see Hans Küng, *Global Responsibility* (London: SCM Press, 1991); Maurice Wiles, Christian Theology and Inter-religious Dialogue, (London: SCM Press, 1992).

[37] See, in particular, Paul M. van Buren, "Covenantal Pluralism?" *CG* (1990/3): 21–27; David Blewett, "Must Jews become Christians?" *CG* (1991/4): 19–21 and Tony Bayfield, "Mission—A Jewish Perspective," *CG* (1993/2): 8–12; John C. Lyden, "Atonement in Judaism and Christianity: Toward a Rapprochement," *JES* 29/1 (1992): 47–54.

[38] Terry W. Bookman, "The Holy Conversation: Towards a Jewish Theology of Dialogue," *JES* 32 (1995): 212–13.

[39] Rabbi Leon Klenicki, "Facing History: Redemption and Salvation After Auschwitz," ibid., 46.

[40] Michael A. Signer, Tikva Frymer-Kensky, David Novak and Peter W. Ochs.

[41] See John 3:36; 14:6; Acts 4:8–12; 1 Timothy 2:5–6. It is striking that while Romans 11 appears repeatedly in the literature pertaining to the dialogical process, statements in chapter 10 (part of the same section of the letter) which make faith in Jesus essential for the salvation of Israelites are studiously avoided.

[42] The following are among the many NT passages which affirm these distinctives: John 14:6; Acts 3:19–4:12; Romans 3:19–31; 1 Corinthians 3:11; 1 Timothy 2:5–6; 1 John 2:1–2.

[43] Peter Beyerhaus, "The Authority of the Gospel and Interreligious Dialogue," *Trinity Journal* 17 NS (1996): 139.

[44] Carlo Molari says as much in an unpublished paper entitled "L'elezione d'Israele nell'autocomprensione Cristiana" presented at the SIDIC Center, Rome (November 4, 1995). Molari writes: "The election of the Hebrew people and of the Christian church are but particular aspects of one and the same call which God addresses in different ways and forms to all nations, to gather them together into the unity of the people of God's children," (ibid., p. 1).

[45] "Such a Christology [which does not claim to represent the totality of revelation] needs to make room . . . for the ongoing validity of the Jewish covenant. A similar approach needs to be developed with respect to the other world religions, especially Islam"; cf. Ewert Cousins, "Judaism—Christianity—Islam: Facing Modernity Together," *JES* 30/3–4 (1993): 417–425.

[46] Wiles takes his cue from Karl Rahner (see Karl Rahner, *Foundations of Christian Faith.* Translated by William V. Dych, (New York: Crossroad, 1982), especially ch. 4). Although Rahner speaks of the universality of the divine offer of self-communication to the human creation, he also insists that saving knowledge of God is available only within the sphere of the Christian faith.

[47] Maurice Wiles, op. cit., p. 68, cited by Tony Bayfield, in "Mission—A Jewish Perspective," *CG* (1993/2): 10.

[48] Tony Bayfield, ibid.

[49] Ibid., p. 11.

[50] Thus Marquardt, in Reichrath, op. cit., p. 58.

[51] Parkes, *Judaism and Christianity*, p. 30.

[52] Pawlikowski, op. cit., pp. 150–151. Pawlikowski suggests the need "to explore whether the realities expressed through the Sinai myth and the Christ myth may be present under different symbols in other world religions," (ibid.).

[53] Williamson, *Guest*, pp. 260–64.

[54] Ibid., p. 126.

[55] Ibid.

BIBLIOGRAPHY

1. Ancient Works

Ambrose
Sermons
Apostolic Constitutions

Augustine
City of God
Sermons
Tract Against the Jews

Barnabas, Epistle of

Clement of Alexandria
Stromata

Commodianus
Instructions

Cyprian
Epistles
On the Unity of the Church
Three Books of Testimonies Against the Jews

Cyril of Alexandria
Commentary on Romans

Cyril of Jerusalem
  Catechetical Lectures
  Didache
  Diognetus, Epistle to

Eusebius of Cesarea
  Ecclesiastical History
  Life of Constantine

Hippolytus
  On Antichrist
  Expository Treatise Against the Jews

Ignatius of Antioch
  Epistles

Irenaeus
  Against Heresies

John Chrysostom
  Demonstrations to the Jews and Gentiles that Christ is God
  Eight Orations Against the Jews
  Sermons

John Damascene
  On the Orthodox Faith

Josephus, Flavius
  The Life of Josephus

Justin Martyr
  Dialogue with Trypho
  First Apology

Lactantius
  Divine Institutes
  The Epitome of the Divine Institutes

Methodius of Olympus
The Banquet of the Ten Virgins

Origen
Against Celsus
On First Principles
Homilies
Commentaries on Matthew and Romans

Tertullian
To Martyrs
Against the Jews
Against Marcion
On Baptism
Exhortation to Chastity
On Modesty
Prescription of Heretics

2. Collections

Classici delle religioni. Turin: U.T.E.T., 1969–

Collana di testi patristici. Directed by Antonio Quacquarelli. Rome: Città nuova editrice, 1975–

Ante-Nicene Christian Library. Alexander Roberts and James Donaldson, eds. 24 vols. Edinburgh: T. & T. Clark, 1867–1872.

Ante-Nicene Fathers. Alexander Roberts and James Donaldson, eds. American reprint, A. Cleveland Coxe and Allan Menzies, eds. 10 vols. Grand Rapids, MI: Eerdmans, 1986.

Luther's Works. vols. 1–30, Jaroslav Pelikan, ed. Saint Louis: Concordia, 1958–1967; vols. 31–55, Helmut T. Lehmann, ed. Philadelphia: Fortress, 1957–1986.

Nicene and Post–Nicene Fathers. First Series, Philip Schaff, ed. 14 vols. Reprint, Grand Rapids, MI: Eerdmans, 1979–1987.

Nicene and Post-Nicene Fathers. Second Series, Philip Schaff and Henry Wace, eds. 14 vols. Reprint, Grand Rapids, MI: Eerdmans, 1983.

Patrologia Graeca. 162 vols. Paris: J.P. Migne, 1856–1866.

Patrologia Latina. 221 vols. Paris: J.P. Migne, 1862–1865. Reprint, Turnbolti, Belgium: Typographi Brepols Editores Pontifichi, n.d.

Pauluskommentare aus der Griechischen Kirche. Karl Staab, ed. 1933. Reprint Münster, Westfalen: Aschendorff, 1984.

The Greek New Testament. Kurt Aland, Matthew Black, Carlo M. Martini, Bruce M. Metzger and Allen Wikgren, eds. Germany: United Bible Societies, 1975.

The Holy Bible. New International Version. Grand Rapids, MI: Zondervan, 1985.

3. Biblical Commentaries

Abbott, T.K. *The Epistles to the Ephesians and to the Colossians*. ICC. S.R. Driver, A. Plummer, C.A. Briggs, eds. Edinburgh: T. & T. Clark, 1897. 5th reprint, 1956.

Barrett, C.K. *The Epistle to the Romans*. Black's New Testament Commentaries. London: Adam and Charles Black, 1957. 2nd reprint, 1967.

Barth, Karl. *Der Römerbrief.* Zürich: Evangelischer Verlag Zollikon, 1954.

Barth, Markus. *Ephesians 1–3*. The Anchor Bible. New York: Doubleday and Co., 1974.

Best, Ernest. *The Letter of Paul to the Romans*. The Cambridge Bible Commentary. P.R. Ackroyd, A.R.C. Leaney and J.W. Packer, eds. Cambridge: Cambridge University Press, 1967.

Betz, H.D. *Galatians*. Philadelphia, PA: Fortress Press, 1979.

Bruce, F.F. *The Epistle of Paul to the Romans.* Tyndale New Testament Commentaries. London: The Tyndale Press, 1965. 2nd ed., 1985.

———. *The Gospel of John*. Grand Rapids, MI: Eerdmans, 1983.

———. *Commentary on Galatians.* New International Greek Testament Commentary. I. Howard Marshall and W. Ward Gasque, eds. Grand Rapids, MI: Eerdmans, 1982.

———. *The Epistle to the Hebrews.* The New International Commentary on the New Testament. F.F. Bruce, ed. Grand Rapids, MI: Eerdmans, 1964. Reprint, 1981.

Burton, E.D. *The Epistle to the Galatians.* ICC. S.R. Driver, A. Plummer, and C.A. Briggs, eds. 1921. Reprint, Edimburgh: T. & T. Clark, 1957.

Calvin, John. *Romans.* Calvin's Commentaries. Translated and edited by John Owen. Grand Rapids: Eerdmans, 1947. Reprint, *Epistles of Paul the Apostle, to the Romans and to the Thessalonians.* Calvin's Commentaries. Edinburgh: The Saint Andrew Press, 1961.

Carson, D. A. *Matthew.* The Expositor's Bible Commentary. Frank E. Gaebelein, ed. Grand Rapids, MI: Zondervan, 1984.

———. *The Gospel According to John.* Grand Rapids, MI: Eerdmans, 1991.

Cranfield, C.E.B. *The Epistle to the Romans.* 2 vols. ICC. J.A. Emerton, ed. Edinburgh: T. & T. Clark, 1975–1979.

Davids, Peter H. *The First Epistle of Peter.* The New International Commentary on the New Testament. F.F. Bruce, ed. Grand Rapids, MI: Eerdmans, 1990.

Delitzsch, Franz. *Isaiah.* Translated by James Martin. Vol. 7 in Commentary on the Old Testament by C.F. Keil and F. Delitzsch. 10 vols. Reprint, Grand Rapids, MI: Eerdmans, 1980.

Dunn, James D.G. *Romans 9–16.* Word Biblical Commentary. Dallas: Word Books, 1988.

Godet, F. *St. Paul's Epistle to the Romans.* 2 vols. Edinburgh: T. & T. Clark 1880–1881.

Grudem, Wayne. *1 Peter.* Tyndale New Testament Commentaries. Downers Grove, MI: InterVarsity Press, 1988.

Haldane, Robert. *The Epistle to the Romans.* 1835–1839. Reprint, London: Banner of Truth, 1958.

Hill, David. *The Gospel of Matthew*. The New Century Bible Commentary. Matthew Black, NT ed. Grand Rapids, MI: Eerdmans, 1972.

Hodge Charles. *Commentary on the Epistle to the Romans*. Revised ed. 1886. 6th reprint, Grand Rapids, MI: Eerdmans, 1965.

Huby, Giuseppe S. J. *San Paolo, Epistola ai Romani*. P. Stanislao Lyonnet S.J., ed. Rome: Editrice Studium, 1961.

Leenhardt, Franz J. *L'Èpître du Saint Paul aux Romains*. Commentaire du Nouveau Testament. Vol. VI. Genéve: Labor et Fides, 1957.

Lenski, R.C.H. *The Interpretation of St. Paul's Epistle to the Romans*. Columbus: Wartburg Press, 1945. Reprint, 1960.

Lightfoot, J.B. *The Epistle of St. Paul to the Galatians*. 1865. 20th reprint, Grand Rapids, MI: Zondervan, 1957, 1982.

Luther, Martin. *Commentary on the Epistle to the Romans*. Translation by J. Theodore Mueller. Grand Rapids, MI: Kregel, 1976.

Marshall, I. Howard. *The Gospel of Luke*. The New International Greek Testament Commentary. I. Howard Marshall and W. Ward Gasque, eds. Exeter: The Paternoster Press, 1978.

————. *The Acts of the Apostles*. Tyndale New Testament Commentaries. R.V.G. Tasker, ed. Grand Rapids, MI: Eerdmans, 1980.

Moffatt, James. *Epistle to the Hebrews*. ICC. S.R Driver, A. Plummer, and C.A. Briggs, eds. Edinburgh: T. & T. Clark, 1924. 3rd reprint, 1957.

Moo, Douglas J. *The Epistle to the Romans*. The New International Commentary on the New Testament, Gordon Fee, ed. Grand Rapids, MI: Eerdmans, 1996.

Morris, Leon. *The Epistle to the Romans*. Leicester: InterVarsity Press, 1988.

Murray, John. *Epistle to the Romans*. The New international Commentary on the New Testament. F.F. Bruce, ed. Grand Rapids, MI: Eerdmans, 1968.

Nygren, Anders. *Commentary on Romans*. 4th ed. Philadelphia: Fortress, 1978.

Perkins, William. *A Commentary on Galatians.* Gerald T. Sheppard, ed. The Pilgrim Classic Commentaries. New York: The Pilgrim Press, 1989.

Sanday, William and Arthur C. Headlam. *The Epistle to the Romans.* The International Critical Commentary. S.R. Driver, A. Plummer and C.A. Briggs, eds. Edinburgh: T. & T. Clark, 1895.

Schlier, von Heinrich. *Der Römerbrief.* Freiburg im Breisgau: Verlag Herder, 1977.

Vine, W.E. *The Epistle to the Romans,* 2nd ed. London: Oliphants, 1948.

Vermigli, Pietro Martire. *Most Fruitfull and Learned Commentaries of Doctor Peter Martir Vermil Florentine.* London: John Day, 1564.

4. Historical and Systematic Theology

Aquinas, Thomas. *Somma contro i Gentili.* Tito S. Centi, ed. Torino: U.T.E.T., 1975.

Ball, Bryan W. *A Great Expectation: Eschatological Thought in English Protestantism to 1660.* Leiden: E. J. Brill, 1975.

Barth, Karl. *Dei Kirchliche Dogmati.* Zweiter Band, Dei Lehre von Gott, Erster Halbband. Zollikon, Zürich: Evangelischer Verlag A.G., 1948.

———. *Dogmatique.* Vol. 1–2. Translated into French by M. Fernand Ryser. Geneva: Editions Labor et Fides, 1954–1956.

Bloesch, Donald G. *A Theology of Word and Spirit.* Downers Grove, IL: InterVarsity Press, 1992.

Boice, James Montgomery. *Foundations of the Christian Faith.* Downers Grove, IL: InterVarsity Press, 1986.

Berkhof, Hendrikus. *Christian Faith.* Grand Rapids, MI: Eerdmans, 1979.

Berkhof, Louis. *Systematic Theology.* 1st British ed., 1958. 3rd reprint, London: Banner of Truth Trust, 1966.

Calvin, John. *Institutes of the Christian Religion.* Translation by Henry Beveridge. 2 vols. London: James Clarke, 1953.

Carter, Charles W., R. Duane Thompson and Charles R. Wilson, eds. *A Contemporary Wesleyan Theology*. 2 vols. Grand Rapids, MI: Zondervan, 1983.

Chafer, Lewis Sperry. *Systematic Theology*. 8 vols. Dallas, TX: Dallas Theological Seminary, 1948. 11th reprint, 1973.

Clouse, Robert G., ed. *The Meaning of the Millennium*. Downers Grove: InterVarsity Press, 1977.

Erickson, Millard J. *Christian Theology*. Grand Rapids, MI: Baker Book House, 1985. 3rd reprint, 1987.

Finger, Thomas. *Christian Theology: An Eschatological Approach*. 2 vols. Nashville, TN: Thomas Nelson Publications, 1985.

Gentile, Panfilo. *Il Cristianesimo Dalle Origini a Costantino*. Collana di studi storici e filosofici. Carlo Antoni, ed. Firenze: Le Monnier, 1946.

Grenz, Stanley J. *Theology for the Community of God*. Nashville, TN: Broadman, 1994.

Grossi, Vittorino and Angelo Di Berardino. *La chiesa Antica: Ecclesiologia e Istituzioni*. Roma: Borla, 1984.

Grudem, Wayne. *Systematic Theology: An Introduction to Biblical Doctrine*. Leicester: InterVarsity Press, 1994.

Hanson, R.P.C. *Allegory and Event, A Study of the Sources and Significance of Origen's Interpretation of Scripture*. Richmond, VA: John Knox Press, 1959.

Harnack, Adolf. *Manuale di Storia del Dogma*. 1st Italian ed. from the 4th German ed. 7 vols. Mendrisio: Casa Editrice Cultura Moderna, 1912–1914.

Hodge, Charles. *Systematic Theology*. 3 vols, 1872–1873. Reprint, Grand Rapids, MI: Eerdmans, 1975.

Jay, Eric G. *The Church: Its Changing Image Through Twenty Centuries*. Atlanta, GA: John Knox Pess, 1978.

Kelly, J.N.D. *Early Christian Doctrines*. 3rd ed. London: Adam and Charles Black, 1965.

Lewis, Gordon R. and Bruce A. Demarest. *Integrative Theology*. 3 vols. Grand Rapids, MI: Zondervan, 1994.

Lindsay, Thomas M. *The Church and the Ministry in the Early Centuries*. The 18th series of the Cunningham Lectures, 1902. 3rd ed. London: Hodder and Stoughton, 1907.

McClendon, James Wm, Jr. *Systematic Theology.* 2 vols. Nashwille, TN: Abingdon Press, 1994.

McGrath, Alister. *Christian Theology: An Introduction.* London: Blackwell, 1994.

Moody, Dale. *The Word of Truth: A Summary of Christian Doctrine Based on Biblical Revelation.* Grand Rapids, MI: Eerdmans, 1981.

Murray, Iain. *The Puritan Hope.* London: The Banner of Truth Trust, 1971.

Noll, Mark A., ed. *Confessions and Catechisms of the Reformation.* Grand Rapids, MI: Baker Book House, 1991.

Oden, Thomas, C. *Systematic Theology.* 3 vols. New York: Harper Collins, 1992.

Oliver, W. H. *Prophets and Millennialists: The Uses of Biblical Prophecy in England from the 1790s to the 1840s.* Auckland: Auckland University Press, 1978.

Pelikan, Jaroslav. *The Christian Tradition.* 5 vols. Chicago: University of Chicago Press, 1971–1989.

Rahner, Karl. *Foundations of Christian Faith.* Translated by William V. Dych, New York: Crossroad, 1982.

Robertson, Archibald. *Regnum Dei.* Eight Lectures on the Kingdom of God in the History of Christian Thought. The Bampton Lectures 1901. London: Methuen and Co., 1901.

Spykman, Gordon J. *Reformational Theology: A New Paradigm for Doing Dogmatics.* Grand Rapids, MI: Eerdmans, 1992.

Strong, A. H. *Systematic Theology.* 3 vols. in 1. Westwood, NP: Fleming and Revell, 1907.

Thiessen, Henry Clarence. *Lectures in Systematic Theology.* Revision by Vernon D. Doerksen. Grand Rapids, MI: Eerdmans, 1979.

Van Gemeren, Willem. *The Progress of Redemption: The Story of Salvation from Creation to the New Jerusalem.* Grand Rapids, MI: Zondervan, 1988.

Whiston, William, translator and ed. *Works of Josephus.* 4 vols. Grand Rapids, MI: Baker Book House, 1974.

Williams, Rodman. *Renewal Theology.* 3 vols. Academie Books. Grand Rapids, MI: Zondervan, 1988–1992.

5. General works, Monographs, Historical Romance

Barker, William S. and W. Robert Godfrey, eds. *Theonomy: A Reformed Critique*. Grand Rapids, MI: Zondervan, 1990.

Barth, Markus. *The People of God. Journal for the Study of the New Testament*. Supplement series, no. 5. Sheffield: The University of Sheffield, 1983.

———. *Rediscovering the Lord's Supper*. Louisville, KY: John Knox Press, 1988.

Baum, Gregory O.S.A. *Is the New Testament Anti-Semitic?* Glen Rock, NJ: Paulist Press, 1960.

Bentwich, Norman. *The Jews in Our Time*. Penguin Books, 1960. Italian translation by Lia Moggi. Gli Ebrei nel Nostro Tempo. Florence: Sansoni, 1963.

Beyerhaus, Peter P. J. *God's Kingdom and the Utopian Error*. Wheaton, IL: Good News Publishers, 1992.

Blum, Erhard, Christian Macholz and Ekkehard W. Stegemann, eds. *Dei Hebräische Bibel und Ihre Zweifache Nachgeschichte*. Festschrift für Rolf Rendtorff. Heukirchen, Vluyn: Neukirchen Verlag, 1990.

Bright, John. *A History of Israel*. London: SCM Press, 1960.

Bruce, F.F. *Israel and the Nations*. Exeter: The Paternoster Press, 1963.

———. *The Spreading Flame*. The Paternoster Church History. Vol. 1. Exeter: The Paternoster Press, 1958.

Bunk, B. "L'élection d'Israel/Analyse Critique de la Position de K.B. sur le Rôle d'Israel dans l'Histoire du Salut." Unpublished thesis. Lausanne: Fac. Théol. Eglise Libre Canton de Vaud, 1966.

Charlesworth, James H., Frank X. Blisard and Jeffrey S. Siker, eds. *Jews and Christians*. New York: Crossroad, 1990.

Clowney, Edmund P. *The Church*. Contours of Christian Theology. Gerald Bray, ed. Downers Grove, IL: InterVarsity Press, 1995.

Collins, R.F. *Studies on the First Letter to the Thessalonians*. Louvain: University Press 1984.

Davenport, Rowland A. *Albury Apostles*. United Writers, 1970. Revised ed. London: Neilgo Publications, 1974.

Davies, Alan T., ed. *Anti-Semitism and the Foundations of Christianity*. New York: Paulist Press, 1979.

de Waard, J. A. *Comparative Study of the Old Testament Text in the Dead Sea Scrolls and the New Testament*. Leiden: Brill, 1965.

Dunn, James D. G. *The Partings of the Ways*. London: SCM Press, 1991.

Ellison, H. L. *The Mystery of Israel*. Exeter: Paternoster, 1966.

Evans, Craig A. and Donald A. Hagner, eds. *Anti-Semitism and Early Christianity*. Minneapolis, MN: Fortress Press, 1993.

Fackre, Gabriel. *Ecumenical Faith in Evangelical Perspective*. Grand Rapids, MI: Eerdmans, 1993.

Feinberg, John, ed. *Continuity and Discontinuity*. Westfield, IL: Crossway Books, Good News Publishers, 1988.

Flusser, David. *Jesus*. Jerusalem: The Magnes Press, The Hebrew University, 1997.

Frend, W. H. C. *The Rise of Christianity*. Philadelphia, PA: Fortress Press, 1984.

Giles, Kevin. *What on Earth is the Church?* Downer's Grove, IL: InterVarsity Press, 1995.

Gonzàlez, Justo L. *The Story of Christianity*. 2 vols. San Francisco, CA: Harper, 1984–1985.

Harvey, Graham. *The True Israel*. Leiden: E.J. Brill, 1996.

Hengel, Martin. *Judentum und Hellenismus*. Tübingen: J. C. B. Mohr (Paul Siebeck), 1973. English ed. by John Bowden. *Judaism and Hellenism*. 2 vols. London: SCM Press, 1974.

Johnson, S. Lewis Jr. *The Old Testament in the New*. Grand Rapids, MI: Zondervan, 1980.

Jules, Isaac. *Genèse de L'Antisémitisme*. Paris: Calmann Lévy, 1956.

Käsemann, Ernst. *New Testament Questions of Today*. Philadelphia, PA: Fortress Press, 1969.

Lacunza y Diaz, Manuel de. *Venida del Mesìas en Gloria y Majestad*. 1811. English translation, with Introduction, of the 11th ed. by Edward Irving. *The Coming of the Messiah in Glory and Majesty*. 2 vols. London: L.B. Seeley and Sons, 1827.

Langmuir, Gavin I. *History, Religion, and Antisemitism.* Los Angeles: Center of Medieval and Renaissance Studies, 1990.

Lapide, Pinchas and Jürgen Moltmann. *Monoteismo Ebraico— Dottrina Trinitaria, Un dialogo.* Brescia: Queriniana, 1980.

LaRondelle, Hans K. *The Israel of God in Prophecy.* Berrien Springs, MI: The Seventh-Day Adventist Andrews University Press, 1983.

Leighton, Robert. *The Whole Works of Robert Leighton, D.D.* Included is "A Life of the Author" by John Norman Pearson. New York: J.C. Riker, 1855.

Luz, Ulrich. *Das Geschichtsverständnis des Paulus.* Beiträge zur evangelischen Theologie. Theologische Abhandlungen. von E. Wolf., ed. Vol. 49. Müchen: Chr. Kaiser Verlag, 1968.

McComisky, Thomas Edward. *The Covenants of Promise: A Theology of the Old Testament Covenants.* Grand Rapids, MI: Baker Book House, 1985.

Moore, George F. *Judaism in the First Three Centuries of the Christian Era. The Age of the Tannaim.* 2 vols., 1927. 3rd ed. New York: Schocken Books, 1971.

Motyer, Steve. *Israel in the Plan of God.* Leicester: InterVarsity Press, 1989.

Munck, Johannes. *Paulus Und Die Heilsgeschichte.* 1954. Eng. Trad. *Paul and the Salvation of Mankind.* By Frank Clarke, 1959. Paperback ed. Atlanta: John Knox Press, 1977.

Newell, J. Philip. "A. J. Scott and his Circle." Unpublished Ph.D. thesis. University of Edinburgh, 1981.

Parkes, James. *The Conflict of the Church and the Synagogue.* New York: Hermon Press, 1934.

———. *A History of the Jewish People.* Penguin Books. Middlesex: Harmondsworth, 1964.

Perkins, William. *The Workes of That Famous and Worthy Minister of Christ in the Universitie of Cambridge, M.W. Perkins.* 3 vols. Cambridge, 1626–1631.

Plag, Christoph. *Israels Wege zum Heil, Eine Untersuchung zu Römer 9 bis 11.* Stuttgart: Calwer Verlag, 1969.

Ramm, Bernard. *Protestant Biblical Interpretation*. Grand Rapids: Baker, 1970.

Refoulé, François. "... *Et ainsi tout Israël sera sauvé.*" Paris: Les Éditions du Cerf, 1984.

Roth, Cecil. *A Short History of the Jewish People*. 1936. 6th revised ed. Hartmore: Hartmore House, 1969.

Ruether, Rosemany R. *Faith and Fratricide*. New York: The Seabury Press, 1974.

Sachar, Howard M. *A History of Israel: From the Rise of Zionism to Our Time*. New York: Alfred A. Knopf, 1993.

Saucy, Robert. *The Case for Progressive Dispensationalism*. Grand Rapids, MI: Zondervan, 1993.

Schaff, Philip. *History of the Christian Church*. 8 vols. Charles Schribner's Sons, 1910. Reprint ed. Grand Rapids, MI: Eerdmans, 1967.

Schmid, Herbert. *Dei christlich-jüdische Auseinandersetzung um das Alte Testament in hermeneutischer Sicht*. Zürich: Theologischer Verlag, 1971.

Scott, Sir Walter. *Ivanhoe*. Nelson Classics. T. Nelson and Sons, 1830.

Sibbes, Richard. *The Complete Works of Richard Sibbes*. A.B. Grosart, ed. 4 vols. Edinburgh: James Nichol, 1862.

Siker, Jeffrey S. *Disinheriting the Jews Adraham in early Christian Controversy*. Louisville, KY: Westminster/John Knox Press, 1991.

Soulen, R. Kendall. *The God of Israel and Christian Theology*. Minneapolis, MN: Fortress Press, 1996.

Toon, Peter, ed. *Puritan Eschatology 1600–1660*. Cambridge: James Clarke, 1970.

Ucko, Hans. *Common Roots New Horizons*. Geneva: WCC Publications, 1994.

Williamson, Clark M. *A Guest in the House of Israel*. Louisville, KY: Westminster/John Knox Press, 1993.

Wistrich, Robert S., ed. *Anti-Zionism and Anti-Semitism in the Contemporary World*. London: The Macmillan Press, 1990.

6. Articles

Atwell, R.R. "From Augustine to Gregory the Great: an Evaluation of the Emergence of the Doctrine of Purgatory." *JEH* 38/2 (1987): 173–186.

Beale, G.K. "An Exegetical and Theological Consideration of the hardening of Pharaoh's heart in Exodus 4–14 and Romans 9." *Trinity Journal* 5 NS (1984): 129–154.

Bianchi, Enzo. "Israele e la chiesa." *Storia cristiana* 10 (1989): 77–106.

Carbone, Sandro. "Israele nella Lettera ai Romani." *Rivista Biblica* XLI (1993): 139–170.

Castellina, Paolo. "La salvezza di Israele: un inno alla sovranità di Dio." *Studi di teologia*. NS. III (1991): 190–198.

Cousins, Ewert. "Judaism–Christianity–Islam: Facing Modernity Together." *JES* 30 (1993): 417–425.

Davies, W.D. "Paul and the People of Israel." *New Testament Studies* 24 (1977–1978): 4–39.

Demson, David E. "Israel as the Paradigm of Divine Judgement: An Examination of a Theme in the Theology of Karl Barth." *JES* 26 (1989): 611–627.

Drane, John W. "Why did Paul write Romans?" *Pauline Studies*. Donald A. Wagner, and Murray J. Harris, eds. Exeter: The Paternoster Press, 1980, pp. 208–227.

Droge, Arthur J. "Justin Martyr and the Restoration of Philosophy." *CH* 56 (1987): 303–319.

Dunn, James D.G. "Echoes of Intra-Jewish Polemic in Paul's Letter to the Galatians." *Journal of Biblical Literature* 112/3 (1993): 459–477.

Evans, Gillian R. "The Beginnings of Christian Philosophy." *The History of Christian Theology*, Paul Avis, Series ed. Vol. 1. *The Science of Theology*. Gillian R. Evans, Alister E. McGrath and Allan D. Galloway, eds. Basingstoke: Marshall Pickering, 1986.

Fuller, Daniel P. "Interpretation, History of." In *The International Standard Bible Encyclopedia*. Fully revised. Geoffrey W. Bromiley, ed. 4 vols. 1982.

Garrone, Daniele. "Il regno di Dio nell'antico e nel nuovo testamento." *Certezze*, 150 (1996): 7.

————. "Protestanti ed ebrei: alcuni nodi del confronto attuale." *Protestantesimo* XVIIV (1989/2): 82–89.

————. "Considerazioni sul sussidio ecclesiastico per il rinnovamento del rapporto di Cristiani ed Ebrei," *Protestantesimo* XLIIV (1989/2): 98–100. Translation of "Christen und Juden. Schwerpunkt-Tagung der Landessynode der Evangelischen Landeskerche in Baden" with notes (Bad-Herrenalb, 1980, pp. 182–183).

————. "Chiesa—Israele: nuove prospettive teologiche," *Protestantesimo* 52 (1977/4): 303–305.

Georgi, Dieter. "The Early Church: Internal Jewish Migration or New Religion?" *Harvard Theological Review* 88/1 (1995): 35–68.

Harrington, Daniele J. "Israel's Salvation according to Paul." *Bible Today* 26 (1988): 306–307.

Hempton, D.N. "Evangelicalism and Eschatology." *JEH* 31/2 (1980): 179–194.

Johnson, S. Lewis, Jr. "Evidence from Romans 9–11." In *A Case for Premillennialism: A New consensus*. Donald K. Campbell and Jeffrey L. Townsend, eds. Chicago: Moody, 1992, pp. 199–223.

Jospe, Raphael. "The Concept of the Chosen People: An Interpretation." *Judaism* 43 (1994): 130–135.

Katz, David S. "The Abendana Brothers and the Christian Hebraists of Seventeenth-Century England." *JEH* 40/1 (1989): 28–52.

Klein, Charlotte. "From Conversion to Dialogue—The Sisters of Sion and the Jews: A Paradigm of Catholic-Jewish Relations." *JES* 18 (1981): 388–400.

Lapide, Pinchas. "Christians and Jews—A New Protestant Beginning." *JES* 12 (1975): 485–492.

Levy, David. "A History of Anti-Semitism." *Israel My Glory* 51 (1993/2): 16–18.

Longenecker, Bruce W. "Different Answers to Different Issues: Israel, the Gentiles and Salvation History in Romans 9–11." *Journal for the Study of the New Testament* 36 (1989): 95–123.

Molari, Carlo. "L'elezione d'Israele nell'autocomprensione cristiana." Unpublished paper presented on 4 November, 1995 at the SIDIC Center, Rome.

Osborne, William L. "The Old Testament Background of Paul's 'All Israel' in Romans 11:26A." *Asia Journal of Theology* 2 (1988): 282–293.

Parmentier, Martin. "Greek Church Fathers on Romans 9. Parts I and II," *Bijdragen* 50 (1989): 139–154; 51 (1990): 2–20.

Pawlikowski, John T. "Contemporary Jewish-Christian Theological Dialogue Agenda." *JES* 11 (1974): 599–616.

———. "Toward a Theology for Religious Diversity: Perspectives from the Christian-Jewish Dialogue." *JES* 26 (1989): 138–153.

Reeve, Simon. "Heartless Haven." *Time*, January 26, 1998, pp. 24–27.

Reichrath, Hans L. "Dei Geschichtlichkeit der Kirche war und ist eine Israelgeschichtlichkeit," *Judaica* 52/1 (1996): 40–58.

Riggans, Walter. "Messianic Judaism: A case of Identity Denied." *IBMR* 16 (1992): 130–132.

Schariah, Zechariah. "Development of epiclesis in the liturgy." Unpublished paper presented at the Doctoral Colloquium, September 1992. Evangelische Theologische Faculteit, Louvain, Belgium.

Schmid, Herbert. "Die Wurzeln des Zionismus im Alten Testament," in *Befreiungsbewegung des jüdischen Volkes*. Veröffentlichungen aus dem Institut Kirche und Judentum 5. Zionismus: Berlin, 1977, pp. 23–29.

Taylor, Howard. "The Continuity of the People of God in Old and New Testaments." *The Scottish Bulletin of Evangelical Theology* 3/2 (1985): 13–26.

Timmer, D.E. "Biblical Exegesis and the Jewish-Christian Controversy in the Early Twelfth Century." *CH* 58 (1989): 309–321.

Trevett, Christine. "Prophecy and Anti-Episcopal Activity: a Third Error Combatted by Ignatius?" *JEH* 34/1 (1983): 1–18.

Van Buren, Paul M. "Covenantal Pluralism?" *Common Ground* (1990/3): 21–27.

Vanlaningham, Michael G. "Romans 11:25–27 and the Future of Israel in Paul's Thought." *The Master's Seminary Journal* 3 (1992): 141–147.

Vleugels, Gie, "*Houtōs*," unpublished notes, Evangelische Theologische Faculteit, Louvain, n. d.

Walker, David. "Thomas Goodwin and the Debate on Church Government." *JEH* 34/1 (1983): 85–99.

Weiss, Andrea L. "Creative Readings of the Covenant: A Jewish-Christian Approach." *JES* 30 (1993): 389–402.

7. Pamphlets

Bicheno, James. *The Restoration of the Jews*, 1800.

Faber, George Stanley. *A General and Connected View*, 1808.

Gli Israeliti: Il Nuovo Amore per Essi, E Il Loro Avvenire. Florence: Le Monnier, 1847.

Priestly, Joseph. *Letters to the Jews*, 1794.

8. Joint Statements

Declaration of the Regional Synod of the Evangelical Church of Renania, January 11, 1980. "Zur Ermenerung des Verhaltnisses von Christen und Juden," Handreichung Nr. 39 für Mltglieder der Landesssynode, der Kreissynoden und der Evangelischen Kirche in Rheinland, Düsseldorf, 19852: 9–11. Italian translation and notes by Daniele Garrone. "Risoluzione sinodale sul rinnovamento del rapporto fra Cristiani e Ebrei." *Protestantesimo* XLIIV (1989): 96–97.

"L'accordo fondamentale tra la Santa Sede e Israele." Jerusalem, 30 December, 1993. *Il Regno-attualità* (1994/2): 1–3.

"The Churches and the Jewish People: Towards a New Understanding." Resolution adopted by the WCC Consultation on the Church and the Jewish People on November 4, 1988. *IBMR* 13 (1989): 152–155.

The Theology of the Churches and the Jewish People: Statements by the World Council of Churches and its member churches. Comments by Brockway, Allan,

Paul van Buren, Rolf Rendtorff and Simon Schoon, eds. Geneva: WWC Publications, 1988.

Tutti i documenti del Concilio, Rome: U.C.I.I.M., 1972.

9. Reference Works

A Greek-English Lexicon of the New Testament and Other Early Christian Literature. Walter Baur, William F. Arndt and F. Wilbur Gingrich, eds. Translated, revised and augmented by F. Wilbur Gingrich and Frederick W. Danker from Walter Bauer's 5th ed. Chicago: The University of Chicago Press, 1979.

A Hebrew and English Lexicon of the Old Testament. Francis Brown, S. R. Driver, Charles A. Briggs, eds. Oxford: Clarendon Press, 1975.

An Analysis of the Greek New Testament. Maximillian Zerwick S.J., and Mary Grosvenor. Revised ed. Rome: Biblical Institute Press, 1981.

An Idiom Book of New Testament Greek. C.F.D. Moule. 2nd ed. 7th reprint, Cambridge: Cambridge University Press, 1959.

Enclyclopedia Britannica. 29 vols. London: Enclyclopedia Britannica (1994).

Encyclopaedia Judaica. 16 vols. Jerusalem: Encyclopaedia Judaica (1971).

Encyclopedia of Judaism. Geoffrey Wigoder, ed. Jerusalem: Jerusalem Publishing House, 1989.

Evangelical Dictionary of Theology. Walter A. Elwell, ed. Grand Rapids, MI: Baker Book House, 1984.

Gesenius' Hebrew and Chaldee Lexicon to the Old Testament Scriptures. William Gesenius. Translated by S. P. Tregelles. Samuel Bagster and Sons, 1847. Reprint, Grand Rapids, MI: Baker Book House, 1979.

Handbook of Evangelical Theologians. Walter W. Elwell, ed. Grand Rapids, MI: Baker Book House, 1993.

A Greek-English Lexicon, 1897. Liddell, Henry George and Robert Scott. 8th revised ed. Oxford: Clarendon Press: 1901.

New Catholic Encyclopedia. 15 vols. New York: McGraw Hill
Book Company, 1967.

New International Dictionary of the Christian Church. J.D.
Douglas, ed. Exeter: The Paternoster Press, 1978.

New International Dictionary of New Testament Theology.
Translated and revised, with additions. Colin Brown, ed. 3
vols. Exeter: Paternoster Press, 1975–1978.

Theological Dictionary of the New Testament. Gerhard Kittel
and Gerhard Friedrich, eds. Translated by Geoffrey W.
Bromiley. 9 vols. Grand Rapids, MI: Eerdmans, 1964–
1972.

Zerwick Max and Mary Grosvenor. An Analysis of the Greek
New Testament. Rome: Biblical Institute Press, 1981.

SUBJECT INDEX

For the names of recent and contemporary authors consulted
during the course of this study, see Bibliography.

Aaron, 117
Abendana, Isaac, 23
Abraham, 5–7, 18, 25, 33–34, 47, 72, 74, 76
Abraham's children, offspring, seed, 16, 33–35, 42, 56
Adam and Eve, 85, 99
Adversus Judaeos, 71, 90, 112, 134
Alsted, Johann Heinrich, 194 (n. 9)
Altar, 106, 124, 130, 135
Allegorism, 82–83, 158–159
Ambrose, 115
Antichrist, 152, 156
Anti-Jewish legislation, 93–96
Anti-Judaism, anti-Judaic, 47, 67, 70–71, 90–91, 97–98
Anti-Semitism, anti-Semitic activity, 22, 124–127
Apostles Creed, 163
Arethas of Cesarea, 54, 55
Atonement, doctrine of, 136, 184, 187
Augustine, 87–89, 115, 135, 159–168, 202 (n. 28), 208
    (n. 114), 209 (n. 13), 214 (n. 86), 215 (n. 97)
Augustinian Tradition, 3, 164
Augsburg, 227 (n. 76)

Balaam, 8–9
Barabbas, 85
Barbarians, 74
Bar Kochba, 69
Baptism, 112, 120, 122–123, 128–129
Bishop, bishops, 93, 101, 103–104, 109, 122–123
Boniface VIII, 166

Calvin, John, 197 (n. 17), 208 (n. 114)
Canon, canonical status of, canonical principle, 73, 77
Catholicity, 124
Children of God, 34–35, 56
Children of the Devil, 33–35
Christ, Christology, 33, 125 *et passim*
"Christian" Europe, 179
Christian unity, 124
Church, ix, xiii, 1–4, 20–21, 29–33, 37, 38, 40, 44–55,
    72–74, 77–90, 99–110, 111–136, 137–142, 148–152,
    156, 159–168, 169–173
Church Councils
    Apostolic Council, 37–39, 129
    Council of Nicea, 95, 125–126
    Council of Chalcedon, 91, 94, 96, 165
    Synod of Laodicea, 94
    Council of Constantinople, 94
    Council of Trullo, 94
    II Council of Nicea, 95
    Council of Toledo, 95
    IV Lateran Council, 95
    II Vatican Council, 31
Church as Kingdom, 159–166
Church as true Israel, 49, 74–75, 134, 167
Church Triumphant, 159, 164–166

Circumcision, circumcised, uncircumcised, 37, 40, 72–73, 76, 79, 112, 129

Clement of Alexandria, 81, 118, 153

Code Napoléon, 24

Code of the African Church, 94

Commodianus, 156, 157

Constantine, Emperor, 124–131

    letter of, 126–127

Council of Christians and Jews, 180, 188, 233 (n. 18)

Covenant

    Abrahamic covenant, 6, 18, 25–26, 38, 146

    Mosaic/Levitical covenant, 6, 103, 106, 117–118, 133

    the Sinaitic covenant superseded, 183

    covenants of promise, 6, 25–26

    conditional covenant, 6

    unconditional covenant, 7

    new covenant, 11–12, 47–52, 103, 118, 120, 138, 146–147

Cromwell, Oliver, 22

Cuninghame, William, 194 (n. 10)

Cyprian, 119–125, 128, 156, 202 (n. 28), 209 (n. 13), 221 (n. 99), 228 (n.80)

Cyril of Alexandria, 115, 158

Cyril of Jerusalem, 131–133, 218 (n. 42)

DABRU EMET, 186

Darby, John Nelson, 194 (n. 9)

David, 7, 8, 11, 17, 26, 140, 146

Dialogue, Jewish-Christian, 1, 195 (n. 15)

    Partners in dialogue, 181, 185, 186, 187, 192

Diodore of Tarsus, 158–159

Disinheritance of Israel, 72–73

Dispensationalism, xiii, 3

Ecclesiology, 3, 99–136, 171–172, 203 (n. 35)
Edict of Milan, 124
Egypt, Egyptians, 7, 8
Einstein, Albert, 23
Elders, 101–102
Esau, Edomites, 17–18, 73, 160
Eschatology, 3, 137–148
    realistic eschatology, 145
    realised eschatology, 139–140, 168
Essenes, 206 (n. 84), 69
Exodus, 7, 26
Eucharist, 110–111, 116, 122–123, 130
    as "sacrifice", 108, 109
    "invocation of God", 110–111, 116

Finch, Sir Henry, 2

Goodwin, Thomas, 2
Greek philosophy, 3–4, 70–71, 153–155, 170
Gregory I, 92–93

Haman, the Agagite, 10
Hebrew people, 1–3, 6, 23–24
Hebrew Scriptures, Old Testament, 71, 73, 77, 82–86,
    97, 140–141, 150
Hebrew world view, 3–4, 170
Hermeneutics, 82, 119, 172–173
Herzl, Theodor, 175, 199 (n. 45)
Hippolytus, 152
Hitler, 25, 178, 193 (n. 1)

Iconoclasts, defeat of, 167

Idolatry, 73
Impassibility of God, 153
Innocent III, 166
Irenaeus, 77–78, 109–112, 135, 151
Irving, Edward, 194 (n. 10)
Isaac, 16–17, 19, 25, 72, 160
Israel, Yisra'e'l, Israelites, ethnic Israel, xi, xiii, 1–4,
    5–27 *et passim*
  assimilation, 25
  "corporeal" and "spiritual" Israelites, 81–86, 96, 99
  election of, 18–19, 27, 61–62, 68
  enemies of the gospel, 15
  future of, 21, 26–27, 50, 81, 145–155
  God's covenant with, 4, 36, 47–48, 146, 171
  hardening of, 26, 57–60, 146
  institutions of, 2, 73, 92, 136
  origin of, 5–8, 15–17
  restoration of, 26, 66, 81, 100, 145–148
  servant of the Church, 78–81
  survival of, 10–13, 21–25
  "the Congregation of evil doers", 132
  unbelief of, 13–15, 57
Israel of God, 42–44, 61
Israel, State of, 1, 25, 45

Jacob, 6–7, 72, 84, 85, 147
James, 38
Jamnia, 70
Jerusalem, 84, 97, 131–132, 142, 148, 160, 228 (n. 78)
Jewish War (A.D. 66–70), 33, 69
Jewish ghetto, 95
John Chrysostom, 36, 89–91
Joseph II of Austria, 24

Judgement, 153–154
Julian the Apostate, 158
Justin Martyr, 71, 74–77, 107–108, 135, 150, 155
Judah, Jews, Jewish people, 7, 10–14, 21–25, 31–35, 50–
    53, 69–71, 86, 92–96, 97, 107–108, 120, 133, 160
Judaism, Rabbinic Judaism, 40–41, 47, 69–71

Kingdom of God, 137–139, 140–141, 148, 229 (n. 95)

Lactantius, 156–157
Lacunza y Diaz, Manuel de, 194 (n. 10)
Law, works of the law, 37–39, 71–74, 107
Leo I, 164–165
Leopoldo I, Granduca of Tuscany, 24
Lord's Supper, 104–105
Louis XVI of France, 24
Luther, Martin, 209 (n. 13), 230 (n. 109)

Medieval ecclesiastical theocracy, 127, 137, 159, 164–
    166
Majority views concerning Israel (see Israel)
Marcion, 82
Mendelssohn, Moses, 24
Messiah, messianic, 26, 39, 49, 97 *et passim*
Messiah of Israel, 97
Messianic Jews, 176, 186, 194
Messianic kingdom, 139, 145, 149, 161, 168
Methodius, 156
Millenarianism, millennium, 137, 145, 148–152, 154–
    159, 161–163
Ministry of the new covenant, 103–117, 123, 127–131,
    133, 170–171
Missiology, 2

Mission to the Jewish people, 134
Mortara, Marco, Chief Rabbi of Mantova, 175

New majority view, 205 (n. 75)
"Nostra Aetate", 31–31, 200 (n. 6), 205 (n. 75)

Old majority view (see also "replacement theology"),
    177, 179, 180–181
Origen, 33, 81–87, 96, 115–119, 153–155

Papias, 149–150
Paul, apostle, 2, 15 *et passim*
People of Israel and the new laós of God, 37–38
Pharisees, 206 (n. 81)
Philo, 81
Platonism, 153
Pogrom, 25
Polemic against the Jews, 30–32, 40–41, 54, 70–71, 89
Priesthood, 102, 104–105, 107, 114, 117, 131, 133
Promised land, 7
Punishment, eternal, 154
Puritan England, 133

Qumran, 203 (n. 39), 205 (n. 74)

Rabin, Yitzhak, 1
Rahab, 9
Reformed orthodoxy, xiii
Repentance, 51
Replacement theology, 2, 29–33, 66–72, 96–98, 169–
    173 *et passim*
Roman Catholic "Jubilee", 136
Rupert of Deutz, 96

Sacramentalism, 124, 128–130
Sadducees, 69
Sacrifices, 104–105, 107–111, 120–124
Salvation, means of, 107, 111, 112–114, 127–130, 132–133, 136
Santuary, most holy place, 130
Satan, 145, 162
Saul, 7
Samuel, 7
Shoah, xiii, 1, 4, 171
Sinai, as "the central and unifying event", 189–191
Soteriology, xiv, 5, 172, 173, 176, 183–188, 195 (n. 15), 221 (n. 101), 231 (n. 1), 234 (n. 34)

Temple, 73
Tertullian, 78–81, 112–114, 119, 128–151
The Sisters of Sion, 231 (n. 119)
Theodosian Code, 92
Theological embroidery, 31, 77
Theological pluralism, 186
Theology, Christian, xi, xiii, 4, 159, 172–173
Theology of recognition, 186
Third Reich, 25
Torah, 41, 73
"Two covenant" theory, 177, 183

"Unam Sanctum", 166

Yohanan ben Zakkai, 70

World Council of Churches, 1, 27, 30, 168
World Evangelical Fellowship, 185

Zealots, 69

Zionism, 25

Zionist Congress (First), zionist movement, 175, 176, 199 (n. 45), 232 (n. 8)

Zanini, Carlo Antonio, 175–176, 231 (n. 2, 3)

CPSIA information can be obtained
at www.ICGtesting.com
Printed in the USA
LVHW011314230322
714164LV00003B/448

9 780830 856893